# CULTURE POLITICS
## THE STORY OF NATIVE LAND CLAIMS IN ALASKA

*by*

KIRK DOMBROWSKI

SYRON DESIGN ACADEMIC PUBLISHING

*Orders and requests for permissions should be addressed to:*
    *Syron Design Academic Publishing*
    *2221 Sheridan Blvd*
    *Lincoln, NE 68502*
    *646-246-5527; syron@syrondesign.com*
        *Or*
    *Kirk Dombrowski*
    *Department of Sociology*
    *University of Nebraska Lincoln*
    *Lincoln, NE 68588-0324*

*This book is available on Amazon.com*

*Cover concept and illustration by Kate Rask.*
*Design and layout by Syron Design, Lincoln, Nebraska.*

*Published by Syron Design Academic Publishing, Lincoln, Nebraska.*

*Library of Congress Cataloguing-in-Publication Data*

Dombrowski, Kirk, 1967-
Culture Politics: The Story of Land Claims in Alaska
Includes bibliographical references and index.
ISBN: 978-0-615-95041-9

1.      Tlingit Indians—Economic Conditions
2.      Tlingit Indians—Ethnic Identity
3.      Tlingit Indians—Missions
4.      Fundamentalist Churches—Alaska
5.      Haida Indians—Economic Conditions
6.      Haida Indians—Ethnic Identity
7.      Haida Indians—Missions
8.      Alaska Panhandle (Alaska)—Economic Conditions
9.      Alaska Panhandle (Alaska)—Ethnic Identity
10.     Alaska Panhandle (Alaska)—Social Conditions

For Gerald Sider...
        teacher, mentor and friend.

*Dombrowski*

# TABLE OF CONTENTS

## TABLES

## MAPS

## PHOTOGRAPHS

# Preface

*Culture Politics* is a significantly modified and updated version of my earlier work, *Against Culture: Development, Politics and Religion in Indian Alaska* (University of Nebraska Press, 2001). That book was written from my doctoral dissertation at the CUNY Graduate Center, and in ways both good and bad, reflects that origin. More than ten years have passed since the publication of *Against Culture*, and I have revisited many of the ideas contained therein with publications that have appeared in academic journals such as the *American Anthropologist, Focaal, Anthropologica, Current Anthropology, The Australian Journal of Anthropology, International Labor and Working Class History, Ethos, The Journal of Historical Sociology, North American Dialogue, Dialectical Anthropology*, and in *A Companion to the Anthropology of American Indians*. As I turn towards a new project on land claims in Inuit Labrador, it seems as if there would not be a more appropriate and opportune moment than the present to put out a revised and updated version of *Against Culture*, now several years out of print, that reflects the rethinking and revision of the 10 years that followed its original publication.

This work is thus significantly updated and includes the elimination of two chapters from the original text, the addition of three new chapters, and a significant revision of three of the remaining chapters. It is in some ways a very different book, thus the new title (rather than publishing a second edition), though the core ideas of the original remain. My hope is that they appear here in sharper focus, more clearly stated and written in more approachable form. Likewise, significant work by other scholars has emerged on these topics in the intervening decade, much of which is incorporated or addressed here as well.

*Against Culture* represented something of a new direction in Native Studies at the time, and one that has since gained significant momentum. In looking back over the original chapters, I am pleased with the way that the work has held up over the last 10 years. My hope is that this book will help sustain the created momentum. Readers familiar with the earlier work will note added development of many themes that were implicit in the earlier text, and hopefully will recognize efforts to make the text more readable, and less of a specialty book. Toward this end, there are very few citations in the current work. Reference to supporting materials has been placed entirely in endnotes, not to minimize the contributions of other authors and material presented here, but to allow the reader to focus more clearly on the work as a whole.

The original study upon which this book is based was conducted between 1992 and 2000, and subsequent writing and archival research. My field research included three summers and one winter in Alaska, plus six months of archival research in New England, San Francisco, and Juneau. Much of this work was historical, little of which is reflected here, but it conditioned the way I later understood the events described. My exposure was centered in the region of Southeast Alaska. There I lived primarily in three villages: Hydaburg, Kake, and Hoonah. Beyond this, I spent time and attended church meetings in Juneau, Wrangell, and Ketchikan. In addition, I spent a couple of months split between Craig, Klawock, and Sitka, and obtained a number of interviews in each of these places.

In the villages I conducted formal and informal interviews, lived in the homes of three different families, and gathered material through "participant observations," meaning that I pulled the lead line and piled corks when fishing, ate Indian food at the several "doins" and "pay-off parties" to which I was invited, and attended church meetings and revivals whenever possible. I accomplished most of my research on Pentecostalism, however, during the four months of my last full field season in 1996; up until that time I was more concerned with issues of political economy—including cannery labor, family politics, subsistence harvests and politics, and wage labor in the timber industry. I became interested in church membership and its importance when two friends invited me to attend a revival with them one long winter evening. We had been hunting that entire day, and I felt as though I already had one foot in the grave. Winter hunting is, to say the least, very cold, and for someone who has done little of it, it is exhausting beyond measure. I wanted to say "no" to the invitation, but surprising myself, I agreed. I had never been to a Pentecostal service; and what I saw at the church came as a complete surprise, although I felt that I knew my hosts, and many other people in the church quite well. To witness their weeping and speaking in tongues—"gifts of the Spirit," I later learned—was, to be blunt, shocking. I knew then that my research was beginning anew.

In other places I encountered virtually the same thing. Many of the people I knew well were members of Pentecostal churches, particularly those individuals on the margins of village and regional sociopolitical life among whom I had spent most of my time. Part of the reason this fact had escaped me was that I had spent time in Alaska mainly during the summer. Church is a winter event throughout the region. During the summer people travel and—more importantly for many of those who attended "radical" Christian churches—pursued subsistence foods. Had I never made a winter field trip, I might never have understood the role church membership played in the lives of many people I saw on a daily basis during other seasons.

Since that time I have tried to understand the importance of church membership—and thus the rise of Pentecostal and other Fundamentalist churches in the region—in terms of the political-economic process I had studied up to that point, and vice versa. More to the point, I have tried to better understand how people thought about and dealt with the political and economic processes in which they found themselves by asking why they found church membership so important.

This was my research. Throughout, it was conducted entirely in English, as this is the first language of virtually every village resident under the age of seventy. Indeed, few younger than this speak the indigenous languages of the area, though at present, classes in Tlingit or Haida are offered in the lower grades in village schools. These programs have met with mixed success due to a lack of commitment by most school boards, a deficiency of available teachers, and continued underfunding by the various federal, state, and local administrations. I do not speak either Tlingit or Haida beyond simple greetings and polite formalities.

One more issue should be made clear for the role it played in orienting my research. Beyond the actual topical interests I pursued—economic development, politics, Pentecostalism—I had come to Southeast Alaska with a specific tactical focus. It animates much of the discussion that follows, and no doubt underlies (in ways I am surely yet to realize fully) the types of questions I asked when I was in the field. Pursuing what seem to me the central unspoken and perhaps almost unspeakable issue of Native American Studies, I went to Alaska seeking to understand how local, village-based inequalities were made, perpetuated, and tied into the larger process of resource extraction that dominates the politics of the region. Behind this lay a belief (still held) that local forms of inequality determine both how people—and peoples—at the margins are tied into a process of global production (a process seldom in their interest) and how they might resist this incorporation. This is, I believe, how and why people so often find themselves "within and against" systems of domination that surround them, as anthropologist Gerald Sider puts it.

Because I did not initiate my research with a focus on Pentecostal churches, the shift to looking at "radical" Christians required certain changes in my overall approach to local differentiation. Nonetheless, the concentration on specific forms of village-level inequality remained at the center of my fieldwork and remains at the center of the anthropology I now propose. This is a risky undertaking, for local forms of inequality are apt to be understood in personal terms, especially when the people reading the stories and discussions that follow inevitably recognize themselves. This is an uncomfortable feeling, made more so by the fact that many of the people for whom this book is written—those on the margins of village life and politics—are unlikely to read it, some because they cannot read, many more because they have more important things to do. In part to protect those whose vulnerability might be further compromised by the work that follows, and to shield myself somewhat from the charges of those who see a discussion of village inequalities as a personal attack, some of the names of individuals whose stories follow have been changed, and where it seemed appropriate, place names have been omitted or altered. To those of my friends who might have hoped to see their names mentioned as a record of their time-consuming, difficult, and perhaps risky assistance, I apologize and try to discharge some acknowledgment her

## Acknowledgements

The debts accumulated in the twenty years since I began this project are numerous. My hosts for several long stays were Joe and Anna Frisby and Owen and Betsy James, and to them I owe the deepest gratitude because they took a chance on me. Wise people that they are, they know that even now it is unclear whether or not it was worth it.

In Kake I would like to thank the entire Jackson clan, especially Mrs. Mona Jackson, Mike Jackson, and Larry Jackson. The people at the Organized Village of Kake tribal offices were always receptive and open, and their guidance was appreciated. Willis Jackson and Archie Cavanaugh gave me my first introduction to churches in Kake, and for their guidance and understanding I am indebted. Ruth Demmert and Gail Jackson introduced me to the Keek

Kwan Dancers and helped me understand how and why people become part of village culture movements.

In Hydaburg I offer special thanks to Lisa Lang and Pugie Sanderson, important and busy people who both found time to talk with me about how villages work, despite the fact that they had little reason to believe my reasons for wanting to know. Algie Frisby was a good friend who helped me get my feet wet and steered me clear of obvious trouble I still managed not to see even after three summers in the village. The late Sylvester Peele offered several open and sincere interviews for which I am very grateful. Adrian and Vicki LeCornu were more than helpful and consistently challenging on these same issues. In Hoonah I wish to thank Paul and Mary Rudolf and the crew of the *Inian Queen*, who put up with my questions about fishing and Native culture. Also in Hoonah, Carl Larson and Harold Dick accepted with patience and good humor my many questions, and Reverends Joe Thomas and Greg Howald were consistently patient and forthright.

Many of the church members to whom I spoke preferred not to be named, especially in villages where there has been conflict, and given the argument raised here, I have decided to use pseudonyms for all. To these individuals, who more than anyone else helped me understand the limits of my own perspective, I say thank you, and note that while the interests portrayed here are not necessarily your own, the representations that follow are made with the hope that they be seen as fair. If they are perceived otherwise, my hope is that the failure is attributed to ignorance or poor research, not a lack of concern. Special thanks are offered to the prayer groups at Juneau and Hoonah, who allowed me to attend their meetings and a joint revival, my very first one. Also to the members of the Assembly of God, Presbyterian, and Four Square churches in Kake, who also allowed me to attend both regular services and a revival. Of the several other ministers and prayer group leaders to whom I spoke I would especially like to thank Pastors Charles Bovee and Glen Wilson of the Southeast Alaska Presbytery and Lieutenant Trickle of the Salvation Army.

Most of the historical work included here is the result of archival work in Juneau carried out in or through the State Historical Library. Special thanks to Kay Shelton, the head of collections, and librarian India Spartz for their patience and guidance. The majority of my fieldwork, including three separate trips in 1995 and 1996, was paid for by a grant from the Wenner-Gren Foundation for Anthropological Research (Grant no. 5876). Without this support, earlier and subsequent research would have lacked any foundation; so to Wenner-Gren, many thanks.

The late Eric Wolf remained throughout a source of inspiration and personal encouragement, as is the work, guidance, and friendship of Joan Vincent. Leslie Gill read the entire manuscript with much care and provided several useful suggestions that have made this a better book. Barbara Price taught me much more than how to write, and later she read this book and offered many helpful suggestions; this book is, without exaggeration, a testament to her patience, help, and faith in me as an ethnologist.

Most special thanks go to Gerald Sider, mentor, adviser, and friend. This book is dedicated to him, with the hope that it represents in some small form the appreciation I feel for all that he has taught me. Most of the good ideas in what follows were prompted by his teaching or drawn from his work. Included in this as well is the debt I owe to the students he gathered around him. I am fortunate to be part of a cohort of anthropologists that included Anthony Marcus, Avi Bornstein, Joshua Moses, Geraldine Casey, Steve Striffler, Gus Carbonella, Leslie Gill, Linda Green, Lindsay Bell, Charles Menzies, Eliza Darling, and Sharryn Kasmir. In more recent years, I have benefited much from conversations with Ananth Aiyer, Bilal Khan, Ric Curtis, Randy Martin, and the editorial collective at *Dialectical Anthropology*. To my many students in Anthropology 340, at John Jay College, CUNY (where most of these ideas were worked into their current form), I thank you for your help and patience.

In writing this book I had the assistance and guidance of Albert Sgambati, my editor. His contribution and commitment to this text was extraordinary. This acknowledgement is in no way adequate for the help he gave and generosity of purpose he showed.

And finally to Colleen Syron, Elizabeth Dombrowski, and Nathaniel Dombrowski, who knows what sorts of things are caught up between these pages: praise, thanks, and love.

Portions of the following works are republished in significantly modified form as part of the following chapters:

- Sections of Kirk Dombrowski (2002) "The Praxis of Indigenism" *American Anthropologist* 104(4):1062-1073, appear in Chapters 3 and 5.
- Sections of Kirk Dombrowski (2002) "Billy Budd, Choker-Setter: Native American Culture and Indian Work in the Southeast Alaska Timber Industry" *International Labor and Working Class History* 62:121-142, appear in Chapter 9.
- Sections of Kirk Dombrowski (2004) "The Politics of Native Culture" in T. Biolsi (ed) *A Companion to the Anthropology of American Indians* pp. 360-382. Malden MA: Blackwell Publishing, appear in Chapters 3 and 9.
- Sections of Kirk Dombrowski (2007) "Subsistence livelihood, Native identity and internal differentiation in Southeast Alaska." *Anthropologica: The Journal of the Canadian Anthropology Society* 49(2):211-230, appear in Chapters 5 and 6.
- Sections of Kirk Dombrowski (2010), "The White Hand of Capitalism and the End of Indigenism as We Know It." *The Australian Journal of Anthropology* 21:129-140, appear in the Epilogue.

*Grateful acknowledgement for the use of these texts is provided here and in the notes to each chapter.*

CHAPTER 1

# Against Culture

In the autumn of 1992, in a village along the Southeast Alaska panhandle, several converts of an all-Native Pentecostal church ignited a bonfire to incinerate "non-Christian" items from their past as a way to demonstrate their new membership in the church and their "spiritual rebirth in Christ." Only those at the bonfire (who are still reluctant to speak about it) know exactly what was burned, but rumors spread fast and fierce that Indian dancing regalia had been set ablaze. Within a day or two, these rumors had reached every village and town in the region, and reporters called or visited the host village in search of more details, and of course more drama. In the weeks that followed, people as far away as Seattle were listening to radio programs and reading newspaper stories regarding the event; almost all the coverage focused exclusively on reports that Native regalia had been reduced to ash. For months afterward, tensions between churches and Native dance groups remained high throughout the region, and even today most Native residents of Southeast Alaska are reluctant to speak of the incident or its inspiration for fear of setting off the still emotionally charged and sensitive issues surrounding the occurrence.

The revival at the center of this controversial event was hosted by an independent Pentecostal church—one that had, at the time, an entirely Native congregation and was led by a locally born Native pastor. At the revival, the self-described "itinerant preacher" Flo Ellers raised the issue of Native culture and, by her own account, challenged her audience to question the place of Native religious and spiritual objects in their eternal salvation. On the other side, non-church members (especially those involved in the current village culture movement) found the events reminiscent of a past incident.[1] In this same village, early-twentieth-century converts to Christianity had convinced fellow residents to burn the nineteenth-century totem poles that stood in front of many of their village homes. While nearly 100 years had passed, this remained an iconic moment in the minds of many Native residents. The recent burnings, therefore, were eerily reminiscent of past attacks on Native culture—and the people who supported it—by outsiders and their converts. Many culture-group members were led to ask, "Have we made no progress in the last ninety years?"

When asked to defend her stance against Native culture, Ellers spoke of her own struggle with the role of culture in her beliefs. After much prayer and thought, she noted, she had come to understand that some elements of Native culture—especially those that had been used in past spiritualist ceremonies (from which at least some elements of today's Native dancing are drawn)—were barriers on her path to salvation. Questioned further on this point, Ellers summed up her understanding by noting that, from what she understood of the book of Revelation, "You won't find any Chilkat dancers dancing in heaven."

Although Ellers was almost certainly not the only preacher to raise the issue of Native culture at this revival or at others, her statement had reportedly set off the burnings that followed. At the completion of the service at which Ellers spoke, several out-of-town attendees supposedly told those around them that they had burned some of their own cultural items at a revival many years before as a way of affirming their own "rebirth in Christ," and had seen the image of a serpent rising from the flames. The idea captivated several young people who had been "born again" at the revival, and they approached Ellers and the pastor of the host church and asked permission to burn some items from before their spiritual rebirth. The ministers consented, saying, "Go ahead, whatever you want to get rid of, get rid of."

Following this, a small crowd gathered in the church parking lot and started a fire in a metal oil drum. They threw many things into the blaze, including rock-and-roll records and cassette tapes, "heavy metal" concert T-shirts, and liquor bottles. Whether or not any older cultural or dancing regalia was actually

---

[1] Unlike church members, who self-identify as such, few village residents are likely to refer to themselves as members of a culture movement. But people in the dance group do identify themselves as dance group members, and when village residents were asked who the key members of the village culture movement or culture group were, no one misunderstood the question. Any movement referred to in the text as such should be understood, however, as an informal group or collection of groups.

burned remains a point of contention. Charred bits of cloth were found, as were coffee cups and windbreaker jackets bearing the logo of the local ANCSA (Alaska Native Claims Settlement Act) "Native" corporation—an intertwined raven and eagle in Northwest Coast style, representative of the two moieties once found among most Southeast Native villages. It is unlikely that any older cultural heirlooms were burned, if only because in most villages, such items are now so rare that few of the young people attending would have had access to them. Some who sifted through the ashes reported seeing burned buttons— the remains of the type of buttons used on contemporary button blankets— and bits of felt, possible from the same type of item. Button blankets are much more common than the older heirloom pieces. Virtually all are recently made by members of village dance groups, and some are made as part of Native culture classes taught in village schools.

The regalia issue dominated the reaction that followed becoming the central focus of people's conversations on both sides, despite the lack of clear evidence. While the revival preachers wouldn't say whether any cultural items were burned—and not one of them, it seems, could have known firsthand as none attended the burning—all defended their firm stance against a range of cultural practices, especially, in condemning the Native dancing that had become very popular in recent years, and which included the making and wearing of costumes—primarily button blankets and headdresses—featuring stylized designs of old clan symbols, laid out in the form of classical Northwest Coast art.

***

Ellers' dramatic stance and the faith and commitment of her congregants place in bold relief the contemporary tensions surrounding "culture" in the everyday lives of village residents throughout the region, and for many, they raise the memory of past tensions as well. Most people are ordinarily more circumspect, but few—perhaps none—are unaffected by the issues and emotions Ellers and her followers have raised. Yet the sources of these tensions are not nearly as clear as one might assume.

The chapters that follow sketch out the complexity of tensions surrounding the burnings, but not for the purpose of simply laying out the troubles of a single town, or even the problems of several towns, for these events might have taken place in any number of Southeast Alaska villages. Rather, the purpose of this book is to point out that, for a class of people world-wide, surprisingly few can easily accommodate their "culture"—the signs, symbols, practices and emotions about the group they belong to, and the place of the group in the world and beyond. This is true for many Alaska Natives, as is dramatically apparent in the "Flo Ellers incident," as the 1992 burnings have come to be called. But it is just as true for ordinary folks everywhere. Most people, in most places, have highly ambiguous relationships with what anthropologists and others have come to term "culture," highly fraught and tense relationships with the very means through which they attach meaning to their lives and to their relationships with one another, and through which they make sense of the world around them. These means can take the form of ceremonies, customs, stories, or even everyday manners, and often reflect patterns of ideas and associations that are at once proposed and reinforced by participation in these same practices, and which become embedded in language and brought out in conversations about everyday life. Even so, the apparent ubiquity of culture can make it hard to see, and its struggles hard to disentangle.

Most anthropologists, and many sociologists and historians, treat "culture" as natural, or as automatic and therefore simple. Generally, they tell us, people are unaware of how or even when "it" (culture) is done. Yet there is little that is natural about culture—people change their ideas, and call into question things they have been taught, whether at the prompting of recent events, the influences of those around them, or the inability of culture to any longer provide them with satisfactory answers to life's problems. Criticism and reflection aren't limited to Western academic faculties—though one might not know this by reading most books about Native Americans.

This idea, that people can be at once a part of a culture and at the same time find it difficult to live with or endure, is a central part of this book. It is, in the eyes of this author, the only way we have to make sense of the Flo Ellers incident and others like it.

Before moving on to the larger situation that framed the Ellers incident, it is worth noting that this is an unconventional stance for an ethnographic account and may catch many readers off guard. Ethnography usually involves an attempt to describe the way of life and worldview of a particular group of people, and to draw from it a series of life lessons that those of us who do not share that culture might benefit from. This is an important function, and much has been gained by exposing the world to alternative life-ways and means for conceptualizing the world. However, much is lost in this effort as well. In the pursuit of holism and cross-cultural understanding, ethnographers have "naturalized" non-western cultures, and in the process rendered them static and often unapproachable. In the intentionally ironic telling of anthropologist Eric Wolf, it has rendered the world outside of Europe as composed of "people without history."

PHOTO 1: *Button blankets at a "give away" worn by the local dance group. This sort of "regalia" is usually made by the dancers themselves. Dance groups perform at many current social gatherings throughout the region.*

This book thus represents a change of focus—a change of analytical objects, if you will—that anthropologists have begun, but which we have yet to communicate very effectively outside our own circles. It follows the lead of ethnologists such as Eric Wolf, or Gerald Sider, whose writing on "living Indian histories" shows how anthropological visions of static culture get bound up with notions of race and place in society. As Sider's retelling of Lumbee Indian history teaches us, academic framings of Native culture as timeless and uniformly shared limits not simply Native peoples' visions of their own past, but also the kinds of presents and futures they can claim in the midst of their ever changing social surroundings. Like Sider's, this account focuses not so much a particular place or group living in that place, but a particular situation. In short, it aims to be an ethnography of a problem, not a people.

This shift of focus has several goals. I hope this change from the ethnography of people to the ethnography of problems will help us move away from the classical ethnographic assumption that presumes a group of people have a fixed collective identity and way of viewing the world, an assumption that is tied to very old but lingering ideas about the link between "race" and "culture." Instead, this book will focus on the questions of when and how the kinds of commonalities that late-coming ethnographers call culture actually come into being. That is, my goal in writing this book is to try to understand how ordinary people come to consider themselves 'a people'—the sort of social entity that can appear to outsiders as tied together by a common culture. As a result, the focus of this book will be the process through which distinctive, particular, and often superficially peculiar cultures come into being, or, conversely, pass into history, rather than an examination of what comes to be seen as the contents of the culture that is the result of that process.

PHOTO 2: *The church where the "Flo Ellers Incident" took place. Note that, despite the fact that this is a public gathering place, the building contains no windows and no indication of its purpose. Unless one is already part of the group, there is no way to learn when the next meeting will be, or to see what is happening during a meeting.*

For historical anthropologists such as Wolf and Sider, this approach involves placing the emergence of particular peoples and customary practices in an extended historical context. By drawing out the shifting political and economic contexts over time, progressive historical anthropologists seek to show both the contingency of conventional anthropological subjects (how specific cultures emerged under specific historical conditions, at particular times, in particular places), and consequently, how the stuff of culture (the ceremonies, customs, relations, and patterns of ideas) comes to be caught up with, and become part of, the political and social changes people faced at the time.

This ethnography is not as historical as Wolf's or Sider's, but it is concerned with the same issues. Conversely, I tend to work backward from the present cultural situation to the context from which it emerged—and very frequently the context *against which* it emerged. As above, the problem this book takes up is the recent emergence of "radical" Christian churches in Native villages in Southeast Alaska. These churches are Evangelical and frequently Pentecostal, and most are very recent arrivals to the region. All practice adult baptism—the hallmark of "born again" Christianity—and all are active in recruiting new members from the region's poorest and most marginal households. More importantly, all have, to some extent, taken a stance against Native culture.

The title of this chapter is thus not just a reference to ordinary people's struggles with sources of meaning in their lives, it also a reference to the radical Christian churches that have sprung up in many Native communities in answer, I argue, to people's growing estrangement from previously available sources of meaning in their lives. The majority of these churches are quietly but insistently and unequivocally opposed to the continuing practice of traditional or even reinvented Native ceremonies and practices. In fact, the phrase "against culture" was first related to me by a Native member of a primarily Native Pentecostal church. "I hate to have to make up my mind," he told me, "but if I had to say one way or the other, I'm against it"—the "it" being Native culture as celebrated in the villages today. Many Native Pentecostal and Evangelical church members feel the same way, though few are quite as open about it.

Not all Native people in these villages are against Native cultural practices— far from it. For very understandable reasons, reasons we will take up again and again throughout the book, many village residents are deeply committed to asserting, reshaping, and expressing a Native culture they regard as both traditional and living. One aspect or side of this dispute cannot be understood without the other. In the end, it is the fact that struggles over meaning and belonging (and thus, as Sider teaches us, struggles over the futures that different means for belonging make possible) become factions in a community which turns a personal, spiritual question in a social, political struggle. This point is important because it speaks directly to why ideas about meaning and happiness inevitably become caught up with politics and social change, and with these, become embroiled in the larger field of political life and economy in which remote Native villages are embedded. Choosing sides of even the most spiritual argument means choosing between one set of actions and another, electing to move toward one future and not some alternative. Emotional struggles and their answers are political acts—all the more so if the actions they entail also require the cooperation of others.

*** 

The situation is, in fact, even more complicated than can be captured by the notion of having different sides of a dispute, for both sides agree on many things. Importantly, virtually all Southeast Alaska Natives use the phrase "our culture" to refer to some elements of their lives and not others. Most often the term "culture" refers to two types of activities: (1) subsistence projects—the processes involved in harvesting and preparing subsistence foods; and (2) the joint participation of members of the community in collective identity projects. It is also used to classify some very arcane abilities or knowledge, such as Native languages or traditional speaking styles, though this is less frequently the case as such skills become increasingly rare.

No one, however—not even church members—would include Pentecostal church membership as part of Native culture, even when referring to entirely Native congregations, or those led by Native preachers like Ellers. In fact, most people—both church members and their critics—continue to view Native culture and Pentecostal religion as hopelessly at odds.

This opposition has partly to do with history. As mentioned above, the village in which the Flo Ellers incident took place had witnessed seemingly similar events before. In the early twentieth century, Christian converts assumed leadership of the village's main political institutions (primarily the school board) and convinced virtually all of the townspeople to take down and burn the totem poles located along the beach in front of most houses. Their reasons were partly practical and partly symbolic. In practical terms, totem poles had in the past been used to house the cremated remains of deceased kin, and some converts feared that these remains could still be used to invoke supernatural harm.

The other reason for burning the totem poles was to demonstrate to mission sponsors in New England and beyond that the town had fully embraced modern ways. Much was at stake. Mission sponsors had purchased industrial sawmills for Hydaburg and Metlakatla, two nearby Native villages, and had also financed several local businesses. In the village where the totem poles were burned, church converts hoped that such an act would signal the sort of conversion that Hydaburg and Metlakatla had undergone, and consequently trigger the sort of support that might be used to gain financing and donations for their own salmon cannery. As will be discussed later in the book, salmon canneries had fully transformed the regional economy by the early twentieth century—changing the way people thought about kin relations, property relations, and political-economic organization in general.

In place of totem poles, the town created a modern boardwalk along the beachfront, completing it with a silver spike forged from a U.S. silver dollar. Pronounced a holiday, the day of the completion of the board walk is still celebrated in the village. Anthropologists have since labeled that which was decimated by the missionaries and their converts as "culture," a term today's residents have taken up as well. Few at the time of the earlier burning would have used this term, though certainly many village residents at the turn of the twentieth century felt that more was destroyed in the fires on that day than simply the totem poles. Thus when, in 1992, revival attendees were rumored to have burned dancing blankets, many residents were instantly reminded of the totem-pole burnings, despite the fact that no more than one or two of today's residents were born when the first burnings took place. Still, similarities between the two situations did much to galvanize after-the-fact resistance to the 1992 burnings and to Ellers—resistance that was used to mobilize support against her and to cancel several future appearances she and others had planned for the traveling revival.

Other church organizations were also prompted into apologies. The Presbyterian Church, the moving force behind the original totem-pole burnings, issued an open apology to Southeast Alaska Natives for its past anti-cultural stance and proclaimed unambiguous support for the current region-wide culture movement. The Presbyterian congregation in the village in which Ellers made her remarks commissioned a traditional wood carving featuring an intertwined raven and eagle in classical Northwest Coast fashion, which is mounted at the rear of the church over the altar. The carving was intended to contrast with the anti-cultural stances of the newer churches, and to demonstrate ongoing support for, and creative integration of, Native and Christian elements that the regional Presbytery has endorsed. Russian Orthodox representatives went on local radio stations to proclaim their own regret for past intolerance and their strong support of contemporary cultural efforts.

Nevertheless, much about the two sets of burnings is distinct, and these differences can help us to understand why the mere suspicion of regalia burning became the central issue in the Flo Ellers incident. To begin, the culture movement of today is very much the public face of this and other villages. Supported by the Native corporations that resulted from state-wide Native land claims of the early 1970s, village dance groups perform at most major village and regional social events. The work they do in teaching and performing contemporary versions of traditional cultural practices plays a large role in the symbolic representation of local identity—much the same as early-twentieth-century Christians had sought to do with Western clothing and Christian singing associated with early Presbyterian and Salvation Army churches.

Just as the original totem-pole burnings had been quietly opposed by a group of non-Christians, primarily drawn from the community's more marginal segments, so too have today's born-again Christians quietly resisted the construction of a contemporary Native identity by village culture groups and Native corporate elites. An like their 19th century alter-egos who quietly resisted the totem pole burnings and the reinvention of the community in external form, today's born-again Christians are themselves also drawn from among the more marginal segments of the community. If anything, the two situations uncannily mirror each other in the most literal sense, as seemingly identical events reversed in orientation. Today's culture movement may have much more in common with the past Christian identity movement than many people would suppose. The same is true for today's church members, whose closed ranks seem more like the 'traditionals' of the past than they do the flamboyant Christians of the earlier era.

There are, however, ways in which these similarities and differences do not form such a neat opposition. Clearly the two sets of burnings do not represent the same problem, and certainly not the same stakes. Much has changed in the villages, and present divisions are very different from those of the past. In comparing the two I seek only to dismantle the easy explanations offered by many at the time—that the recent burnings were simply the result of long-standing, wrongheaded beliefs or bad theology on the part of the Christians who fail to understand the nuances of Native belief systems. There is much more to the recent burnings and resulting confrontations.

If the burnings of 1992 can be usefully compared to those of the past, it is not because Christians automatically oppose Native culture. Most culture-group members throughout the region are also members of Presbyterian, Salvation Army, or Russian Orthodox churches, and most attend church with at least as much regularity and sincerity as their suburban counterparts in the continental United States. Rather, the real purpose behind comparing the two situations is that the early burnings point us to what must be considered the central theme of the chapters that follow: the fact that, whatever the differences between the two events, divisions over culture within this village and in virtually every Native village in the region, continue to play a critical role in the relationship between small communities and the larger political economy that surrounds them.

This is a crucial point, which we will return to in the chapters that follow. Throughout, the purpose is to explain the connections between local divisions such as those between the culture group and Pentecostal church members, and the ongoing political economy of Southeast Alaska. In schematic terms, the guiding assumption of this book is the idea that, to understand Pentecostal church membership in Southeast Alaska today, one must examine it as part of the broader interrelationship within and between village communities and their political and economic surroundings—particularly as some in the community seek to manage culture with an eye towards what is going on outside the community. In short, what anthropologists and those around them have come to call "culture"—local meanings and the local ways used to produce and reproduce these meanings—is intimately caught up with wider social processes, which often increase and intensify political and economic differences within Native villages.

***

That being said, a word of caution is in order. If much of what we call "culture," and equally, much of what we call "religion," is caught up in the process of local difference making, it is not because church membership or culture-group membership is simply a crude reflection of other, more primary social divisions. This was not simply a question of rich and poor, although it is true that many of the members of new, more radical Christian churches come from the economic margins of the community and many of those most active in the various culture programs are from families or households that have benefited from the land claims agreement that helped revive the importance of Native culture in the region. People in Alaska—and everywhere else I have been—join churches to save their souls, and they join traditional dance groups to discover their identity. Neither of these activities, or their accompanying hopes, desires, or cosmologies, is reducible to some calculus of political or economic gains and losses, and studies that have concluded this are misguided and generally wrong. Far more often, when marginal people join radical churches they simply add to the stigmatization and marginalization they already suffer.

Yet church membership or religious conversion is not simply a quest for existential meaning—for some more rational and less contradictory system of beliefs—the sort of explanation that supposes that everyone will subscribe to what makes the most sense, or makes them feel the most important. As Susan Harding points out, people tend to join religious groups after having already learned the language and way of viewing the world practiced by the group. The gradual, habitual adoption of the language of Pentecostalism only gradually makes sense of the world. Most people first begin going to one of the new churches for companionship, or because a relative or spouse is going, or because they are bored, or because there is free food available after the service. Once there, they begin to hear the language of belief and piece it together, bit by bit. Gradually, Harding tells us, a series of implied connections, say between God's plan and a single event in one's life, becomes plausible. The more one learns of these implied connections, the more one begins to think like a convert, and almost always, the more one notices the absence of competing forms of connection and causality. According to Harding, one learns the language of conversion and becomes dissatisfied with one's own past explanations at the same time.

At some point in this process, conversion makes sense. This can seem rather sudden, but it is not. Any recent convert might tell you (as one told me): "I had a growing feeling that God had a plan for me but it took me a while to accept that. Once I did, then I could immediately feel the Grace of God on me and I became born again, brand new." As Harding teaches us, by the time people decide to "believe," they already have gained the ability to render the world in a new way, and in the process already discovered a great deal of dissatisfaction with their ideas about connection, causality, and meaning that they had previously held.

Of course to learn the language of conversion, one must be involved and immersed in a community that speaks that language. The same holds true for culture in general. What makes the stuff of culture *and* religion necessarily social is that it requires learning and interaction with people capable of rendering the world in its own terms. Once this is possible these same connections require people to act on the world in specific ways, with specific intentions. What makes culture and religion intrinsic to the local (and larger) divisions that we usually call politics is that none of these things—belief, identity, cosmology— is ever something that can be accomplished entirely on one's own. In contrast to the popular assumption that issues of conscience are entirely personal, belief and cosmology are always social entities, and always involve acting with, upon, or against others.

In part this is because they are taught to and learned from others. More than this, it is because each of these things is framed by signs and processes that do not operate according to the easily identified categories of individual and social. People assign meaning to the world around them that allow them to live with it and in it, just as the people around them are both engaged in their own meaning making and are caught up within the webs of significance spun by others. For a long time anthropologists and psychologists have been content to call the meanings people come to agree upon or share, "culture," and those meanings a person does not share with those around them, "personality." Yet this division has done little to clarify how people both make meanings, on the one hand, and then, conversely, come to be subject to meanings made by others. Nor does it tell us very much about how or when some people choose to throw off some meanings and not others.

Instead of holding too closely to notions of personality and culture in the conventional academic sense; or asking what sort of personality or personal situation might lead one to convert to a radical church; or what sort of collective cultural signs might predispose one to a particular (perhaps Pentecostal) set of religious signs and meanings; this book will instead be concerned with religion and culture insofar as the elements that make them up come to be part of specific social strategies to make the world meaningful and thus livable, strategies that necessarily involve and invoke action upon, with, and against other people. Thus we return to the point that this approach goes in the opposite direction from those studies that see cultural meanings as lasting and fixed. Instead, beginning with the extraordinary contingency of even our most meaningful and central beliefs, this book seeks to ask how such meaning is created, continued, or constrained. All of these processes of meaning making and beyond involve power and relationships with other people, and so it seems questions of culture come, inevitably, to involve questions of power as well.

*\*\*\**

Alaska Natives—or Native Americans in general—are not special in this regard. All people, everywhere, act against their culture, without ever ceasing to value it or live within its emotional and interpersonal grasp. Some anticultural feelings—feelings that express the failure of culture to provide a meaningful, livable life, even for those who accept it—are expressed in simple, individual, destructive ways like alcohol abuse and other forms of substance abuse, or even in their most extreme form, suicide, both of which played a role in the Flo Ellers incident and in nearly every conversion story I was told. Such processes are prevalent in Alaska, but they are by no means limited to Native villages.

Other anti-cultural stances are both more social and more aimed at reforming the parts of culture that are most difficult to bear. African American reactions to segregation in the South are perhaps the best examples. Barred from participation in many community institutions, black Americans rallied around the institutions they could control, and in so doing transformed these institutions anew. This was the basis for the mobilization of black Christian churches in the South during the era of Jim Crow segregation—institutions that were later able to combat segregation in a way and with a force that suburban churches in the North could not even imagine. In so doing, African American churches simultaneously shifted the focus of Protestant Christian religious practice away from the smug self-assurance of Max Weber's famous *Protestant Ethic*-style Baptists to a redemptive theology of suffering and salvation, now seen in black Baptist churches everywhere.

Yet if there is no difference between the ambiguous relationship Native Americans or Alaska Natives have with their culture and what ordinary people everywhere normally feel—no real difference, for example, between what it feels like to be "Indian" versus what it feels like to be "black," or "Latino," or "poor," or "illegal," or "a welfare mother"—there is still a significant difference in how these feelings might be expressed, either to those in power or to each other, or even to oneself. To understand just what this difference is, one must consider, briefly, the notion of subculture, which reveals critical hidden agendas within our ordinary popular and anthropological conceptions of culture.

The term "subculture" has become popular as a way to describe the dynamics of being within and against culture. Subcultures are generally taken to be groups that have found the culture they live within—the ways, that is, in which meanings are created and meaningful lives lived—to be unsatisfying, unfair, or most often, unattainable. Their response, however, has not been to overturn their culture entirely, but rather to co-opt, subvert, and redefine elements of the dominant culture and refashion these elements into alternative systems of meaning, or alternative ways of living meaningful lives. The notion of subculture elucidates the fact that most people find ways to live differently within, and even against, a set of meanings and institutions they find impossible to live with—and that they can do so without entirely (or even mostly) abandoning those same meanings and institutions.

In this way, African American subcultures in the United States have, for generations, made use of elements of the dominant culture to express resistance, autonomy, and, perhaps most importantly, ways to live meaningful lives otherwise denied to them. Notably, however, most of the elements of this subculture have been drawn, directly or indirectly, from the dominant culture. Christian churches are a very good example of this, but so are many contemporary elements as well—from hip-hop to all-black college fraternities. All of these are, to a certain extent, posed against mainstream American culture, but none are so radical as to make a complete break with that culture. Hip-hop fully embraces the commodified, market-driven dynamics of the recording industry and of American business practices in general. Black churches have continued an American tradition of gender bias and exclusion in their leadership.

Issues of subculture work very differently for Native Americans and Alaska Natives, however. In fact, there are no Native American subcultures, at least according to most people's—and most Natives'—understanding of the term. The reasons for this are complex and have much to do with the fact that Native Americans have historically been allowed to participate in the American political economy *as Natives* only as long as they have maintained a clear and organized cultural distinctiveness.

This is a complex point, and warrants careful explanation, so let us pause a moment to consider the reasons why this is so: When I write that Native Americans have sought to participate in the economy "as Natives," I mean that Native Americans have sought to be involved on the basis of being a collective group of current or past owners of a host of resources used in the economy, and thus whose role in the economy should be based on that ownership. Of course, Native American individuals have been free to participate *as individuals* in the Euro-North American economy since the first days of European colonialism on the continent, though almost always on the basis of their ability to labor rather than their ownership of important resources. At times, in the past, they have been able to participate in the labor economy as collectivities, for example, during the 18th century fur trade, or the 19th century buffalo trade, but even here their ownership was denied and undermined even as their ability to work the land collectively was exploited. Gradually, this all ended as well, as the treaties of the 19th century eroded the recognition of collectivity itself, and the resources formerly held by Native American Nations/Tribes appropriated.

Not all collective claims to resources were eliminated, and not all of those resources taken, but the conditions of continued collective participation changed through time. By the mid-20th century, Native Americans were generally only allowed to participate in the American economy *as Natives*—again, as collectivities with hereditary, distinctive claims to disputed, important resources—only where they maintained extraordinary sorts of distinctiveness. Native ownership is continuously re-rooted in visible, stereotyped, difference. This special status has been the basis for both Indian gaming and mineral development—two cases where collective tribal autonomy has often allowed outside industry to operate within Native communities and skirt state laws prohibiting gambling in the first case, and environmental laws aimed at long-term public protection in the second. As discussed later in the book, under the Alaska Native Claims Settlement Act (ANCSA), Native village-based timber corporations have since the 1970s been able to harvest timber in ways that would not be possible on federal lands, and they have received considerable support from the timber industry as a result.

Where Native American distinctiveness has become unclear or intermixed with other sorts of distinctiveness—like race or class—participation *as Natives* has been denied, although, importantly, individuals within these groups have remained free to participate as individuals in ways open to other minority groups and persons of color. James Clifford has discussed the importance of distinctiveness for the Mashpees in what became one of the first and most important contemporary recognition trials in recent Native American history. As Clifford shows, in this case, Native persons were denied participation *as Natives* because they did not seem different enough—or, perhaps as importantly, because they lacked a significantly different social organization and culture that would have made them useful as Natives. Tellingly, even while being denied status as Natives, they were repeatedly and unabashedly confirmed via their treatment by the court in their status as people of color.

One result of this insistence on stable, identifiable and organized sorts of difference is this: Native Americans have been required to maintain a very different relationship with "their culture" than have other subordinated peoples in the United States. Native American groups, to remain such, must maintain clear barriers between their own culture and that of mainstream America. While Protestant churches can become a mainstay of an African American subculture, these same churches have never been seen as part of Native American culture—even in congregations composed entirely of Natives and led by a Native preacher, as was the case above—not even by the Native members of these churches.

This is the collective fate of Native Americans. Claims to resources are tied to the demonstration of tangible cultural difference. Yet for individual Natives, as well, there are differences between being part of an American subculture on the one hand and being part of Native American culture on the other. As has become clear in the history of race in America—and as my African American students are fond of pointing out—you cannot stop being "black" just because you want to, as ongoing issues of police profiling all over the United States make clear. You can stop being "Native," meaning you can lose your right to participate as a "Native" in America's political economy. This happens to most Native Americans who fail to maintain tribal membership with a federally recognized tribe. Like those groups who have failed to keep up the requisite cultural distinctiveness, individual Native Americans without tribal affiliation are allowed to participate in the American political economy as persons of color, but not as people with special claims to contested resources.

All of this means that the ordinary ambiguity that virtually all people feel toward their culture—toward the sources and systems of meaning in their lives—must be lived differently by Native Americans than by others. For Native Americans to be against their culture, they must risk losing their claim to being "Natives" in ways that matter materially as well as culturally or socially.

Pentecostal and Evangelical church membership, I will argue, is part of the process through which many Southeast Alaska Natives live against their culture, without leaving their communities or giving up their right to collective participation in community resources. As will be discussed later, Pentecostal church membership offers people an institution through which many of their own feelings about the failure of current identity projects can be expressed. It is worth recalling that whether or not contemporary dancing regalia was thrown into the fire that afternoon, it is quite certain that ANCSA corporation windbreakers and coffee cups were. This, it has been argued, is perhaps because these jackets and coffee cups bore a Native design; it is also possible that individuals were expressing a sense of alienation or betrayal felt by many marginal individuals and families toward the land settlement and the two classes of Natives it has created. In either case, however, it is clear that in many people's eyes, the current identity movement is very much caught up in the ongoing issue of resource development and corporate ambition.

Beyond this, church membership in one of the new, radical churches, allows Natives members to continue with those elements of their culture that many depend on for simple survival—subsistence hunting, fishing, and gathering, and the relations these activities entail. In fact, Pentecostalism's silence on these issues stands in strong contrast to that of the culture movement, for whom subsistence has been, in effect, reduced to an icon of Native culture: while the culture movement's stance on subsistence has brought much attention to the issue, it has also turned subsistence into an identity issue, and not necessarily a survival issue. For many individuals and households dependent on subsistence livelihood, this change has proven costly. Native timber corporations have logged much of the land claims area that some households have relied on for food, further exacerbating the differences between those in the community who depend on access to resources to make a living, and those who make a living through recently recognized ownership of resources in the area. It is no coincidence that those most dependent on subsistence foods for their livelihood are among the more marginal members of most Southeast communities, and are also the most likely to wind up in one of the newer Pentecostal churches.

Taken together, Pentecostalism provides Native church members the sort of dramatic break that the notion of subculture provides other groups—but which are, ordinarily, denied Alaska Natives and Native Americans alike. In many ways, Pentecostal practice involves the adoption of an entirely new language and way of seeing the world—one in which being a Native American has little or no significance. This is a radically different status than what is normally associated with Native American identity—which is increasingly all or nothing. Jesus, church members will tell you, became a living man for everyone, regardless of who they were before. All you have to do is put yourself in his hands and you will be saved, no matter who you are or what you have done. This dramatic denial of *culture* per se—not just particular cultures—has special appeal to people whose particular culture has become an unbearable and unavoidable burden, and for whom any available, alternative culture is likely to prove just as unlivable. For this reason, many Pentecostal converts will tell you that they are not just against Native culture, but against *all* culture.

In the early 1990s, as the household economies of those on the margins of Southeast Alaska's Native villages gradually collapsed under the weight of a diminishing commercial fishery and rapid environmental degradation at the hands of their own Native corporations, the appeal of churches that were "against culture" proved strong. The Flo Ellers incident is one example of this, but in reality most church members just quietly went about their business: attending church, going fishing and hunting, and trying to simply "hold on," both emotionally and financially, as the business of being Native in Alaska took off. Looking back, it seems amazing that so many held on long enough for the churches to form. Today, in 2013, many of these same communities have seen large outmigration, as those who could not hang on simply packed up and left. But that is the end of the story, and we have yet to get to the beginning.

*Map 1*

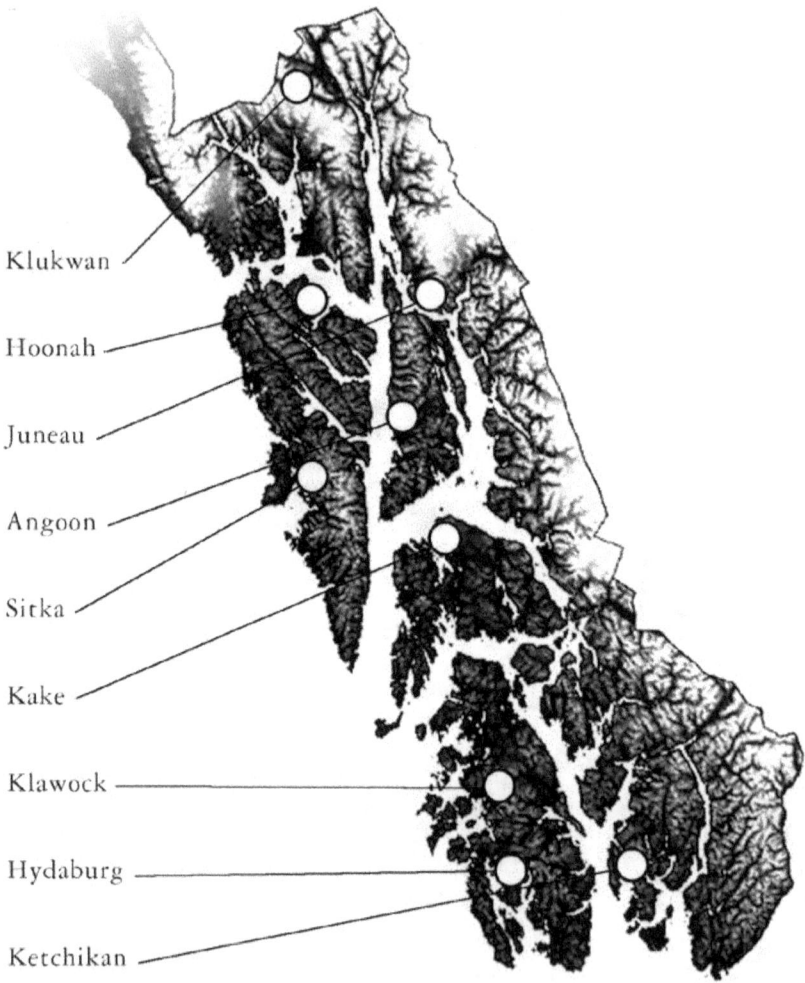

Klukwan

Hoonah

Juneau

Angoon

Sitka

Kake

Klawock

Hydaburg

Ketchikan

CHAPTER 2

# Politics on the
# Other Side of the Mountain

*Southeast Alaska has become a favored spot for cruise ship tours. The area is almost entirely an archipelago, the islands, actually submerged mountains with deep waterways, temperate rain forest, and post-glacial scenery on all sides. The sheer cliff-faced mountains meet the water in dramatic fashion, between them the fjords and "canals" large enough that the glaciers or forests can be viewed up close, without leaving the ships, and often without even going outside.*

*The area's artistic and mineral history fuels the accompanying tourist commodifications. The waterfronts of the main tourist towns—Ketchikan, Juneau, and Sitka—are dense with shops catering specifically to approximately half a million passengers who visit each year. Most of the plastic totem poles they sell are actually mass-produced in China and the dried smoked salmon is processed in smoker factories in Washington or Oregon. Little of the jewelry is produced locally or from local materials. There are even a few shops that specialize in jade jewelry, capitalizing on the notions of precious materials and distant indigeneity despite the South American origins of their products and design motifs.*

*The cruise ships tend to travel the larger north-south canals. Few visit the smaller, Native villages along the outer edges of the islands. Rather, the stock-in-trade of these tours is the scenic wilderness that lines the fjord walls of the canals. When traveling by plane to and from any of the smaller villages, or on the ferries that service them, one sees clearly the paths of the cruise ships. Their routes are marked by long stretches of old-growth forest on the mountainsides that face the canals through which the cruise ships pass. These same mountains are often clear-cut right up to their peaks on the sides opposite the scenic passages, leaving vast fields of stumps and the rotting remains of low-grade felled timber.*

*The canal side is a camera-ready forest facade, the other side a virtual lunar landscape.*

*The forest facade is not extended to the work-a-day ferry routes that service the Native villages on the outer coast. These ferries carry fewer tourists, although some still feature guides from the U.S. Forest Service who give brief presentations on the villages they pass. The guides stick to the sensational and superlative whenever possible: "the oldest Russian settlement outside Sitka," "the tallest totem pole in the world," "the hiding place of Kaatlean." The stories seem radically out of touch with what appears outside the windows. Some listeners on the ferries are sufficiently romantic to retain the nearly impossible illusion; others are not, though for them the parody does not dissolve, but rather seems to move to a higher level.*

*"Aren't any of the old houses left?" one asks. "No. There are in Juneau and Ketchikan," referring to the replica Native longhouses which are actually quite new, constructed for the cruise ship tourists. For many tourists, especially those who have never visited before, the villages no longer seem very accurate representations of themselves— sensibilities heightened by these same longhouses and totem poles mentioned by the guide, which are meant to look like a imagined Native village. The ferry traffic in the outside villages is too light and the villages too poor for this kind of tourist investment. The ferries are seldom in a village for more time than it takes to unload and reload the cars and trucks and a handful of people coming or going from one of the large towns.*

*Yet many of the ferry passengers leave feeling as though they have seen the "real" Alaska, for one indirect result of the façade—and it applies not just to the remaining trees, but also to the tourist longhouses and the entire physical landscape—is that it delineates a world that lies "behind" the natural orchestration, one imbued with potential for exposure.*

All landscapes are social landscapes; all relationships are social relationships. Standing, for example, in Hoonah and looking across the bay at the long swath of clear-cut land, village residents see not only the place where trees once stood, but the means—the social means—by which the trees were removed. This can mean many things, because timber harvesting is a complex process and an even more complex business. For some, the social life of timber consists of their own labor and the others they worked with, labor used for cutting or hauling or loading the timber; perhaps for building the road that allowed it to be trucked out; or time and effort spent caring for children while a spouse or grown child worked the woods across the bay. For others, the denuded hills recall the political relationships whereby it became expedient—perhaps important—to cut timber, and to cut that patch of timber in particular at that time. These relationships are colored by hope and disappointment that rests on particular people, and particular processes, promises broken or kept, hopes that were dashed and made again. They rest on simple relationships of need, and the needs of one's neighbors that made clear cutting one's own land make sense. This can be true even when what was cut shortened or narrowed one's own future. Others can look and see only the social and personal costs: the loss of former hunting, berrying, or fishing grounds, and the family times they made possible.

All these visions raise questions about the relationships people have with other people. After all, ownership of a tree is never an agreement between a person and a tree. It is an agreement between some people and some others about who can and who cannot cut down and use that tree. Other relationships may determine when the "owner" will choose to (or be forced to) cut it, while still other relationships will determine to whom that owner will be able to sell the resulting timber, and at what price.

PHOTO 3: *One of the new traditional houses built for tourist displays in one of the larger towns. These towns receive many visits from cruise ships, and the tourist business is an increasingly important part of the local economy.*

The outline of this present chapter is a somewhat historical, a narrative put in place as an effort to aid and assist the reader's understanding of how the present came to be the particular, peculiar way that it is. For people now living within the landscape it describes, however, the relationships discussed here are all present, all known and felt at the same time. By this I do not mean that people lack a knowledge of the order of events, for many know it quite well; rather, I mean simply that for people living in the villages today, the relationships discussed here are structured and interrelated in other, far more pressing ways than simply which came first, and which came last.

Native residents maintained a high degree of social and political autonomy during this time, as they had under the Russians previously. It was not until the late 1870s, when several salmon salteries were refitted to pack sockeye salmon in cans that Alaska began to command the attention of politicians in the United States. It was canned salmon that brought the future, and it was through the salmon industry that the region's Native peoples began to see hints of the colonialism that would follow. In the next six decades, cannery production and cannery politics would dominate the social landscape of Alaska, from the largest cities to the smallest villages. Without exaggeration, canned salmon not only determined the state of Alaska; it also made Alaska a State.

By 1900, sixteen canneries were operating in Southeast Alaska and by the second decade of the twentieth century Alaska would out-produce all of Canada and the rest of the mainland United States combined. This level of production quickly outstripped local labor, and canneries began to import large numbers of white and Asian workers from the West Coast to man the boats and packing lines of the area's many canneries. At its peak it was estimated that twenty thousand laborers spent the packing season in the territory, working in 116 canneries, and packing 7 million cases (over 300 million pounds) of canned salmon, mainly for export to the industrialized East Coast and England.[2]

Throughout the cannery period the majority of Southeast Alaska's Native population worked for the canneries, although, like the seasonal workers from San Francisco and Seattle, few worked year-round. Canning was limited to the summer months of July, August, and early September. During this time, the canning lines would run continuously from 6 a.m. to midnight, with maintenance and restocking done from midnight to six. Women worked inside the cannery on the "slime line" where fish were cleaned and arranged for processing, particularly after much of the rest of the processing was mechanized in the 1890s. Others might have worked filling the lid machine or on the patching table, where cans imperfectly filled by the machines were finished off by hand to make the required one-pound weight. The remaining

---

[2] See Daniel B. DeLoach, *The Salmon Canning Industry.* Corvallis: Oregon State College, 1939; Homer E. Gregory and Kathleen Barnes, *North Pacific Fisheries with Special Reference to Alaska Salmon.* New York: American Council, Institute of Pacific Relations, 1939.

inside work—loading fish into and out of the various bins, maintaining and operating the machines, and heading and gutting the fish—was all done by the "China gang," labor imported from China by way of San Francisco. After the Chinese Exclusion Acts of 1902, most of the Chinese laborers were replaced by Japanese, Mexicans, and later, primarily Filipinos. Despite the ethnic changes of the shore gang, the division of labor within the cannery remained the same.

Most of the Native men fished for the canneries in company-owned boats. A few held jobs maintaining the physical plant, but the majority of the management and engineering jobs were held by whites. All of the shoreside crew worked the same hours: twenty-hours a day. Management justified this by saying that the fish would not keep if left in bins, so the plant had to operate as long as it had fish. Yet the demands made on fishermen for a continuous supply were just as great, ensuring that there would always be so many fish that there would be no choice but to operate around the clock.

PHOTO 4: *One of the old canneries from the turn of the 19th century. The equipment in the foreground was, at one time, used to boil the canned fish.*

The rule of thumb for cannery superintendents was that the total annual "pack" had to exceed thirty thousand cases of salmon to create the acceptable profit margins for cannery owners. This was not always met, and canneries did frequently open and close, often reflecting insufficient packs in off years. Although just as often, plant closings represented the efforts of one cannery to eliminate local competition for fish by purchasing a competitor and closing it down. What's more, once the goal of thirty thousand cases was met, virtually everything produced thereafter would go toward profit. This was because the greatest proportion of the costs involved in producing canned salmon was not the fish, cans, fuel, or even labor, but rather the fixed costs of fish traps, canning machines, plant maintenance, and especially the transportation of all of these things to and from Alaska. These costs varied little with the size of the eventual pack. Once they were met, the profit on every case produced was nearly the sale price of that case. It was not uncommon for successful plants in areas with a good supply of fish to return two to three times their initial investment in a single season.

During summer months, while working at the cannery, many Native families would move out to the cannery location, even when canneries were built close to the villages in which these families spent the winter. In addition to building large houses for white managers and bunkhouses for the Asian workers, most canneries constructed a row of small houses—generally single-story houses measuring eight by twelve feet with mud floors—for use by Native families working for the cannery. Most houses were reserved for those families where the husband fished on a company boat and his wife worked on the line. Single men or women found housing by bunking with relatives in one of the small houses, meaning that three, four, or even five adults shared the small space, often with the children of the primary couple, and perhaps an older relative who could keep an eye on the youngest children and prepare meals for those working. However crowding was less of an issue than might be supposed. Almost all of the adults worked long hours.

Many of today's elders remember these houses, some of which still stand alongside now-collapsing canneries throughout the region, with surprising fondness. Often time these were the first houses in the region with electricity, supplied for the season by cannery generators. In addition, cannery camps were places where Western novelties like movies, new foods, music, and even alcohol, dancing, and gambling, were in ample supply.

At the close of the cannery season, Native families would purchase their entire winter supply of food staples and clothing from the cannery store. Very few stayed on at the cannery past the packing season. Rather, entire families would load their summer possessions and newly purchased sacks of potatoes, sugar, coffee, pilot bread, and rice aboard smaller boats and head back to their permanent homes, or to fishing camps on the outer islands.

For the latter, autumn meant another form of commercial fishing. This involved fishing the outer islands for fall salmon, usually coho and king salmon, to sell to the remaining salmon salteries located in the region. Trolling required families to move into new areas to fish on a regular and evolving basis, and subsistence patterns changed to meet these new circumstances. People would still "put up" some smoked fish for their own use, and pick berries or hunt deer. A lot of this work reflected past practices, but by the 1910s, old clan property lines were giving way to the pragmatics of a short subsistence season and the opportunism of migrating families who were combining subsistence with commercial work.

Most of these families did not return to their winter homes until late October and early November. This caused many children to miss the entire fall school session, and missionary teachers and some local leaders called for an end to the "camp" system on this basis. This early conflict between those families still dependent on subsistence resources and seasonal cash income (small-boat owners, crewmen, and anyone without year-round employment) and those able to remain in the village year-round (usually the large-boat owners with good cannery connections, store owners, or government employees) polarized many villages in ways that prefigure later and even current divisions.

\*\*\*

In the late nineteenth century, canneries tended to be built near existing villages, especially early on when clan property forms were still understood by whites and Natives to be at least potentially enforceable. This was particularly true in northern areas where several large Native villages represented a desirable labor force and a potentially intractable obstacle to cannery superintendents who would otherwise have invaded the area. In these areas, canneries remained particularly dependent on locally supplied fish for the first decade or two of their existence.

By the late 1880s, however, as canners became more assured that their own notions of property would be protected by an increasing U.S. military presence, they began to set up production near choice sockeye streams and to encourage nearby Native groups to relocate. At times the summer subsistence territory of a single clan would become the site of a new, multi-clan village when other groups began to forgo their own subsistence territories for labor at the cannery. Several Southeast Alaska Native villages—Kasaan, Hoonah, Kake, and

Klawock—remain at or near these sites today.

Other permanent villages were formed when Presbyterian missionaries encouraged, and in some cases forced, migration and consolidation of one or more groups. Villages like Haines and Metlakatla were formed as "model villages" with missionary and government support. Hydaburg was created in 1912 from three Haida villages: Klinkwan, Sukkwan, and Howkan.[3] In this case, local dependence on missionary service for schools, financial support, mail and steamer service that had built up over the previous three decades was used to coerce families from the small, dispersed villages that had been built nearly a hundred years before to hunt and trade sea otters to Yankee traders, to take up residence at a single new location. When this was done, none of the old-style communal houses that had characterized villages throughout the regions were built. Rather, under missionary instruction, only single-family, European-style houses were constructed along a single boardwalk—at one end of which was the church and mission home, at the other, the cannery.

Along with new villages and house styles came new forms of political organization. Continuing the example from Hydaburg: when the new village was built, it was suggested by the local mission pastor and the government paid school teacher that a city council be formed. Inter-clan cooperation had always been a concern in Tlingit and Haida villages throughout the region, and Howkan and Klinkwan had both had village-governing bodies drawn from the leaders of the resident clans. In Hydaburg, however, the idea of a village-wide election for a village council was a relatively new idea. Missionary demands that the council business be carried on in English further alienated clan heads. In the end, the elders from the three communities decided to let the younger men lead the council. According to anthropologist Daniel Vaughan:

> When the annual election came up, the first group of [clan] leaders, sensitive to criticisms of their traditional meeting style, asked voters to elect younger men to office. The next group of councilmen were people of the age to have attended school in either Klinkwan or Howkan schools. The Haida lay-preacher [Sam Davis] was elected mayor. This council conducted town meetings in the "new way," bearing some semblance to parliamentary procedure… This new council also requested that all business of the town be transacted in English (*ibid*, 135-6)

---

[3] James Daniel Vaughan, "Toward a New and Better Life: Two Hundred Years of Alaskan Haida Culture Change." PhD dissertation, University of Washington, 1985.

In other villages, traditional clan elders continued to hold sway in the selection and function of new councils. Yet in the cannery-dependent villages, outside influences and internal divisions made older, clan-based councils relatively ineffective, and these too soon passed away.

The wider social changes came rapidly. By the 1910s virtually all of the region's villages were company towns for almost half of each year, and individuals with close ties to the canneries were able to exercise informal power over others in the village. The cannery owners themselves also held considerable power over the fates of these villages. Decisions not to open a particular packinghouse in a particular year could cause families to move away, diminishing the impact of local leaders without any obvious change in formal organization. This was the case in places like Ketchikan, where thorough immersion in the cash economy undercut the authority of local leadership without replacing it with any novel body or structure.

In other areas, new sorts of entities such as school boards held sway and gradually replaced other forms of organized politics. In Kake, the local school board was nearly able to eliminate the "camp" system of autumn fishing and subsistence production by issuing fines of twenty-five dollars for each child taken out of school. Where households had once moved together from one remote area to the next while trolling for fall salmon for the remaining salteries and gathering subsistence foods along the way, the requirement that all children attend for the entire school year meant that whole patterns of life would have to be abandoned. The steep fines effectively confined most families to permanent residence in the village by the late 1920s. After this only men went away to the camps, and their time there became less frequent and less lengthy. Smokehouses were built in Kake for the first time during this period as well, much to the dismay of many older villagers who found the practice of processing fish in the village, in the words of one resident, "unsanitary."

These changes put in place new versions of social difference that, in one form or another, would dominate the next 100 years. The division of Native villages into those whose means for survival was linked closely to the land, versus those whose livelihood derived from connections to the world beyond the village, emerged early and stayed long. Or perhaps the lines were not so clear, even early on. After all, families out in the camps were still "fall fishing" for export, though the process allowed them to put up foods for their own use at the same time. Connection with, and dependence on, an outside economy applied to both those who moved full time to the cannery towns and those who merely circled around them. Still, there was a difference—if only in the fact that those who resisted full time settlement still maintained some level of control over their own livelihood, and some measure of insulation from the ups and downs of commodity production for a world market.

Meanwhile, where Native-run village councils were fighting a different kind of battle for autonomy, with some able to win formal political power in the face of cannery resistance—usually through extremely careful and persistent use of legislation meant for white colonists in larger towns. Thus by the 1920s, a number of Native villages were able to gain official territorial status as incorporated towns, and with that the right to tax business within their boundaries. In their turn, canneries were able to circumvent this authority by invoking jurisdictional conflicts between the territorial administration and federal governments.

This was the case in Klawock. In the early decades of the twentieth century, the village council had been able to win municipal incorporation under early territorial laws. This allowed them to tax the local cannery, one of the first in the region, which lay within the municipality. This small outfit had grown considerably in the intervening three decades, becoming a large outfit owned by a California-based firm. Despite its size, in response to incorporation the cannery simply abandoned its buildings and moved across the harbor to an area outside the municipal boundaries but within 200 yards of the original location, and thus within rowing distance for the village laborers. Subsequent efforts by the community to expand the municipal boundaries were blocked by the federal government, which had in the decade before claimed almost the entire Southeast Alaska archipelago as a national forest. In the end, the cannery paid no taxes and the village remained dependent on missionary support to keep a school open year-round.

\*\*\*

Permanent village locations and the creation of a regional Native high school in the 1910s encouraged another novel sort of political body that *did* gain region-wide influence for Natives. The Alaska Native Brotherhood (ANB), formed in Sitka early in the cannery period, was founded by several missionary-educated Tlingit and Tsimshian Natives. Their original intentions are unclear, though fraternal organizations were popular throughout the United States at the time and no doubt had been encourage by missionaries for their "civilizing" potential.

Very soon after its founding, however, the ANB became active politically, mainly under the direction of William Paul, a Native lawyer from Wrangell whose mother had been an early Christian convert and educator. With the ANB's financial backing, Paul litigated a number of important cases concerning Native rights. One of them gained Southeast Natives the right to vote several years before Native Americans in the lower forty-eight states were granted that right by Congress. Another gave Natives the right to send their children to territorial public schools, putting an end to the "two school" system in Alaska. By the late 1930s the ANB was active in labor politics as well.

Paul's left leanings had led him in this direction early on, and it is likely that the ANB was pulled along with him rather than vice versa. Under his direction, by 1940 the ANB had won the right to be the collective bargaining representative for many of the cannery workers and most of the fishermen in Southeast Alaska. At this time the ANB began to offer "associate status" to anyone who wished to join, and soon there were many more non-Native associate members than there were Alaska Natives. Throughout, however, Paul and a central core of longtime members remained in control of the organization.[4]

The ANB, as representative of the fishing union, took as its main goal the outlawing of fish traps owned and operated by canneries. These traps were placed near stream mouths and convenient pinch points (e.g., where schools of fish must pass through a narrow area between islands) in the same locations by the same canneries, year after year. By the 1930s, more fish were caught in traps than by boats. For Native fishing labor, traps were a visible threat as the traps required few operators and functioned continuously once set up. The ANB, under Paul, called for the outlawing of traps altogether; the cannery owners resisted, and despite the fact that the issue was taken up repeatedly by U.S. Congressional committees over several decades, no injunction was ever issued. Eventually the fish-trap issue would tip the balance of local opinion in favor of statehood in Alaska, and a fish-trap injunction was the first law passed by the newly formed Alaska State Senate. But this was not until 1960, after almost thirty years of steady advocacy.

Long before this, the declining importance of fishing to cannery operations

4 Philip Drucker, (MS) Field notes from Southeast Alaska dated 1957, "Interviews with William Paul and others on the Alaska Native Brotherhood and its early formation" Juneau: Alaska State Historical Library. Philip Drucker, *The Native Brotherhoods: Modern Intertribal Organizations of the Northwest Coast.* Bureau of American Ethnology Bulletin 168. Washington DC: Bureau of American Ethnology, 1958.

was matched by the declining power of the ANB in labor arbitration. The ANB had never made advocacy for shore-side workers a priority in their negotiations, despite the prominent role Native women played in this work. Beginning in the 20s, Seattle-based unions had been organized among the Filipino crews, often affiliated with national and prominent West Coast unions. When fishing declined, as traps became more numerous and the price of fish continued to fall, the ANB was left without a role in the regional economy, and thus without a place in the region's politics. By the late 1940s, the ANB was out of the labor-organizing business, outmaneuvered by Seattle-based unions and compromised by internal disputes.

***

The political gap left by the decline of the ANB did not last long, however, though this time the impetus to organization did not arise locally. In 1936 Congress extended the Indian Reorganization Act to Alaska, attempting here, as elsewhere, to create more uniform means through which to monitor and transform Native communities in the United States.

The IRA offered several routes for political organization, and only a few Southeast Alaska communities chose to reform, or re-create, tribal councils along the lines laid out by the IRA Act. Instead, most villages had by the 1940s already adopted village or city councils in parallel to non-Native towns in the Territory. In these places the adoption of a tribal council system was seen as duplicating existing town and village councils, while endangering the equal footing with their non-Native neighbors that Native communities had earned under Paul and the ANB.

Instead, most Southeast communities favored the formation of economic or cooperative associations as vehicles to secure loans and coordinate BIA commercial and financial interaction. The means for this process, and money to support it, were part of the IRA legislation, and were heavily favored by the Juneau Area office of the Bureau of Indian Affairs. So by 1950, IRA cooperative associations existed in Hydaburg and Klawock, and IRA councils with business charters were formed in Kake and Angoon. All four used this status as means to purchase canneries in their respective communities. The time seemed right. Competition had made the canneries more affordable, and age had made them salable—both good and bad news for the communities who bought them. Mixed blessing aside, many Natives felt that at last they were in charge of the economic engines of their own communities. Few, either in the communities or among their bureaucratic sponsors recognized that this control came at a time when these engines were sputtering to their eventual demise.

Proof was not long in coming. Following local purchase, none of these ventures was financially successful, and by 1960 they had accumulated nearly $5 million in debt, nearly one quarter of the total BIA cooperative debt for American Indian communities across the entire United States. The fishing industry in Southeast Alaska had suffered a considerable downturn throughout the period following World War II, with smaller catches, fewer fish landings, diminished production, and demand for canned salmon decreasing worldwide. Despite this, the BIA's Juneau Area Office had encouraged the cooperative associations and IRA councils to keep them running, regardless of whether they made or lost money. Their motives, as well as those of the various councils were complex. No doubt many in the BIA saw the canneries as key elements in their effort to complete the transformation of Southeast Native villages to a full-scale wage economy. These goals were at once lofty and self-serving. Running the cannery meant a modern economy where the electricity in most villages need not be turned off at the end of the cannery season, or where individuals didn't have to leave villages seasonally for wage or subsistence work as far away as Washington State or California. It also meant personal gain for well-placed Natives in the BIA bureaucracy who stood to benefit from boat loans and management jobs at the canneries themselves. In either case, however, the Juneau Area Office went to great lengths to keep the canneries in operation, including the gradual assumption of total control of all four Native-owned cannery operations.

In 1960, with the single largest economic asset in the villages fully under BIA control, Native political power in the region reached a nadir. Cooperative associations formed in the villages in the early 1940s under the IRA were largely defunct. The ANB was out of the labor-organizing business, and household economies were sliding as well—for as statehood approached, nonlocal cannery owners closed up operations in anticipation of the coming fish-trap ban, the final nail in the canning industry coffin. Fishing had been declining for two decades, and despite the brief boom that followed statehood and the fish-trap ban, the market for canned salmon was shrinking—further lowering the price of fish. During this time many Native families left the smaller villages that had been formed nearly 80 years earlier, some for the larger towns in Southeast Alaska, like Sitka, Ketchikan, or Juneau, and others for faraway Anchorage or Seattle. Hoonah showed a decline in population by one-third in the late 1940s and 1950s. In Klawock, it was nearly half.

PHOTO 5: *Older houses along the main street of Hydaburg. The state of local housing by the mid-1970s had reach crisis proportions.*

The exodus threatened the survival of many villages, jeopardizing such population-dependent programs as school lunches and public utilities services, as well as the survival of those few small shops and suppliers found in every village. Ironically, the exodus did little to combat the housing shortage that characterizes most villages even today. This had begun with the lack of new housing during the war, and in the economic decline that followed. As families left the communities, housing built during the early cannery period quickly deteriorated, making it difficult for families to return if and when they found life outside the village wanting. For most, return to the village was impossible until the regional housing authority began construction in the mid-1970s.

The answer to this decline was far from obvious, and few at the time would have placed much hope in its speedy accomplishment. Still, for many, the answer lay around every village in the region: land claim.

The issue was not new. Land claims had originally been advanced by the ANB at a regional convention in 1929, and in just about every year that followed. The issue was highly contentious, however, with some groups advocating a cash settlement in return for settling a lawsuit, and others hoping for a land settlement or reservation in the form of those in lower 48 in exchange for a cessation of claims throughout the rest of the region. Some local leaders, such as William Paul, felt that the land claims should be advanced by local clans and clan leaders—the aboriginal titleholders according to many historic sources—rather than villages.[5] The BIA preferred the village-based claims approach, as did the majority of the post-Paul ANB leadership. As a result of these divisions and the general reticence of the U.S. federal government to see the problem of Indian Country extended to Alaska, no progress was made in advancing a single set of claims for several decades.

Hydaburg, partly as a result of its distinct tribal status—most Hydaburg residents are Haidas, while virtually the entire remainder of the region is Tlingit—followed a BIA initiative to support "model villages" and opted for reservation status in the late 1930s. The land swap arranged by Secretary of the Interior Harold Ickes included the surrender of over 1 million acres on Prince of Wales and neighboring Islands by the Haida for a 101,000-acre reservation in and around Hydaburg. Much of the logic of the swap rested on ownership rights of the water that bordered the specified reservation lands, giving the Haida rights to three successful but privately owned fish traps to supply their own struggling cannery. But pressure from the fish-trap owners caused the reservation agreement to be overturned in a court decision less than a year after the agreement.

Shortly after the land claims issue was introduced, it created such dissension within the ANB leadership that it had nearly paralyzed the institution. At the time the ANB was at the height of its union power, and the paralysis threatened this success. As a result, in 1939, discussion of land claims was banned from the floor at ANB meetings and a separate body was formed to pursue the claims. The new group was known as the Tlingit and Haida Central Council. When formed it was composed of many of the same individuals as the ANB Executive Council, although the groups diverged over the next several years.

The land suit was finally brought to court by the T&H Central Council in 1957, and in 1959 it was decided in favor of Southeast Natives. The cash award, however, was postponed through a series of negotiations between the Justice Department and the BIA. The eventual award was quite small—$7.2 million for the entire Southeast Alaska panhandle—supposedly the value of the land assets lost to the federal government through the legislative creation of the Tongass National Forest in the first decade of the century. This was drastically

---

[5] Curry-Weissbrodt Papers. (MS) Correspondence and collected documents of the lawyers representing the Central Council of the Tlingit and Haida. Microfilm. Juneau: Alaska State Historical Library. *Also* Central Council of the Tlingit and Haida Indian Tribes of Alaska (CCTH), "Historical Profile of the Central Council, Tlingit and Haida Indian Tribes of Alaska." Juneau: CCTH, 1992.

undervalued by nearly all accounts, and despite the fact that the award was not made until 1968, it included no interest or adjustment for inflation.

The small payout only exaggerated other problems. Prior to the award's reception, there was little agreement on its disbursement. In the end the leaders of the Tlingit and Haida Central Council decided to retain the entire award amount and use the money to start a centralized tribal administration. This body would act as a tribal representative to the federal government/BIA and apply for a self-governance relationship within the federal bureaucracy. This decision was bitterly disputed by the ANB, which had always considered itself the central representative of the Southeast Alaska Natives, a position that many saw as being usurped by the Central Council. Lawsuits and appeals followed, but eventually the ANB lost in its bid for tribal recognition, and the Tlingit and Haida Central Council (or "T&H" as it has come to be called) emerged as the largest Native political power in the region, particularly in relation to the federal government and federal Indian programs.

Following recognition in the early 1970s, T&H created two separate branches of its own organization: the Tlingit and Haida Regional Housing Authority and the Tlingit and Haida Regional Power Authority. The former was designed to act as a subcontractor to the Central Council, building low-cost, HUD-sponsored housing in Native villages throughout the region. This was and is generally considered a success, and T&H houses now make up perhaps half of the total available village housing in all Native communities in the region. Yet even this was far from simple. The majority of the houses built by T&H are still owned by the Housing Authority, and residents pay rent based on their annual income. After making consistent rent payments for twenty years, residents are supposed to gain title to a house. This, however, seldom happens. Extensions on the payments are added each time the Housing Authority comes in to renovate the houses, and most houses are so shoddily constructed that renovation is a near-constant need.

For families living in these houses, the added repairs mean additional years of payments before they receive title. Beyond this, an unbroken residency of twenty years is rare for families anywhere in Alaska (and perhaps anywhere in the United States), especially in areas with highly volatile economies; and each time a family leaves, the status of past payment lapses. If they move back to the village, they must begin the twenty-year effort anew. More costly, perhaps, is the fact that for those who leave, past payments that might have gained equity in any other sort of ownership system necessarily revert back to that status of "rent" and are, in effect, unrecoverable in any form.

The Tlingit and Haida Power Authority now produces the electrical power in most villages through diesel generator plants built in the late 1970s. Not surprisingly, most of the T&H houses are heated with "electric heat." This too has been viewed as a success, with steady utilities now a given in all the communities served by the Central Council, and T&H now a fixture in many elements of village life throughout Native Southeast Alaska.

PHOTO 6: *The new houses built by the Tlingit and Haida Housing Authority. These houses, and hundreds like them, have helped alleviate the housing shortage, and increased the role of the tribal body in the lives of most Native residents of Southeast Alaska.*

Here too, controversy followed. T&H's combined political, housing, and electrical control became an issue for villages seeking some independence from the regional body. In the early 1970s, when village economies had reached what must be considered the low point of the last fifty or perhaps even 100 years, most village IRA councils and cooperative associations delegated what little tribal political authority they retained after the land claims process to the Central Council. When acting on behalf of most of the region, T&H's role in many federal programs was enhanced, and it was as such that the creation of the Housing and Power Authorities was possible. As the delegate of largely defunct cooperatives and IRA associations formed in the 1930s and 40s, T&H could claim a larger client-base in its assertions for federal support. In return, it maintained the official tribal roles and managed the registration process.

However, by the mid- and late-1980s a new generation of leaders had emerged in most villages, and an entirely new economic landscape had been created through the Alaska Native Claims Settlement Act, or ANCSA (discussed in Chapter 3). These leaders sought some independence from T&H, which by then had grown into a large institutionalized bureaucracy. For T&H, the loss of delegated authority over local tribal communities would mean a significant loss of clout in their relation with the federal government, and perhaps their dissolution as a centralized political body altogether. Movements in Hoonah, Yakutat, Hydaburg, Klawock, and Craig in the 1980s and 1990s, as well as the early exclusion of Kake, Ketchikan, and Sitka from T&H jurisdiction, made a gradual dissolution of the tribal administration a real possibility.

The result, many village residents suspect, has been a considerable amount of foot-dragging on T&H's part in promoting village self-government. Others have cited stronger (albeit entirely circumstantial) evidence of collusion between branches of T&H to punish those who seek some measure of village independence. More compliant tribal members seem to receive faster repairs or modernizations on their houses, according to some residents. Self-governance advocates, on the other hand, say that they wait far longer to get housing and repairs in the houses they eventually receive. Regardless of whether or not this is true, this perception is a basic political dynamic in many villages.

All in all, it remains clear that the Central Council is the paramount political entity in most tribal-federal relations for Southeast Alaska Natives, with the remnants of local tribal councils and cooperative associations, including the largely defunct ANB, mostly sidelined in the process. Its practical role in providing heat, electrical power, and housing to many villages has underwritten the retention of its own political power. At present, "city" governments formed through legal channels available to all communities (Native and non-Native) via the constitution of the State of Alaska handle most of the local administration, with budgets going primarily to supporting local public schools and minimal public services, such as water and trash pickup. Tribal business is carried on through T&H, including support of General Assistance Relief (the strictly Indian arm of the welfare system), the Housing and Power Authorities, and through T&H's role in seeking and receiving broader federal assistance for community development. Without exaggeration, T&H controls most of the money through which village economic and social transformation can and does take place.

\*\*\*

When Alaska achieved statehood in 1959, its dominant industry—particularly in terms of employment and individual or family (rather than corporate) income—was fishing. Although logging accounted for an important source of jobs, it lacked fishing's broad political base in the region. Furthermore, lumber had been stymied in its attempt to join the world market by the extreme distance of Alaska to the major timber processing industry in Washington State. These conditions would last three more decades, leaving fishing as the largest, and only hope for the majority of Alaska residents, Native and non-Native.

At the time of the debate about statehood, the fish-trap issue had come to be understood as local fishermen's opposition to "outside" cannery interests. In reality the sides were never quite so clear. Many of the boats that fished in Alaska, then as now, came seasonally from Seattle or Bellingham in Washington State. Likewise, by the 1960s many canneries were owned by people who lived in Alaska, and sometimes lived in the same villages in which their canneries were located. Even so, demographics and political momentum were tilted in favor of fishermen, and the first law passed by the newly elected State legislature was a total ban on fish traps. Within a year all of the traps were gone, and in effect so was the chance of the canning industry's survival. As canneries were forced to meet boat owners' demands for higher fish prices, the cost of canning salmon increased and its place on the dinner tables of European and East Coast working-class families declined.

Compounding the difficulties of an already challenged industry, the trap ban did not stem the decrease of salmon stocks. Instead, the brief boom for boats that followed the ban invited a renewed capitalization of the fleets, with larger versions of the Alaskan "limit seiner" catching even greater amounts of fish. Between 1960 and 1971, boat landings rose to three or four times their pre-ban level, then fell to well below half their peak.[6] By the mid-1970s, overcapitalization and decimated stocks were so apparent that the Alaska legislature was pressed to limit fisheries throughout the state.

---

[6] George W. Rogers, Richard F. Listowski, and Judith Brakel, "Final report: A Study of the socio-economic impact of changes in the harvesting labor force in the Alaska salmon fishery." Institute of Social and Economic Research, University of Alaska-Anchorage, 1972. *Also* Stephen Langdon, "Transfer patterns in Alaskan limited entry fisheries" Final report for the Limited Entry Study Group of the Alaska State Legislature, 1980. Data cited here is from tables 6, 8, and 9, pp. 20-29.

The means adopted was a limited-entry licensing system, enacted in Alaska in 1974-75. A limited number of permits were issued to individuals for participation in a particular fishery. Seiners had to have a seine permit, trawlers had to have a trolling permit, and so forth. An individual could hold licenses in more than one fishery (trolling, gill netting, purse seining, long-lining), but no more than one license in any single fishery. The principle behind the strategy was to fix the fishing effort by capping the number of individuals and boats pursuing various, distinct fish stocks. These permits being limited in number had two critical economic impacts on fishing families and villages. The first was to depress the value of seine boats (still the most important element of the fleet in Southeast Alaska), especially those sold without a license, for without a license the boat was essentially unusable. The second was to create a commodity market in licenses. As a commodity, the right to fish and make a living in fishing became alienable and could be lost through sale; something Southeast Alaska residents had never known before.

With the depressed value of seine boats, Native fishermen suffered a setback in their single most accumulated item of capital. This, coupled with the alienability of the license, led to a rapid decline in the number of limited-entry permits held by village residents. Between 1975, the first year of the program, and 1979, the year of the first comprehensive study, Southeast Alaska residents lost one in four of their fishing licenses, and nonresidents gained almost as many. Three-quarters of those that were lost were transferred through sale or purchase, and half of these acquisitions were financed, either by a bank, the original owner, a processor, or the state loan program. In short, most of those buying permits were doing so with borrowed capital.

In his report at the time, anthropologist Steve Langdon noted that the purse seine permits required the most financing because they remained the most expensive, averaging more than $50,000 in 1978. Financing was further complicated by the fact that the limited-entry law was unclear as to whether permits themselves could be used as collateral for loans. Banks often required collateral in the form of boats and nets or real estate, while fish processors often did not require collateral of any kind. On the other hand, those fishermen who became indebted to processors accepted radically limited marketing options, in effect becoming clients of the fish buyer who held the note on the license. For purse seiners, the level of "processor" financing was the highest, with fish buyers financing one of every five transfers. In plain terms this meant lower prices and, with lower prices, a more tenuous place in the fishery.

In Southeast Native villages, few fishermen held the necessary non-fishing collateral to obtain a bank loan. The cycle of outmigration in the villages further aggravated these trends. Throughout the 1960s property values had declined directly in proportion to the limited job opportunities available to residents, further depressing house values and thus the ability of those remaining in the villages to obtain financing for boats or permits. At the same time, the brief fishing boom and the statewide oil boom in the 60s and early 70s had the opposite effect in the larger, predominantly non-Native towns. There, for most of the 1970s, property values rose and financing for corporate ventures increased. This meant that even for those licenses that were sold or transferred within the region, most moved from Native villages to the larger towns of Ketchikan, Sitka, Wrangell, or Petersburg, and as such, from Natives to non-Natives.

In the first three years of the limited-entry permit system rural residents, statewide, lost one out of five of those permits originally issued in 1975. Southeast Alaska took an extremely hard hit, with well over half of the purse seine permits in non-village residents' hands within three years after enactment of the law. This trend continues. By the late 1990s there were few purse seiners left in most Native villages. A few still fished from Hoonah, one or two from Klawock, but none from Hydaburg or Kake. Those few that remain in Hoonah supported the salmon and salmon roe (fish egg) export trade to Japan. Indeed, by the late 1980s about half of all U.S. salmon production in Alaska was exported to Japan, and while Alaska continues to produce about 40 percent of the world's salmon, those species most available in the Southeast are favored mainly for their roe. It is not uncommon to see Southeast Alaska processors disposing of thousands of pounds of salmon carcasses that have been stripped of their eggs, the actual meat of the fish no longer being sufficiently valuable to justify processing. The vulnerability of an industry with a single market has been felt recently by several sharp depressions in fish and fish product prices that have little to do with the Alaskan supply and are caused mainly by recent competition from Chile and Russia.[7]

The decline of commercial fishing in most villages marked a deterioration in two elements of local sociopolitical organization, one informal and the other formal. "Family boats"—those fishing operations whose owners are captains and who employ members of their own families as crew—were once the

---

[7] G. Knapp, P. Peyton, and C. Weiss, "The Japanese Salmon Market: An Introduction for Alaskans." Juneau: Alaska Department of Commerce and Economic Development, Division of Economic Development, 1993.

predominant arrangement among Native-owned purse seiners. The loss of a permit in such circumstances meant not only the loss of jobs, but the likely dissolution of a form of local corporateness that had been around since the early cannery days.

At the formal level, village IRA councils and cooperative associations, most of which had been set up in the 1940s as vehicles for obtaining boat loans for their members, found themselves bankrupt by their holdings of boats whose value diminished significantly once a permit was sold. Since that time, most councils have quietly arranged the sale of boats for which they hold the note, often at a significant loss on the original loan, with the tacit agreement of the BIA's Juneau Area Office. Without boat loans, the raison d'être for most cooperative councils has diminished and even disappeared, and without a local lending agency, the possibility of purchasing of a working purse seiner and permit by any village resident is now a distant memory.

\*\*\*

Many of the political entities discussed thus far still operate with limited authority or scope in most villages. ANB halls are found in most villages, though these have fallen into disrepair in many places because of a lack of dues-paying members. Young people no longer join the ANB as a means of public recognition. Some local chapters have turned to bingo to help finance local activities and to maintain the hall itself. In some villages the ANB hall still serves as the site of most village-wide functions: wedding receptions, retirement parties, "payoff parties,"[8] or dance group celebrations. At these events, however, ANB members seldom play a prominent role based on their status as such. In other villages, larger functions are held in the school gymnasium, marking a shift in the orientation of the village from the ANB to the state-financed school.

The IRA councils and related cooperative associations have, in all but four villages, turned over most of their relationship with the federal government to the Tlingit and Haida Central Council. Some still meet, but their authority

---

[8] This is the term used throughout much of the region for what were called "potlatches" in the anthropological literature. In this case, the name comes from the fact that some people in the community will take responsibility for the funeral and burial of a deceased family member. The purpose of the party is to reciprocate for this. In some villages, where moieties are still recognized, one "side" is paid off by the other side. For the most part, though, these are entirely family affairs, in the sense of "family" discussed in Chapter 4.

within the villages has attenuated. What relevance they retained after the failure of the canneries was lost through the limited-entry system, which left most bankrupt. Very recently, some have tried to gain back some of the responsibilities (and subsequent authority) given over to T&H, which has in turn resisted these efforts; at present, no new village councils or associations have managed to achieve any formal recognition by the federal government.

The Tlingit and Haida Central Council continues to be the main regional Native power. This has come through the associated Housing and Power Authorities and their role as intermediaries to the federal government. Grants and programs for economic development, general assistance, emergency relief, and a host of miscellaneous federal programs like Small Business Administration loans have allowed T&H to maintain a hold over dependent villages—which is, ironically, increased by the escalating dependency of most villages on federal programs. By taking a percentage of the monies gained through all of the programs, the Central Council pays for a fairly large administrative staff. These jobs are used to establish alliances with important families (the topic of Chapter 4). Village representatives to T&H and City administrations under the Alaska Constitution remain important as a source of employment in all villages, and here the wheels of patronage turn most predictably.

Administration budgets for most town and village governments are relatively stable and most income is earmarked for specific fixed costs (e.g., schools, past village debt, ongoing programs such as building roads or dumps, and, of course, village administration), the allocation of which is often overseen by the either the State government or T&H. Little of any village's budget is left for discretionary spending, and what little there is, is mostly reserved for capital outlays—garbage trucks and dock or town oil tank repair, for example. Mayors and village administrators have few options and derive very little power through the control of local spending. Rather, most of their sway is gained through their ability to influence hiring in their administration—police or village public safety officers, garbage collectors, local construction and maintenance staff, clerical workers, town inspectors—and in state- and federally-sponsored programs such as public schools or Head Start. With full-time, benefit-guaranteed employment scarce in every village, these jobs are a priority for everyone. For this reason, mayoral races in some villages will be quite heated, despite the fact that the village administration has little real power to set policy or exert authority over village life in any structurally significant way.

At different times, each of the political entities introduced in this chapter—

missionary school boards, town councils, IRA councils and cooperative associations, city governments, the ANB and ANS, and the Tlingit and Haida Central Council—has seen moments of considerable local influence. The gradual erosion of this influence has usually followed as the political economy once again shifted in a new direction. The ebb and flow of capital in what remains a resource-rich area has fostered and undermined several markedly different forms of political and social organization. Many of these still exist in a formal sense, though at present most of the power lies with the ANCSA boards of directors, to which we will turn presently.

Underlying this ebb and flow, and the changing political forms it created, lies a more hidden story of changing lives and livelihoods, layers of "traditional" social orders repeated reconfigured by outside interests while survival strategies for the most marginalized by those changes go largely un-noticed. This caused not only resentment by those dependent upon a cohesive continuous structure but in many ways completely cut away the system by which they were tied to the village. Viewed in this light, the popularity of a new order introduced by the Evangelical churches that followed all of these changes might be seen not so much as "rejectionist" but more as an attempt to regain what many in the village believed had been unjustly lost. And without a doubt, the greatest of those losses, was ANCSA.

CHAPTER 3

# The Alaska Native Claims Settlement Act

*Norman is a well-known carver from a Tlingit village at the base of the panhandle. He works silver as well as carves wooden hats and masks, in traditional styles. Most of his work is sold locally, mainly within his village. He is a son in one of the largest and most powerful families in one of the larger Native villages in the region, and just about everyone in the village on speaking terms with his family wears some piece of jewelry he has made. He also attends the biannual cultural gathering of Southeast Alaska Natives—called Celebration—that is held in the state capital, sponsored by the ANCSA regional corporation Sealaska. This year, once again, he has a table in the hall set aside for Native craftsmen to display and sell their work.*

*Because of the unusual venue, Norman has brought with him a smattering of work to suit many audiences—white and Indian tourists, dance group members, and serious collectors. One mask is priced at seven hundred dollars, which would pay for his entire trip, though he doubts it will sell.*

*Cruise ship tourists pour through the hall, but often the prices surprise them. They settle for a T-shirt or a machine-cut silver bracelet stamped out in a shop in Seattle, or maybe Korea: the kind they sell at the airport. Norman isn't jealous. "I'd prefer they got what they were looking for, rather than buy something of mine just to buy it." Other people, mostly*

*Natives, pass through the hall. Many of them are dancers from one of the region's village-based dance groups. There is, in fact, at least one dance group in almost every village these days, and some villages have more than one. They sing traditional songs and perform traditional dances. They also make and buy dancing regalia, which consists of button blankets (blue and red felt blankets embroidered with pearl-colored buttons in the shapes of traditional animal motifs), carved and woven hats, armbands, carved knives, necklaces, and other jewelry. The dancers tend to make some of their regalia, especially the blankets, and buy other items from artists like Norman. On his table he has several spruce-root and carved cedar hats, and rattles inlaid with mother-of-pearl that are carved in traditional animal shapes. These he hopes will interest the dancers. All are made in the style of older pieces, which is something virtually all dancers consider a crucial element of their regalia.*

*As we stand talking, a hat catches the attention of a passerby. Though Native, he is not dressed in dancing regalia as many of the others are. He holds up the hat and looks at the design. It's a carved hat, cut entirely from a single piece of red cedar. The shape is simple— a "Chinaman's hat" Norman calls it—narrow and almost pointed at the peak, flaring out at the sides. On the front is painted a raven design in typical Northwest Coast fashion, in two dimensions with selected anatomical features reduced to broad, symmetrical lines and placed in semi-symmetrical fashion.*

*"You stole this design," the man charges, quite unexpectedly. "You can't use this. It's not yours. It's my clan's."*

*Norman sits quietly. He is much older than the visitor; already a large man, he swells somewhat. But he doesn't say anything. The man continues to accuse: "This raven is ours, our rights." His companion, a woman in her mid-forties, appears excited but does not join in. The visitor looks at the price tag: $400. He puts it down. "You can't sell this. It's intellectual property of our clan."*

*The last term startles me, though not because it is unfamiliar. The cultural heritage wing of Sealaska, the regional Native corporation has been pursuing intellectual property rights for Native designs and design styles for the past two years. This is a new twist, however, for the main purpose in pursuing these laws has been to keep non-Indians from copying and mass-producing classical work for the "airport art" market favored by the cruise ship visitors. A dispute between Natives is different, and not just because it will never be fought out in court.*

*After the man leaves, Norman takes the hat off the table. When I ask him where the design came from, he tells me he copied it from a book. "That's the way everybody does it," he explains. "All of the old pieces are in museums. It's the only way to see if you're doing it right."*

Since its inception in 1971, the Alaska Native Claim Settlement Act has been the axis around which virtually all Alaska Native politics have turned. It was, and is, the largest Native land settlement in the history of the United States. Despite its size, however, the impact of ANCSA on ordinary folks in the villages throughout the Southeast might have been far less. Meant to incorporate dispersed communities with declining economies into the global system of trade and commerce, its initial impact was small. What ANCSA did do, from the very beginning, was change what it meant to be Indian or Native in Alaska. Some of this change was for the better, some quite clearly for the worse.

ANCSA is a law—not a treaty—enacted by the U.S. Congress to settle and extinguish all of the outstanding land claims of Alaska Natives. It involved a cash payment to Alaska Natives of over $980 million and the retention by them of 40 million acres of land, with all of the remaining land in the state of Alaska becoming the property of the federal government and the state itself. Yet unlike past agreements and treaties, the vehicle for these changes were not the tribes, communities, clans or organizations making the claims. Rather, ANCSA sought—in ways that presaged the mass privatization of government functions that would dominate the Reagan years of the 1980s—to "fix" the land claims issue in Alaska through a corporate format, creating out of these villages and organizations a series of for-profit corporations.

Prior to the 1960s, the federal government had shown little initiative in examining or settling Native claims in Alaska. As discussed above, Southeast Natives had advocated for, and eventually sued and won, a land settlement with the federal government in return for lands taken to create the Tongass National Forest, which to this day makes up much region. This process took decades, however and marked the only place in Alaska where resources warranted entering into the messy field of indigenous land rights, in the view of the federal government. This changed, however, when large reserves of crude oil were discovered in Prudhoe Bay on Alaska's North Slope. The discovery, coupled with rising oil prices on the world market, prompted intense corporate pressure for a clarification of claims; pressure heightened by a decision of progressive Secretary of the Interior Stewart Udall that held up development of these oil fields until claims were addressed statewide.

\*\*\*

ANCSA is unique in U.S.-Native relations. It was passed shortly after the end of the "termination" period, and while it bears the imprint of the desires that had underlain termination efforts, it nevertheless pursued this strategy through novel forms of Native recognition. The legislation was framed by three tenets: (1) Congress' unwillingness to create new government-to-government relations or to recognize new "Indian territory" in Alaska; (2) its need to quickly and finally resolve outstanding land disputes then slowing the development of crude oil resources on the North Slope; and (3) its desire for a way out of costly social welfare programs for primarily Native rural Alaska.

To accomplish these goals, Congress settled all outstanding Native claims in Alaska by creating a series of for-profit, quasi-publicly held corporations whose stockholders would initially be composed entirely of Alaska Natives, and then awarding these companies the land and cash compensation sought by Native advocacy groups. In this way a "village corporation" was created in most villages with primarily Native populations in the state, and shares were distributed to current and former Native residents of each community, as well as to the descendants of former residents. Each of these corporations was awarded a portion of the initial cash settlement and a significant parcel of land that was held, like all corporate holdings in the United States, privately, that is, as fee simple property.

Significantly, neither the cash payments nor the land awarded under the Act went directly to the Native organizations, tribes, clans, or villages whose claims the Act sought to settle and extinguish. Rather, Alaska Natives throughout the state only gained control over the rewards of the claims process indirectly through their participation in the development of natural resources by their ANCSA corporations.

Each village corporation in the Southeast region was allowed to choose 23,040 acres of land, in most cases contiguous to the village itself, for development. Those villages whose surroundings were off-limits or unsuitable for development—like Angoon and Klukwan—were allowed to choose parcels from islands with no permanent Native populations. This meant that these parcels were hundreds of miles from their own villages, and inevitably in areas used by Natives from other villages for subsistence hunting and fishing.

Most village corporations in Southeast Alaska chose parcels with valuable stands of old-growth timber with the intention of using that timber for commercial development. Mineral resources were seldom considered during the initial selection in the Southeast, because the subsurface rights to the village corporation land were not held by the village corporation itself, but rather by the regional corporation.

Regional corporations were the second tier of companies set up by ANCSA. Under the terms of the Act, the state was divided into twelve regions, and twelve regional corporations were created. Shareholders in village corporations located within a particular region were issued shares in the respective regional corporation as well. In addition, some who were not village shareholders (most often because they missed enrollment, or were residents of villages denied village corporations) were enrolled in regional corporations as "at-large" shareholders.

Beyond to the twelve regional corporations formed throughout the state, a thirteenth corporation was set up for those Natives not then residing in Alaska and unlikely to return. This corporation was given a share of cash awards but no land. The remaining twelve regional corporations were awarded more or less the same amount of land as the combined total of their particular region's village corporation holdings. Thus for every 23,040 acres issued to a Southeast Alaska village corporation, the regional corporation Sealaska was issued 23,040 acres as well, usually contiguous to the area selected by the village.

Throughout the state the regional corporations were awarded the subsurface rights for their own land and for the lands of the village corporations within their region. This was meant to facilitate the development of North Slope oil reserves by fixing the negotiating power for drilling rights with a single board of directors—that of the Arctic Slope Regional Corporation. In this way, the oil companies hoped not to have to negotiate with those people, families, and villages most affected by the search for oil beneath their homes or traditional hunting areas. Instead, a single contract could be worked out with the regional corporation for development beneath all village lands, regardless of the individual village residents' opinions about the arrangement.

In the Southeast region, the distribution of settlement funds preceded the selection and conveyance of land. Half of the total cash award was paid out to the regional corporation immediately after the passage of the Act, with the rest staggered over the next ten years. Sealaska, the regional corporation for the Southeast region, was expected to redistribute a portion of this award to the village corporations and to pay out a percentage in "dividends" to its shareholders. The funds received by the village corporations and those remaining funds held by Sealaska were to be used to set up the corporate infrastructure and begin the development process on the land awarded by the Act.

The latter was made more difficult by the delays in the conveyance of the land to the corporations, however. Less than 1 percent of the 540,000 acres awarded to Native corporations in Southeast Alaska was conveyed by 1979, eight years after the Act. Oil drilling and development on state and federal land had begun right away, however, and most Natives could see the "other side" of the agreement reaping the benefits of the settlement. This led to great pressure in the first decade of the Act for a show of results by Sealaska and the other ANCSA corporations. At the village level this pressure was manifest in the elections for corporation directorships. Individuals in every village ran for board position on the promise to distribute settlement monies to those in their communities and were made corporate board members on this basis alone. In most villages this meant a distribution (as "dividends") of initial village corporation cash assets from the cash portion of the settlement to shareholders even before corporations had developed a single acre. As a result, when the conveyance of land did begin after 1979, the vast majority of the village corporations were strapped for cash, and many had to pledge their timber holdings for loans necessary to begin the development process.

On the shareholder side, the desire for some show of results was understandable from a number of standpoints. During the 1970s, commercial fishing in Southeast Alaska had reached a historic nadir. The cannery boom that had created many of the small villages in the early 1900s was by this time completely defunct, with only a handful of the more than one hundred former canneries still in operation. Beyond this, the limited-entry permit system was causing many formerly prosperous families to sell their homes and holdings and move out of the villages. Household incomes throughout the region dropped significantly, and many longtime fishing families lost their boats. Indeed, one of the reasons why some individual Natives chose to enroll in the regional corporation Sealaska as at-large shareholders, rather than receiving shares in a village corporation, was that at-large shareholders were paid more in the initial distributions than were shareholders in the village corporations. Individuals who elected to take this route received double checks in the initial distribution, and still receive dividend checks from Sealaska that are half again or even twice the amount received by village corporation shareholders.

Locally, the problem with profitability did not stem from a lack of individual or collective familiarity with the for-profit nature of the corporations, as some have argued. All Southeast Alaska communities had been involved in commercial ventures—commercial fishing boats, cannery labor and wage work, general stores—for generations. Rather, it had to do with both historical and structural issues that confronted Southeast villages in the early years of ANCSA. Two issues in particular had a critical impact on the success of village corporations.

The first issue, mentioned above, is that the monies awarded the village corporations in the early years of the Act were often spent or distributed before the land was officially conveyed, leaving many village corporations without the start-up capital needed to begin an efficient timber-harvesting operation. In fact, most villages in the Southeast region did not receive their ANCSA-allocated land until almost a decade after the Act. When the land was finally conveyed, many village corporations lacked the funds to begin a harvesting operation. Some opted to subcontract their harvests to outside firms, but such firms were under no pressure to hire Native labor from the village whose timber they were harvesting. These strategies were unpopular with shareholders living in the village who hoped that ANCSA would replace livelihoods lost as fishing had declined.

Other village corporations went into debt in order to purchase the necessary equipment to begin their own harvesting operation, often borrowing money from Asian timber-marketing firms who would then have considerable control over the sale of the timber. In many villages, such as Hydaburg, these options were tried sequentially. First, a timber-harvesting project was begun, based on borrowed funds. When this failed to produce dividends, an outside contractor was brought in to run the harvest. Taken together, debt burdens and limited marketing options ensured that few village-based timber operations ever made a profit, though for three or four years many did employ large numbers of village residents at relatively good wages.

***

While seemingly a boon to communities struggling from the collapse of fishing, the job programs formed through ANCSA actually led to considerable conflict between shareholders in many village corporations. This led to the second reason why many village corporation timber operations failed, though to understand the source of these tensions we need to step back to a discussion of how village corporation shares were issued initially.

In 1971, shares in village and regional corporations were allocated according to very loose notions of village or regional residency. Individual Natives had three options for ANCSA enrollment. They could enroll as a resident of either the village or city in which they were resident at the time, a village in which they had lived in the past, or a village in which their parents or ancestors had lived. All of these were acceptable, as long as an individual enrolled in only one village corporation and consequently only one regional corporation. Indeed, many village corporations encouraged nonresidents to enroll in their corporations, for the initial cash distributions from the regional corporation to the village corporations were determined largely on a per capita basis. Thus the more people who signed up with a village corporation, the larger that corporation's piece of the initial pie.

The result of this process was that even in the immediate aftermath of the Act, many village corporation shareholders were not residents of the village in which they held shares. These nonresident shareholders were a minority in the first years following the Act, but the decline of the salmon fisheries and the demographics of the shareholder system meant that each year the relative proportion of nonresident shareholders increased.

For some nonresident shareholders, especially those who had left only recently, having timber operations run by the village corporation meant the possibility of a job and a return to the village. But for those now established in a new city and a new life, such relocation was not feasible. For them any village corporation investment in jobs-related programs was simply a squandering of funds that ought to be distributed as dividends.

The conflict of interest between resident and nonresident shareholders grew more tense when village corporation timber operations proved unable to turn a profit while simultaneously depleting large amounts of village liquid and solid (i.e., timber) capital. At that point, and this included most Southeast communities in the early 1990s, nonresident shareholders began voting for board members who would shut down the village corporation timber operations, sell the timber on the stump, and distribute any proceeds to shareholders.

Resident shareholders regarded these attempts at dissolution as selfish and extreme, and more poignantly, as attempts to drive them from the village, but this had little impact on the results. Presently, nonresident shareholders own the majority of shares in most village corporations, and most villages have gotten out of the timber business (and the job-providing business) altogether.

The original rationale behind ANCSA was that shareholders would encourage their corporations to develop the land awarded them, thereby providing jobs and economic stimulus for the local communities. This, in turn, would reduce the welfare needs of these same communities and allow supposedly "isolated" peoples to participate in the larger economy. It would also, and not coincidentally, hasten the development of Alaska's dispersed but considerable natural resources. At the same time, it was thought, ANCSA would avoid creating any new reservations or any new government-to-government relationships by not recognizing any new tribes or awarding land compensation to any already recognized tribes. And, finally, to ensure that the regional corporations would take up the welfare responsibilities of the government, the Act stipulated that 70 percent of all profits earned by the regional corporations would be redistributed among the other regional corporations. This way, oil revenues in the North and timber revenues in the Southeast would be used to help communities in other areas of Alaska where resources were less abundant and welfare/general assistance was more burdensome to Alaska and the federal government.

ANCSA thus laid the groundwork for several critical inter- and intra-community dynamics and tensions. It allowed Natives to participate in the larger economy as Natives—that is, as individuals with claims to significant resources based on prior occupation/ownership—only through the corporate/shareholder format. In recognizing Native claims broadly, however, ANCSA created lasting resentment by non-Native Alaskans over the "special treatment" of Natives.

Within Native villages, the shareholder provision awarded shares only to those alive at the time of the Act (i.e., 1971). Those born afterward, locally called "new Natives," have no claim on the village corporations that dominate the political economy of their villages unless they receive shares through gift or inheritance from the initial shareholders.

Every village thus had "two classes of Natives," as residents put it, shareholders and non-shareholders. Moreover, by awarding shares to former residents of communities and their descendants, many (for Southeast Alaska, now the majority) of the shareholders in village-based corporations were not, or are now no longer, residents of these villages. These three divisions—between Natives and non-Natives; between shareholding Natives and "new Natives"; and between resident and non-resident shareholders—have dominated the implementation of the land settlement in ways that go far beyond the vision of the original legislation. In the process, they have created divisions that, while a part of those described in the last chapter, exaggerated and intensified existing divisions between those trying to forge a livelihood from the land, and those whose futures lay with the twists and turns of the larger economy.

A decade after the fact, these tensions dominated Native politics throughout the state. And ANCSA may have died then; the benefits seen by most village residents were small, often amounting to nothing after the initial disbursement of settlement funds. The gains were too small, and the legal morass too large, and many, likely most, Natives thought it better to scrap the Act and start over. This might have actually happened had ANCSA not created one other division among Natives, one that would figure significantly in later attempts to re-open ANCSA for "fixing." Once opened, the problems associated with the original legislation we not fixed. Rather, the Act was expanded, and an avalanche of new changes were begun that dwarfed those of the original settlement.

\*\*\*

Outside of Southeast Alaska, with its large areas of old-growth forest, and the North Slope, with its vast oil reserves, most regional and village corporations in Alaska have had difficulty making a profit, or even breaking even. In those areas where ANCSA was a bust, people resented the "corporate" format of ANCSA and blamed North Slope and Southeast Natives' for their willingness accept the terms of the Act at the expense of those with less readily available resources to exploit. By the mid-1980s such tensions had come to a head, and resource-poor communities began pushing for the "tribal option."

The idea behind the tribal options was simple. As corporate entities chartered like any other corporation under the rules of U.S. commerce, the shareholder of a local village corporation could, in theory, elect to dissolve the corporations and turn over its assets to still-existing or newly re-created tribal governing bodies. These bodies would then be free of the corporate format and rules associated with profit sharing, board elections, the exclusion of new Natives and the raft of divisions and complications that ANCSA had introduced. In effect, it would mean that communities would "get back their land," as people like to say, and decide how best to manage it for themselves.

Whether these efforts would have worked is a difficult question. At large and non-resident shareholders would likely have felt very differently about the turning over of assets, though given the lack of profit by most corporations, it is unclear whether many would have bothered to care. Then there is the issue of the subsurface rights, which most village corporations did not hold. How would tribal governments deal with the fact that regional corporations could still mine or drill for oil on their land?

Government lawyers, weary of the reintroduction of Indian country to Alaska, and with it the complex, government-to-government relationships they sought to prevent in Alaska and escape elsewhere, argued that such efforts would require a change in the original legislation. Politicians argued that it would require a unified voice on the part of Alaska Natives, something they knew would be difficult for advocates of the tribal option to muster, and something they moved quickly to prevent.

Those on the resource rich end of ANCSA were also not without complaints, however. For them, the profit-sharing provision of the Act created a legal imbroglio that had angered directors and managers in those few areas where success under ANCSA seemed possible. The profit sharing provision, part of the original 1971 legislation dictated that 2/3rds of the profits of any regional corporation had to be redistributed to the other regional corporations. While clearly an attempt to spread the oil money of the North Slope around the state, wealthy regions felt as though their profits were being used to replace government welfare programs, robbing them of the opportunity to reinvest and create sustainable development programs—something, they said, to take the place of the oil and timber they had at the time, but that they were using up at a rapid pace. The profit sharing provision had already caused considerable damage by the mid-1980s. Jealousy and suspicion, plain corporate greed, and the complexities of modern business accounting conspired under the Act to prompt regional corporations to find ways to avoid payouts, encouraging their neighboring corporations to hire lawyers and bring a lawsuit. The result was that much of the profits gained by those few successful corporations wound up in the hands of non-Native lawyers, causing further resentment between have and have-not regions.

As a result, with the tribal option lurking in the background and wealthy regions pushing for change, by the mid-1980s Congress was forced to take up ANCSA again. Had they not, everyone recognized that a raft of lawsuits and complex legal entanglements would soon cripple what little effect the original legislation had created. The result of this is what have come to be called the 1987 Amendments (though they were actually passed by Congress in 1988).[9]

***

While ostensibly created as a remedy for number of problems in the original legislation, the 1987 Amendments, perhaps more so than the original Act, served to amplify its original effects.

The first purpose of the revisions was to fix a concern common to both sides of the profit sharing and resource debate: the potential sale of ANCSA

---

[9] US Public Law No 92-203, 85 Stat. 668 (1971) (codified as amended at 43 U.S. Congress 1601-1641(1988)).

corporate shares to non-Natives. The original ANCSA legislation had called for exclusively Native shareholdership for the first twenty years, meaning that shares of a village or regional corporation could only be sold or given to someone who was already a shareholder, or a descendent of a shareholder. According to the original Act, after 20 years this was to change, and voting shares were to become available to anyone who would be interested in purchasing them, regardless of ethnic or racial categories, or his place of residence.

By 1987, the 1991 moratorium on the exclusion of non-Natives was rapidly approaching, and the potential alienation of corporation land frightened many village residents. This helped bring a unified Native voice to Congress, at least on this issue. The possibility that Alaska Natives could face the same fate that had repeatedly befallen Native Americans throughout their history—whenever group resources were privatized and distributed, they were lost, and misery, poverty and landlessness followed—had caused much worry throughout Alaska. Thus the original impetus for the 1987 legislation was to alleviate this possibility by turning over to the shareholders themselves the decision of whether to allow the sale of shares to non-Natives. In this way, only by shareholder vote could the rules about the alienability of corporation stock be altered.

Had the amendments stopped there, however, the deeper issues of the resource divide and the tribal option would remain open. And, as one might guess under such complex and competing forces, much more than the shareholder moratorium changed once Congress reopened the can of worms that ANCSA had created.

Of the two issues—the profit sharing provision and the tribal option—Congress saw the second as the more threatening. Their solution was to try to split the solidarity of the Native community in Alaska by finding ways to make existing corporations more profitable, thereby reducing the tribal option to a minority position in the State as a whole. In so doing, they sought ways to make village corporations more profitable, which would help keep any new proceeds out of the profit sharing morass. For Southeast Natives, this double strategy proved profound, as Congress specifically identified local, struggling Southeast Native timber resources as their target.

In the eyes of Washington, Southeast village corporations seemed ripe for enhancement, as most were sitting on large tracts of potentially valuable timber. All they needed to do, it was thought, was to get this timber to market, and local profits would show Southeast residents that dissolving their corporations and turning these lands back over to largely defunct tribal governing bodies was a bad decision. With both Southeast and North Slope Natives to stay the course, advocacy for the tribal option would be allowed to die a slow, isolated death.

PHOTO 7: *A logging ship loading timber from local ANCSA corporation lands. Though barely visible due to the size of the ship, individual "longshorers" can be seen standing on the logs that are rafted beside the vessel for loading. Longshoring remains an important source of income for many village residents.*

The problem was that most of these village corporations had expended all of their potential startup money, and few had any experience in timber harvesting. To make matters worse, prices in the global market for timber had fallen precipitously over the prior 15 years, so much so that the two largest timber harvesters in Southeast Alaska—the Ketchikan Pulp Corporation and the Alaska Pulp Corporation—were both struggling to maintain profitability, even given their enormous federal timber subsidies. Alaskan timber, it would seem, was the victim of the mass opening of new sources of timber in Siberia, New Guinea, and Southeast Asia. Southeast Native corporations had simply come at the wrong time. Coupled with the lack of capital, the falling price of timber meant that squeezing a profit out of local ANCSA companies was more difficult than might be guessed by their ostensibly large holdings.

The solution, it turned out, was not to make a profit at all. Rather, it turned out that the best way forward, was to make as big a loss as possible.

***

To set the stage for the ANCSA amendments, Congress began by passing a revised provision in the 1986 Tax Code. The key to this change was the creation of what have come to be called "Net Operating Loss" (NOL) provisions.

The first element of the NOL legislation was to extend to Southeast ANCSA corporations a tax loophole used in the past by many non-Native timber corporations to enhance their profitability. The loophole essentially allowed timber corporations to count a loss in the value of their standing timber between the time of purchase and the time of harvest as operating losses (similar to ordinary operating expenses such as the depreciation of timber harvesting equipment). As this loss in timber value would be tax deductible, it could be used to lower the declared level of profits for the timber corporation, and therefore to lower its tax bill. Large companies like Weyerhaeuser had used this provision for years, in effect allowing tax dollars to insure themselves against losses that would come from holding large timber assets over long periods of time.

The change in the 1986 tax laws allowed ANCSA timber corporations to count the difference in the market value of their timber between the time it was conferred (usually between 1972 and 1982) and the time that timber was harvested, as an operating loss as well. This was a bit duplicitous, because the Native corporations had not actually paid anything for the timber they held (other than the loss of hope and future that ANCSA had produced). It had been awarded to them as part of the settlement. Still, because of the significant drop in timber values over the period between receiving it and 1987, many small, village-based ANCSA corporations could show enormous fictive or "paper" losses—at times exceeding $100 million for those corporations who had yet to cut significant portions of their ANCSA allotments. For Sealaska, the loss was even higher.

These losses, though somewhat fictive, could potentially serve as huge tax shelters against profits gained by Southeast corporations. The problem, though, was that few of these corporations had ever earned a profit, and with timber prices continuing to slide, few were likely to do so in the foreseeable future. Losses are only assets when they can offset taxes. Short of that, they are worth little.

In response, the 1987 Amendments to ANCSA carried a provision that allowed ANCSA corporations with enormous paper losses to sell these losses to more profitable corporations. This was the genie in the bottle that rapidly remade the regional economy, and which ramped up the effects of ANCSA well beyond those ever created by the original legislation. In one stoke of the proverbial legislative pen, Congress turned large paper losses into enormous assets, crushed the tribal option, and set the stage for a massive environmental change that likely forever altered the social life of Native villages in Southeast Alaska.

For profitable non-Native corporations, the possibility of buying transferable losses was attractive. Many were willing to pay as much as 30 cents for each dollar of loss acquired, thereby saving 40-50 cents in taxes for every 30 cents spent. ANCSA village corporations selling losses could thus expect to see a return of $30 million for a paper loss of $100 million, while the corporations buying losses could expect to save $40-$50 million in taxes for a $30-million purchase. It was a "win-win" situation (although it cost the federal government $40-$50 million in lost corporate tax revenues).

The only downside for the ANCSA corporations was that, for the NOLs to be actualized, the timber had to be harvested (since the loss was calculated at the time of harvest). For Southeast ANCSA corporations, this meant consenting to the clear-cutting or sale "on the stump" of their entire timber holdings. Most did, resulting in what must be considered one of the largest timber boondoggles of all time.[10]

\*\*\*

The impact of the NOL legislation was immense. Most of the "NOL money," as it is referred to locally, was distributed as "dividends" to shareholders. As we will see in Chapter 5, non-shareholders—new Natives and landless Natives, who are already usually the more marginal members of the communities—received none of this money, but had to bear the brunt of the ecological damage caused by the clear-cutting. Indeed, non-shareholder residents of any village are often among those most dependent on hunting and gathering for daily subsistence and, thus, as a result of the devastation

---

[10] The local regional corporation, Sealaska, used some of the profits from its own NOL sales to purchase the entire standing timber holdings of many of the village corporations within its region. This helped them to actualize their losses, and to transform itself into one of the largest timber-holding corporation in Southeast Alaska. Sealaska is now in the process of clearcutting these lands.

prompted by this legislation, faced significant new challenges in their ability to simply subsist. Further, as many village corporation boards are now controlled by nonresident shareholders, they are reluctant to use much of the money generated by NOL sales for job creation or other village-sustaining initiatives that might partly compensate marginal households for the loss of livelihood that the clear-cutting created. As a result, poorer residents bear the majority of the consequences of this policy with the knowledge that the long-term prospects of continuing to live even as marginally as they do now are decreasing dramatically, as a result of corporation activities.

***

Not all of these changes found village residents lying down. Local reaction against ANCSA and its amendments since the late 1980s has been constant and has taken many forms. There have been, for example, moves within communities to award shares to "new Natives," though none have yet to be successful.

Similarly, much early resistance to ANCSA centered on the "subsistence" provisions within ANCSA, and their modification in the Alaska National Interest Land Conservation Act (ANILCA). Both of these issues we will return to below. Yet neither effort gained the attention of industry and federal officials more that recent struggles blossomed from the NOL boom, for neither had the potential to expand the reach of the original ANCSA legislation. And neither of these issues—new Natives or subsistence—shows how quickly industry and state officials are willing to take dissatisfaction with ANCSA and turn it into more of the same.

Rather, he story of the 1987 Amendments has been repeated over and over again in the last two and a half decades, each time growing out some complaint, and each time transforming that complaint into a rationale for greater and greater timber harvests.

A case in point is the "landless Natives" issue that arose just after the NOL heydays. Here, the struggle to force a new settlement for the landless Natives once again revealed the way in which resistance to the Act has been subverted by Congress and used—or in this case, almost used—to further the original aims of the Act.

To take up this story, briefly: the individuals who composed the landless Natives were, primarily, the Native residents of five predominantly non-Native Southeast Alaska communities: Ketchikan, Petersburg, Wrangell, Tenakee

Springs, and Haines, and together they comprised over twenty percent of the total ANCSA shareholders in the Southeast region. It is unclear still, why these communities were not allowed to form village corporations like their neighbors, despite a federal report commissioned for the purpose of discovering the cause. Yet because of the "special treatment" shown Southeast Natives throughout the ANCSA process,[11] by the early 1990s, Congress was reluctant to reopen ANCSA for a segment of a group that, on the whole, many in Congress felt should not have had a role in the Settlement in the first place.

Nevertheless, in 1988, fresh off the NOL victory, members of the five landless communities joined together to form the Southeast Alaska ANCSA Land Acquisition Coalition, Inc. (SAALAC). This organization, located in the tribal offices of the Central Council of the Tlingit and Haida, had as its purpose the creation of ANCSA village corporations for Natives in each of the five landless communities and the awarding of land under ANCSA to these corporations. With 3,500 potential members, it was thought that SAALAC could use its own enrollment and sympathy from other Native villages to bring pressure on Alaska's congressional delegation to force yet more change into the original legislation. It turns out that little force was required.

In these efforts they were, at least initially, supported widely by Natives throughout the region. They also found what might at first seem an unexpected ally in the large corporate timber and pulp producers located in Southeast Alaska, and the two largest Native timber corporations in the state: Sealaska and the ANCSA village corporation for Klukwan. Each of the latter gave $400,000 to the newly formed organization to help with its lobbying and enrollment process. More support came from Alaska's congressional delegation, and, in related form, from non-Native timber interests. Indeed non-Native timber interests, while initially suspicious of ANCSA, had by the early 1990s come to see Native claims as a way around declines in their own timber harvest allotments, which were under threat from the more environmentally friendly Department of the Interior and Congress.

Some explanation of the change in industry support is necessary, for it figures largely in the events that followed. Prior to the late 1980s, and continuing in

---

[11] Southeast Natives on the whole had been included under ANCSA only by special provision, having accepted a prior Court of Claims settlement in the late 1960s that, in effect, foreclosed future settlements or awards. As the result of a last minute compromise, however, Southeast communities were recognized by ANCSA, although they were awarded less land per community than were Natives elsewhere in the state. In contrast to the population-based formula used to award much larger plots elsewhere in Alaska, each Southeast village, regardless of size, was awarded relatively small, 23,040-acre plots.

diminished form up to the late 1990s, timber harvests in the Tongass National Forest in Southeast Alaska had been dominated by the long-term contracts of the region's two large timber processors: Alaska Pulp Corporation (APC) and Ketchikan Pulp Corporation (KPC). Since the 1950s, both had harvested timber through road building contracts under a system in which the U.S. Forest Service allows the harvest of a certain number of acres of timber in exchange for roads built in the Tongass by the harvesting companies. The roads serve no practical purpose other than to access future timber harvest areas and thus are essentially an industry subsidy: pulp producers get paid in timber to build the roads they need to haul it out. The result is that the two large pulp companies in the region have for decades been able to obtain timber from public land they do not own for little more than the cost of harvesting it.

Harvest levels were set early on with the awarding of long-term, fifty-year contracts for road building to each of the pulp companies: 192 MMBF (million board feet) annually for KPC and 104 MMBF for APC, or two-thirds of the total allowable harvest in the Tongass. The U.S. Forest Service, APC, and KPC justified such high harvest levels by alleging that a pulp mill must work continuously to avoid near complete breakdown (due to the use of highly corrosive materials) and thus must be guaranteed a constant supply of wood.[12]

The early 1990s represented a significant change in timber politics in the region, however. Coupled with the overall glut of timber on the world market, the 1987 Amendments to ANCSA had allowed for timber harvests on an unprecedented scale, further depressing pulp prices and quickly accelerating the already precipitous downward spiral of the regions large pulp producers. Beyond this, the ecological devastation caused by the sudden rush to harvest NOL timber prompted significant backlash from environmentalists. Nationally, the appointment of environmentally concerned administrators to federal positions set the stage for an environmental showdown, with the Tongass at its center. The first result was the Tongass Timber Reform Act (TTRA) of 1990. This law forced the Forest Service to abandon the road building contracts for APC and KPC, and allowed for the creation of zones within the forest that would be excluded from timber harvests and reserved instead for wildlife, tourism, and Native subsistence. These timber-harvest-free zones, established under the TTRA, were called "LUD 2s," short for "land use designation 2," and by the mid-1990s comprise a significant portion of the Tongass. With a shrinking resource base, a glut in world markets, and increased

---

[12] Bill Shoaf, *The Taking of the Tongass: Alaska's Rainforest*. Running Wolf Press, 1998.

competition abroad, the timber industry in Alaska was, by the early 1990s, facing a radical change, and with it a feeling a genuine panic.

The rise of SAALAC, the landless Native coalition that had begun with considerable local support, presented timber corporations and toadying politicians with the possibility of circumventing timber harvest ceilings created by the TTRA. By the mid-1990s, existing village-based ANCSA corporations had shown timber interests that land awarded to Natives would not disappear from the timber market—far from it. If anything, ANCSA corporations had shown willingness to clear-cut their entire holdings in the interest of windfall profits during the NOL days. What is more, ANCSA corporation lands were private holdings. This meant, in effect, that the environmental regulations used to govern harvests in the rest of the Tongass did not apply to Native lands. This alleviated potentially costly harvest problems such as wide stream buffers, landslide protection buffers, environmental impact studies, and endangered species protection—in short, the entire package of environmental regulation meant to safeguard public lands from corporate development and destruction.

As such, harvests on Native lands would be, potentially, even more financially "efficient" for timber processors than similar harvests on public lands. Toward this end, Alaska Senator Frank Murkowski drafted a "Landless Native Allocation Act" in October 1994 (Senate Bill S. 2539). The proposed Act contained several provisions, including the creation of village ANCSA corporations in the five landless villages. In addition, because these communities had missed out on the initial cash distribution that accompanied the original 1971 Act, Murkowski proposed awarding the new village corporations land allotments according to the population-based formula used elsewhere in Alaska, rather than the flat-rate 23,040 acres received by other Southeast corporations. Thus, the two largest landless villages would each receive over 160,000 acres, and the other three smaller villages would receive between 69,000 and 140,000 acres.

Because this large amount of land—over 600,000 acres in all, as much as the original ANCSA allocation to all of the original Southeast village corporations and Sealaska combined—was unavailable in the areas immediately surrounding the five landless communities, and because all of these communities are actually small cities with significant white populations thought by Congress to need room to grow, it was proposed that the lands awarded to the landless communities under Murkowski's bill need not be located near the communities themselves. This meant that lands for the landless would have to be drawn from areas near other Native villages, a point that would factor significantly in subsequent Native resistance to the bill within the region.

Likewise, S. 2539 specified that the lands selected could not be among those already designated for commercial timber harvest under the long-term contracts of the large pulp corporations. As such, these new land commitments required the reallocation of much of the forest, especially those areas (LUD 2s) designated for environmental protection, Native subsistence, and "balanced use" under the TTRA, many of which were set aside specifically because of their significance to other Native communities.

PHOTO 8: *Modern-day paper manufacturing machines at the Ketchikan Pulp Corporation. Timber politics have dominated the local economy for years in Southeast Alaska, a testament to both the decline of the commercial fishing industry and the continued immersion of the region in industrial resource production.*

And finally, S. 2539 contained a provision requiring timber harvested on land allocated to these five communities to be sold to timber processors located within the region. This meant, in effect, that all of the timber from the new allocations would have to be sold to APC or KPC, or one of the other small processors.

If any question remained, this final provision exposed the Act for the industry land grab that it actually was, and prompted an outcry from conservation advocates and several Southeast Native communities.[13]

In the end, S. 2539 never received a floor vote in the Senate and it was withdrawn later that year when the Alaska Senate delegation proposed a more bold move—the return of the entire Tongass Forest to the jurisdiction and management of the State of Alaska. This too failed, but like the salmon returning upstream, it seems to repeat itself each year. The most recent proposal, put forward in February 2013, was labeled the "H.R. 740: Southeast Alaska Native Land Entitlement Finalization and Jobs Protection Act." This proposal once again revived the population proportion argument put forward in S. 2539 in an attempt to dramatically expand the lands allocated to Sealaska. It also contains provisions to allow Sealaska to choose from several hundred thousand acres of previously off-limits sections of the forest, i.e. the same LUD-2s discussed above. At the time of writing, the fate of this bill is unknown.

***

There is little doubt that, regardless of the fate of S. 2539 or HR 740, such efforts to "fix" ANCSA will continue, and in each case advocates will cite Native communities and their needs as the raison d'être, even while advocating processes that ultimately destroy many Native village residents' ability to "be Native" in the ways that make sense to them. For many, this way includes the ability to live and work the land for subsistence, and in so doing raise a family in the company of each other, in the place their ancestors lived and thrived for generations.

The case is important for several reasons, not least for the environmental havoc it created. But just as importantly, and in parallel with the original ANCSA agreement, the politics of Native land settlement in Alaska reveal a new direction in government/Indian/industry relations that has subsequently become common in other places like Canada or Australia. *In particular, after centuries of removal and confinement, ANCSA and it amendments reveal how prepared industry has become to act in support of the issue of "indigenous" rights, even to the point of greatly expanding the list of recognized "indigenous" communities and the claims of these communities.*

Throughout, timber corporations and those like them were driven by very conventional business goals: the overriding desire to further development aims and industry profits. This is, in itself, not surprising. What's new is that they see

---

[13] Vance A. Sanders, "Murkowski's Landless Bill." *Ravens Bones Journal* v. 3, n.1 (1995): 3—5.

"indigenous" recognition as a way of possibly circumventing existing curbs on this process, whether these curbs are moral, historical, or environmental. Indeed, if any sentiment characterizes the ethos of ANCSA, this is it.[14]

***

At the height of this process, in 1996, the regional ANCSA corporation Sealaska sponsored a large cultural fair called "Celebration." It was here that Norman was confronted by the visitor to his booth about the intellectual property rights of his art. The timing is significant. Both the festival itself, and the confrontation over intellectual property, point to the ways that Native identity and culture are ambiguously caught up in the same processes that produce windfall cash from the sale of losses and their accompanying environmental destruction.

In the program for Celebration '96, the chair of the Sealaska Heritage Foundation used his opening letter to explain that Celebration is a "new tradition." His point was aimed at some segments of his audience more than others. For many younger Southeast Alaska Natives, and even some middle aged and older, Celebration is the only large-scale Native cultural event they have ever participated in. Thus for those in the Heritage Foundation, and others concerned with keeping up more "authentic" traditions, some clarification seemed justified. He writes:

> *Every other year we gather again, and Celebration '96 is the eighth such gathering. Celebration is strong, but we must remember that it is a new tradition. In the Old Way, a clan from one side was usually host to another clan from the opposite side. For example, an Eagle clan would host a Raven clan, or a Raven clan would host an Eagle clan. Those who danced together as hosts or guests were from one clan or one side. Since the old times, people from each clan have scattered far and wide in search of work. Some clanspeople now gather as single-clan dance groups, but most groups at Celebration '96 represent many clans. Some are Tlingit, Haida, or Tsimshian, but some are combinations. As times change, our people have adapted.*

New traditions are not specific to Alaska or to Natives, of course; most of

---

[14] See also: Kirk Dombrowski, "Culture and praxis in post-modern times." *Focaal* v. 56, n. 1 (2010): 81-89; and Kirk Dombrowski, "Reply: what's changed (since 1975)?" *Dialectical Anthropology* v. 32, n. 1 (2008): 43-50.

what passes for tradition in the twentieth century is not much older than that. Nevertheless more is at stake here than the "invention of tradition," however useful this notion has been for other purposes.

Given what most people say and think about tradition, the notion of a "new tradition" would seem an oxymoron. In ordinary language, traditions are traditions because they are thought to have been practiced the same way for a long time. Something that is new, therefore, cannot be a real tradition.

As a matter of fact, the history of traditions is far more complicated than simple chronology implies. The notion of tradition is always linked to questions of domination and resistance, rather than, or in addition to, questions of age and continuity. Traditions can be (and most often are) those things that allow a group to stand apart from and often against its larger social setting; the traditions of virtually all ethnic communities and of classes within these communities fall into this category. Kilts, in this sense, matter as much for the fact that the English *don't* wear them as the fact that the Scottish *do*.

Many traditions (including Scottish kilts) are thus not very old, or have taken on their current meaning only when placed in a new social arena where their presence stands out. In this way, "tradition" invokes a second and perhaps more accurate etymological history: tradition is that which stands outside of and against the current political order—linked in meaning to "betrayal," as Raymond Williams points out, and to "traitor."[15] Traditions are, in this sense, those things which set their participants apart from some situation they are both a part of, and wish at least partly to resist. "New" traditions are, in this sense, just new means for doing this.

The flip side of this is that the label "traditional" has often been used as a stigma—a way to identify something that is out of place in changing times. Historically, this stigmatizing label likely came first to Native Americans, and only later was it seized upon as a way of mobilizing and creating differences that could be used to counter those same stigmatizing forces.

Alaska Natives, like most other Native Americans, have at times been forced into such alterior status, defined by outsiders as "traditional" peoples and forced to take up the ambivalent stigma of tradition in their own self-defense. When they do, they inevitably invoke charges of romantic glorification and political expediency by those around them; of using identity purely for the sake of resistance, according to Adam Kuper or Francis Widdowson, two

---

[15] See Raymond Williams, *Keywords: A Vocabulary of Culture and Society*. New York: Oxford University Press, 1985, pp. 318-9.

anthropologists that have recently decided to "unveil" these processes.

However such tactics were never Native peoples' only chosen option, nor was traditionalism uniformly accepted as the best strategy. The number of model villages in Alaska provides ample evidence of other strategies, for example. In places like Kake, Hydaburg or Metlakatla, colonial forces were taken at their word, thorough changes enacted, and whole ways of life reinvented. In these places, "backward" traditions were done away with, and "modern" ways taken up in earnest. Today, however, these places look a lot like the other Native communities in the region. Having taken colonists at their word, and allowed them to set the terms for what was and was not acceptable tradition, later generations have found the results disappointing, to say the least.

Where traditionalism has become an important identity for resistance, it is at least partly the result of people's choosing, and convincing others to do the same, long after the non-invention of tradition didn't pan out the way that colonial powers envisioned. In doing so, Natives have often—and knowingly—given credence to an "otherizing" strategy practiced by colonists continuously for centuries.[16] More than simply marginal, Native peoples who embrace tradition have come to be seen and come to see themselves as "outsiders" or "others"—as something quite different in kind from those arriving on the steamer. To the extent that this helped justify a colonializing mission, self-differencing processes were something that colonial powers were only too happy to support. This has caused many Native communities much pain—as outsiders used tradition to justify inferior schools and health care, to the forcible removal of Native children from their communities, to the housing of hazardous wastes on Native lands, to the relocation of whole tribes.

At the same time, this alterity has also been the source of many Native groups' ongoing resurgence. It is what gives some tribes the right to open gambling casinos in states whose laws otherwise forbid it, or to run tax- free stores catering mainly to non-Natives. In Alaska, Native corporations can harvest the timber on their ANCSA settlement allotments without much regard to federal regulations for the environment or endangered species. For this reason, as discussed in detail above, many timber processing companies have favored the allotment of more land to Southeast Native corporations, as unregulated harvests usually mean cheaper prices for timber processors.

Alterior status was perhaps more easily justified by both Natives and

---

[16] See Gerald Sider, "When parrots learn to talk, and why they can't: Domination, deception, and self-deception in Indian-White relations." *Comparative Studies in Society and History* v. 29, n. 1 (1987): 3-23.

government administrators when Native Americans were more obviously "Indians"—that is, when their lives revolved around a set of social institutions, symbols, and mutual relations more obviously in contrast with the wider society into which they had been absorbed. Today, such differences are more costly and not available to all. The resources required to continue to be seen as "Indians" are often beyond the reach of many groups, like the Lumbees or the Mashpees, and certainly beyond the reach of those more marginal individuals and families among already-recognized Indian tribes—like the Haidas and Tlingits of Alaska. New traditions can remedy this, by placing alterity in the hands of those who need it, but who could not afford the high price of more authentic traditions. Hence the concept of the button blanket, which is traditional in the sense that it harkens back to items made from buttons traded during the early colonial period, but which can be produced in arts and crafts classes, at costs well below those required to make Chilkat blankets, for example.

No doubt some sense of this drives Celebration itself. But even here the process assumes much that ANCSA itself makes increasingly impossible. For those just making it, a trip to Juneau, with its high priced hotels and expensive foods, is impossible. For them, even new traditions may prove unreachable. In contrast, and as will be seen below, prayer groups come to them, in their villages and in their homes. And for those groups, no tradition, not even new and inexpensive tradition, is required.

\*\*\*

For some village corporations, the NOL provisions in the 1987 legislation meant sudden, vast windfalls and an abrupt end to advocacy for the tribal option. However, this has done little to quell the tensions between resident and nonresident shareholders in Southeast villages. In fact, it may have aggravated these tensions by raising the stakes. Since the early 1990s, most nonresident shareholders have sought an immediate distribution of NOL money. Village residents have sought the use of some money for the creation of village-sustaining industries (mainly in the fish-processing business). Yet, as mentioned above, nonresident shareholders now make up a majority of the voting stock in virtually every village corporation. As a result, in all villages the "NOL money" as it was called, has been distributed in monthly amounts of $500 to $1,000 for every holder of one hundred shares (the number of shares issued a single individual in the original 1971 distribution).

In those few villages where a portion of the money was used to develop industries, such as Kake, these operations have struggled (as have all fishing-based operations in Southeast Alaska), and most have yet to produce a profit. In these cases there are today renewed calls by nonresidents for a liquidation of corporate assets and a full distribution of corporate resources.

The one certain and undeniable result of all this is that, at present, virtually all Southeast Native villages have cut or sold their entire original timber allocations and distributed or spent virtually all of the capital proceeds from both the harvest of timber and the sale of NOLs. And despite the seemingly vast sums distributed to shareholders, many village households now foresee a severely limited economic future. Hoped-for revivals in the region's fishing industry have all but passed by Native villages, and the number of commercial fishing operations in the region's poorest towns is generally now fixed at zero. As mentioned in the previous chapter, the "forest primeval" visible from the cruise ships is all that remains of once usable hunting and fishing grounds, leaving most villages stranded in what has become, ironically, an economic and subsistence desert amidst a tourist-scape of lush rain forest.

In response to the very real possibility of renewed village abandonments, the federal government has begun to propose a series of land swaps—the trading of parcels of clear-cut land owned by village corporations for new land with still-standing timber. Not surprisingly, there is considerable support from the timber industry to continue to allocate such new lands to ANCSA corporations. Inevitably, though, the new lots of land offered in the swaps are always smaller than those for which they are traded; resulting in a gradual reduction in Native holdings throughout the region.

Piece by piece, year by year, the amount of land in the hands of Natives, and the usability of that land to sustain a subsistence livelihood, is disappearing. As swapped lots come to border those lots already clear-cut at the edges of the villages, the long run result is the complete denuding of forest resources for vast stretches in those areas formerly used most heavily by village residents.

Making matters worse, many of the region's younger individuals missed entirely the distributions of NOL money, having been born after 1971. Some of these individuals, now in their mid-twenties and thirties, have families as well. Tellingly, no accommodations were made in the any of the ANCSA legislative amendments for the issuing of new shares to Natives born after 1971. This has left these individuals without a vote in the collective use of lands around the villages in which they live, and largely without claims on the central political entities for Natives in Alaska, the village and regional ANCSA corporations themselves.

The result is that many residents of Native communities in the region find themselves in a collapsing economy, largely run by nonresidents, that is overwhelmingly beholden to a single, rapidly depleting industry, i.e. commercial timber. From the perspective of these individuals, and many others who failed to benefit from the land claims in ways that most had hoped for and even taken for granted, ANCSA, its amendments, and the entire packet of NOL legislation looks more like a program to limit the possibility of being Indian in Alaska than a recognition of Native presence and value.

By limiting special-status political-economic participation to those who are shareholders, ANCSA has ensured that, of all those who claim Native status and identity, only a fixed number of individuals will be allowed to participate *as Natives* in the ongoing negotiation of village life. By not issuing shares to the new Natives, ANCSA shareholders have participated in this exclusion, though notably, most would deny that they had limited anyone's ability to "be Native."

The same might be said of the timber swaps now underway. Here one can see quite plainly that the long-term result of a series of such swaps is the gradual diminution of lands held by Natives, and thus of people's ability to "be Native"—at least in a way that shapes, rather than is simply shaped by, the surrounding society. As Native corporation holdings in the area are reduced to insignificant levels, and as more and more people who consider themselves Native find themselves left out of any say in the management of village and regional corporations, the long-term dynamics of ANCSA become clear.

In each case, "being Native" under ANCSA is increasingly limited, both in power and, more devastatingly, in time. As a greater proportion of Native residents in the region are excluded from shareholder status, people find that their claims for being Native outside ANCSA depend on a host of identity issues, and not on the control of significant social and material resources. In this way, ANCSA turns out not to have been an assimilationist vehicle at all, but one of gradual, increasing marginalization. And it is a process in which, as both the new Natives and land-swap issues show, Natives themselves are encouraged to participate.

In contrast to this appraisal, many Alaska Natives would object to any characterization that equates being Native with participation in corporate development activities, and many have opposed ANCSA for this reason. Yet the alternatives available to those who seek another way of being Native are increasingly circumscribed by the evident hopelessness of ANCSA. In place of new traditions, these individuals would point to older traditions of self-sufficiency and subsistence fishing, family connections, and the spiritual relationship with the land that all of these allow and encourage. Yet these too are circumscribed by ANCSA and the history of colonialism in Southeast Alaska. As we turn to questions of family and food, those limits become evermore clear. Here too, difference and differentiation has taken root, and belonging become contingent on radical reformulations of what it means to be Native. When that too is unavailable, people are pushed toward radical reformulations of what it means to be a person, and a member of a community.

In this way, the same forces that are driving culture are driving family, and splits between families, and even the Evangelical and Pentecostal movements that are opposing that culture. These divisions, and the lunar landscape of denuded rainforest that now stretches for miles around most communities, are the true legacies of ANCSA, its amendments and expansions included.

## CHAPTER 4
# The Ins and Outs of
# Village Social Life

*It's the summer of 1995, and I have returned to this village after two years to find that it now has two Indian Reorganization Act (IRA) councils. For the past decade, including during my first visit in the summer of 1993, there had been none. Actually, this isn't quite true. When there had been no IRA council here, the regional tribal government—the Tlingit and Haida Central Council—had been delegated as the village's official tribal representative. So in effect, even when there was no IRA council there was still a tribal governing body. And now, when there are two tribal councils in the village, it means there are, in effect, three.*

*The "radicals," as they half-jokingly called themselves, formed first. They consist of the former city administrator of the village; his wife; an elder (and one of the few remaining Native language speakers in the village) who has lived most of his life in a nearby, predominantly non-Native city; the president of the local ANB chapter; a logger who was born in the village and has lived here occasionally but has moved around quite a bit as well; and finally, an out-of-work totem-pole carver who has lived all his life here and occasionally worked in logging. Altogether there are five men and one woman.*

*Their reason for forming, they say, is to take back control of the IRA council from T&H, which as the regional tribal body is currently their tribal representative, recognized as such by the federal government. In the late 1970s or early 1980s (no one from this group is quite sure) the village IRA council had turned over its management and representation responsibilities for the Native residents of the village to T&H. At that point, whenever it was, the local council ceased to meet regularly, and eventually stopped meeting at all. The radicals have collected statements from several past council members acknowledging that they have not met in many years.*

*The radicals are largely self-appointed. For, as they immediately make clear, there are no up-to-date records of tribal enrollment, and thus it is impossible to have an election. At their first meeting they began collecting signatures for enrollment, and they now plan an election at midsummer. Until then, they refer to themselves as the "Tribal Council of the K— Tribe."*

*This name has historical political significance. The original village delegates from here that attended the formation of the Tlingit and Haida Central Council in the late 1930s signed their enrollment in T&H on behalf of the K— Tribe, not on behalf of the local IRA council. This, others point out, was because there was no local IRA council here at that time. It was formed later, in the late 1930s or early 1940s, as part of the implementation of the Indian Reorganization Act in Southeast Alaska. By assuming the title "K— Tribe," the radicals are seeking to impose an alternative notion of legitimacy on themselves and, as importantly, on T&H and the federal government as well. Had they assumed the old title of the IRA council, they say, it would have signaled some acknowledgment of the federal government's right to dictate the political structure of the group. What they wanted to avoid, they said, was any acknowledgment of the IRA as a basis for tribal organization or sovereignty in the village. Likewise, by taking up the name K— Tribe they assumed the mantle of the group that had originally lent its authority to T&H, and which could now take it back, presumably without regard to the wishes of that body.*

*Not surprisingly, the radicals met with instantaneous resistance from T&H. Soon after word reached Juneau, T&H sent representatives to the village to help organize a meeting of what they claimed to be the current board of the local IRA council. But because there was no currently elected board, the first priority of the T&H representatives was to appoint an elections committee that would enroll new members and update the membership list. They picked two women, which might have been a surprise to anyone not acquainted with the realities of village politics here. However, each of these women is at the center of a nexus of relatives and dependents—a "family" in local terms—and so each is in a position to bring to bear considerable local political weight. At the same time, neither woman has in the past been directly involved with the local IRA council, so both can potentially seem like nonpolitical outsiders. In reality, they are anything but outsiders.*

*The first is an older woman who was at the time of her nomination the Native language teacher at the school (meaning that she gave weekly classes on local history, language, art, and lore). The second is a younger woman who has lived for a time outside the village, but who now lives here. Both are educated, influential members in their families, of which there are currently four in the community. By choosing central figures in two of the four families, half the battle was already won. Where none of the "radicals" holds such a position in any of the remaining families, the rest of the victory is not far behind.*

*The enrollment lists—the one begun by the "Tribe" and the second collected by the re-formed election committee composed of these two women—function like a straw poll, with each side trying to enroll as many people as possible so as to appear the largest and most legitimate. People sign up for one, then change their mind and go over to the latter. Some remain on both lists.*

*Where the radicals had a month-long head start, their list was at first far ahead. That changes quickly, and now both lists are nearly the same size, and there is considerable overlap. And the defections from the radicals' list grow each day. After some initial resistance, the radicals seem to realize that they are outmatched here and that their best bet is to try to win an election based on the combined list of enrollees. If they can muster enough town support, they now feel, and win a T&H-sponsored election, no one will be able to question their claim to represent the village. On the other hand, T&H has already made it clear that they supported a different set of candidates...*

*It is now August, and it perhaps comes as no surprise to the Tlingit and Haida Central Council that it is the younger of the two women appointed to the election committee who turned the tide against the radicals. Her appointment made sense in two ways. She is bright, articulate, college-educated, and has served as the village representative to T&H in Juneau in the past. Even more importantly, she is on her way to becoming the central figure in the village's most important family.*

*Virtually single-handedly, she enrolled well over half of the adult population of the village, including a number of people who had originally enrolled with the "Tribe." This added further legitimacy to the T&H-sponsored election—at least in the eyes of the Central Council and the federal government—for it means that the radicals cannot claim that their supporters were barred from the election. Just as importantly, though, she found a group to run against the radicals—all of whom favor a continued relationship with T&H.*

*Having lost the enrollment battle, the radicals opted to run as a slate, and most in town now view them not as a rival organization, but simply as the opposition in an election largely managed by T&H. The question of legitimacy has been dropped in favor of an election based on family connections, and the radicals are largely seen as marginal to the several important families in the village...*

*A month later and it is done. In the end, the election was one-sided in favor of the slate of candidates favored by T&H. The radicals say they will continue to meet as "the Tribe," but with no additional enrollment and continuing defection among those already enrolled, enthusiasm has dampened...*

*When I return again to the village in 1997, several members of the radicals have been "run off," meaning they were forced to move away from the village, according to those who remain. Just as likely they left to find work, though this is itself often a political matter. The new IRA council continues to request help from T&H for achieving independent status.*

*This help has been slow in coming, though programs designed to promote greater local self-governance have now become a regular part of the T&H patronage cycle. Local council / board members now attend regular self-governance workshops, sponsored and paid for by T&H, and are allocated money that can be spent locally, perhaps to hire someone to work as a coordinator for self-governance issues. While outwardly promoting the very thing the radicals sought, these programs do the opposite—further entwining local political aspirations in the web of patronage that links the federal government to the regional tribal council (T&H) to the leaders of local families. It isn't clear to me whether Tlingit or Haida people ever shared the views of some Native Americans, that time is cycle in which the end is the beginning of the same, but it is not hard to see how elections like this could awaken those kinds of feelings if they did.*

The term "family" is actually used by Southeast Alaska village residents in two related but very different ways. It is used to refer to a household or nuclear family in the same way that it is used elsewhere in the United States. More commonly, though, it is used as a political term to describe large, extended kin groups, usually amounting to between four and eight in any Southeast village. These families—extended bilateral and affinally linked groups of three or more generations—have emerged intermittently over the past one hundred years. At certain times they have been the most important element in village social structures.

Not everyone in a village belongs to such a family. Some people, usually poor or displaced residents, may not be considered part of any family as such, even if they have relatives in a village. Other people can be considered part of a family and even central members of a family even if they share no actual kinship links with others in the group. Obviously, families have little to do with the types of blood or marriage links we normally associate with the term, or with anthropological notions of kinship more generally.

Part of the confusion comes from the fact that kinship has always been important in Native villages in Alaska, and many still speak of "uncles" and "nephews" as special relationships, reminiscent of past matrilineal linkages and clan affiliations. But today's local social organization is quite different from the clan and housegroup organization common in the past. Today's families do not resemble Tlingit or Haida clans or housegroups in organization, recruitment, or corporateness. Instead, families are shaped in large part by those same forces that have consistently destabilized other forms of social organization in the region and villages, from missionaries to boat loans to tribal council elections.

As will become apparent, families have emerged where other forms of social organization have disappeared precisely because families have as their basis no permanent or lasting foundation. They are ad hoc organizations, loosely structured by notions of biological relatedness and extended kin ties. They can shrink and grow, and they can emerge from nowhere as situations, opportunities, and problems arise. As a result, ever since the massive and continuous reorganization of the region began in the early twentieth century, families have gradually become the important, at times dominant, political units in every village in the region. The shifting nature of the family unit should not be mistaken for a lack of political importance, however. Large families can dominate village politics. In fact, this seems to be the crucial factor for defining those groups that may be considered a family.

PHOTO 9: *A modern Alaska "Limit Seiner," one of the few that still fishes from one of the Native villages.*

This point is unique, and it requires some clarification. Briefly stated, families must exercise power to be considered real families. Indeed, the very nature of the linkages—general notions of bilaterality and in-married relatives—means that an almost unlimited number of potential families could be assembled in any one village, for the necessary linkages are so loose that almost anyone can demonstrate some link to any number of such groups. Those families that are real (in the sense that they are recognized as corporate groups by themselves and others) act together to assert or dominate some aspect of village social life. Families, like Nuer clans of classical anthropology, are most visible only when in pursuit of a goal.

This structure causes tensions to arise between families, for in any village there are limits on the number of political "goals" as such, as well as a constant need on the part of families to re-create themselves in pursuit of one goal after another. Thus "family politics" have the potential to wreak havoc on many local institutions: school superintendents and police chiefs are perhaps the best examples of this. I was told that one could be a police officer in any of the larger Native villages for as long as one wanted, but that no one will ever last more than one or two years as chief. This is because, in effect, families realize themselves (in the sense of becoming real or concrete, and becoming conscious of themselves as such) through political activity, and getting a police chief or school superintendent fired is one of those activities. As such, political activity is important as much for its constitutive functions as for the goals pursued. Individuals in Hydaburg once described to me the removal of a school superintendent as simply a family "flexing its muscles." To extend this metaphor, other families can in turn "flex their own muscles" by trying to block this same goal.

The repercussions of this system of social organization are manifold, and they affect in important ways the political institutions introduced in the Chapters 2 & 3. Thus in one village, the present mayor (now in his third term) is a non-Native resident originally from Texas. It is widely acknowledged that much of his election success stems from the fact that he is not affiliated with any one family. Were he to be recognized as a member of one of this village's several important families, there is little doubt that the other three would join together to prevent him from being elected to a further term. Knowing this, he maintains cordial but intentionally distant relationships with the leaders of all the families in the village. Ironically, it is his lack of clear support that keeps him in charge.

What turns this broader social tension into tensions within families is the fact that the exercise of power in these circumstances (i.e., where power must be exercised for it to be held) inevitably means that the crucial political economic issues described in Chapter 2 necessarily provoke a state of near constant struggle over the gains and losses associated with the coming and going of the cannery system, or the rise and fall of the ANB, or election to contemporary tribal governing bodies. This has a large effect on those who live their lives at the margins of the community—those whose fates are tied most closely to the political footballs that are kicked around between families. In these circumstances, some members of every family pay a higher price than others for the continuous political recreation of local social organization.

These limits are built into the system as well. When a family secures a government job for one of its members as an act of political will, it secures a job for only that member, the benefits of which will never reach all of the members of the family that secured the job. In this way, no family is ever capable of meeting the needs of all of its members, and often is incapable of meeting the needs of even most of its members.

PHOTO 7: *A crewman on one of the last "family boats" fishing out of Hoonah. I was lucky to be able to make a couple of trips on this boat, and to see a version of family enterprise that once described much of the industry in the region.*

Yet few families are in a position to free themselves from this situation by eliminating marginal members. The reason for this is quite simple: most families exercise power through voting. Numbers matter when electing village councils, mayors, IRA council members, ANCSA board members, ANB representatives, and so on. Even apart from formal elections, large numbers can also be important for the sheer magnitude of their collective participation in churches, Native dance groups, or even town meetings, where large crowds add up to influence. For these reasons, a family must be large to be powerful.

For family leaders, this means recruiting even those with marginal kin links to the family and unsure status within the village.

For those on the margins, participation means at least the potential to gain some favor. In the dire economic circumstances in which most households function, this potential is about all that many of those on the edge can hope for. As a result, less central members of families often remain members of these groups despite the lack of any immediate benefits.

The implication of these two dynamics is that any family will be made up of people with very different needs, hopes and expectations. Because past political and economic dynamics have combined to make all villages stratified, families are highly stratified as well. As such, powerful families are diverse, socially and economically—a diversity that bestows upon them a form of internal economic dissention that lends to their ever-changing makeup, and more than a few inevitable shouting matches. The reasons are clear and the solution elusive. To draw the lines of a sufficient breadth to become a real family, family leaders pull in individuals and households with very different political and economic needs, needs that drive these marginal individuals to seek out powerful patrons or families that might meet these needs. In the end, every family thus contains members with very different but sometimes very immediate political and economic expectations.

By way of an example drawn from contemporary politics, when a family is forced to choose—to throw what few resources even the most successful of them have—between subsistence rights on the one side and jobs in logging on the other, either choice will negatively affect some of their members. What's more, either choice will probably cost the family some members, as those whose livelihoods are no longer possible will likely leave the village. The family in question, to be a family, must choose. If individual members choose differently and for themselves, then the family ceases to be a "real family" and becomes just a group of relatives. When this happens, members are likely to leave and align themselves with other relatives or in-laws, knowing that their former family no longer possesses the unity to demand jobs and patronage, and hoping to gain by re-affiliation a better hearing for their needs or expectations. This is, in effect, how new families form and how all families try to grow in size, and thus in influence and power.

\*\*\*

One result of all this is that movement in and out of the villages has been a part of village life and family dynamics for decades. Family members who leave the village are still considered relatives and may be called on for help, as when college-age children board with relatives in Seattle or Anchorage. However, members who leave the village lose much of their influence in a family, and unless they are willing and perhaps even plan to move back to the village, they are unlikely to have any say in the use or sale of family resources, such as a family house or parcels of land. Likewise, those who leave are unlikely to have any say in family decisions regarding village or corporate politics, or the renegotiation of family alliances undertaken in their absence.

Despite this political coordination, families are seldom even remotely economically corporate. Some assets, such as old houses, tend to remain within families, but family-run businesses have a short life expectancy. In just about every village, one learns of family stores that went broke by extending too much credit to members of its own family, who later could not or would not repay. In commercial fishing, the once-common family boats are now very rare, partly because of the decline of the fisheries, but especially because of the inability of family boats to cut back on crew expenses as efficiently as non-family boats.

In the past, important families have been able to gain seats on tribal, village, or IRA councils, only to find that the demands made on the council members for jobs and patronage far outweigh the ability of the entire council, let alone a single councilor, to deliver. This has threatened the very existence of successful families, and some have disappeared as a result.

Note that this does not indicate a change in actual kinship relations or how they are reckoned, but rather reflects the many options open to any individual or household. For given the very general, loose means through which family affiliation is constructed, every individual has a number of options as to which family he or she will belong. In this way, families can disappear without a single member actually passing away or leaving the village. Likewise, some families remain strong despite the near constant loss of individual members to outside jobs or other opportunities, usually through more strategic use of patronage and efforts aimed at recruiting marginal members.

In the vignette that began this chapter, one of the "radicals" (the out of work totem pole carver) actually belonged to the same powerful family as the younger of the two election organizers, yet the differences between their respective places within the family could not be more stark. In part this difference came from kinship—the election organizer was the daughter of a former fishing boat captain that had been a major force in village politics for years, while the totem pole carver drifted in and out of several families and had left the community for several years to work on the Trans-Alaska Pipeline in the early 80s. But there was more to it than this.

In many ways the differences between the centrality and marginality of the two members of the same family involved their different levels of connectedness to outside political-economic dynamics. Put another way, one of the key differences lay in what they were able to broker back to the community from entities such as T&H, or friendship with one of Alaska's senators. At the heart of this is the fact that family politics turn on the ability of family leaders to simultaneously bridge the gap between rich and poor members and to selectively alienate members whose demands conflict with the potential of the family to sustain itself as a powerful entity, even while they also maintain an ability (normally not shared by other members of their family) to bridge the gap between what is happening in the village, and what is happening outside. When done well, a family can assume long-term, quasi-corporate existence and considerable local power.

\*\*\*

**The Ins:** The Jamisons are the current descendants of a former Native schoolteacher, Clara, who was born in Southeast Alaska in the late 1800s. The current Jamison family is among the most powerful families in its village, and until recently, had dominated village politics for more than three decades. Yet none of their power comes from any status in pre-colonial systems of clan or housegroup relations. The late Clara Jamison was an orphan and was raised, with her mother's brother's consent, by a family of missionaries. Later, as a young woman, she married a white man, one of the early settlers in the region. He had been a sawmill operator associated with a mission group in the village where she was born.

Her status, and the status of the family she started, came from her connections with the world beyond the village. Clara Jamison was one of the first individuals from the village to get a teacher's license, and she taught in the village where she was born for more than forty years. Her husband died long before she did—indeed, she passed away only recently, well into her nineties.

Beyond her connections to the world outside the village, Clara Jamison was also an authority on village matters. She spoke fluent Tlingit and had been instructed by her uncles (on her mother's side) in much tradition and folklore before moving in with the missionaries. It was her place between the village and the larger political economy in which it was embedded that allowed her to make critical political and social connections with the world beyond the village. The power of these connections was apparent at her memorial dinner, which attracted people from all over the region, including one of Alaska's senators.

Together the couple had four children, three boys and one girl. Two of the boys remained in the village; the daughter and one son moved away to Anchorage, where they still live. Evan, the elder of the sons who remained in the village, is a fisherman, one of the few commercial fishermen left there. He was and is a "highliner"—the owner of a commercially successful boat—and the status he gained from this allowed him to become mayor of the village several years ago. Today, to remain financially successful in the shrinking fishing industry, he has withdrawn from village politics and now fishes nonstop for eight months each year. He holds limited-entry permits in several fisheries outside the region and a purse seine license for local waters. He and his wife have no children. She remains in the village while he is away fishing, but she is not from there and remains apart from family politics.

The younger brother, Henry, works in the village as a maintenance man on village-owned buildings. He got this job when Evan was mayor of the village and has kept it ever since. Like his brother, he is well known in the community, though less commercially successful or politically prominent. He has never married, and has no children. Both brothers are known for their local knowledge and their use of subsistence resources. It is a common sentiment around the village that on any given day you will see one or the other heading out of the village at the crack of dawn to collect cockles or mussels, pull a crab pot or two, net some shrimp, gather wood for the stove, or go hunting on one of the nearby unlogged islands.

Evan was mayor for several terms. He was also involved in the IRA council when it gave over the majority of its responsibilities to T&H in the late 1980s. Many people in the village resent him for this. Even greater resentment concerns the IRA council's financial dealings during the time that Evan was a central member. The village IRA council then owned a cannery and some facilities, which they had originally purchased in the 1940s. The cannery had functioned off and on into the 1970s, generally subcontracted to a processor who would then hire people from the village as laborers and buy fish from local boats. As with many village canneries at the time, the point was not to make money, but to provide employment to community and a market for local fishermen, from the village perspective at least. From the lease holder's perspective, the point was to make money. Needless to say these two perspectives were frequently at odds.

Since the leasing system was always more of an employment scheme and a means for allowing local boats to "stay local" than it was a commercially aggressive business, the IRA council that actually owned the cannery seldom received much financial compensation from the contractor. Membership on the IRA council at the time, however, allowed council members to have a say in which contractor ran the cannery, and thus they were in a position to assure their own and their family's continued role in the fishery—for like cannery owners in the past, IRA councils and cannery contractors in the 1970s often provided the financing for fishing boats and materials. Evan had obtained his boat on a loan from IRA council, originally, but purchased other limited entry permits with loans from the contractor who ran the fish plant. The fact that he had played a large role in the selection of the contractor did not escape the notice of other families, of course, though their reaction took some time to come together.

Other benefits came to the Jamison's as well. After limited entry, when the number of boats fell and the canned salmon market, already depressed, was dealt its final blow, the cannery had been refitted for several successive purposes: to process shrimp; as a cold storage for the fresh fish market; and as a fish-egg packinghouse that sent salmon roe to Japan. While times were troubled for many families, control of the IRA council at this time meant at least the possibility of having some family members hired on during the refitting or as workers at the plant when it did operate. The increased number of products handled by the plant meant a boon for any fishermen who could deliver across a range of fisheries. The contractor would later point out, financing the acquisition of permits across these different fisheries was a survival tactic for the business, and nothing more.

At the time, it was unclear to most people in the village where the funds for the refitting of the cannery came from and what role individual council members had in choosing those contracted to run the operations. There has arisen some suspicion (though I emphasize that I have no knowledge of actual evidence) that several board members, including Evan Jamison, were compensated as a part of the deals that were struck.

All of this would likely have gone the way of small town gossip and past family rivalries, except that the contract holder for the fish processing plant, in the end went bankrupt and sued the IRA council for money invested and opportunity lost. His claim was that the community had failed to deliver the amount of fish (across several fisheries) necessary to sustain the operation at a profitable level, which resulted in a breach of contract. The arbitrator found in favor of the contractor and awarded the contractor the right to collect from the local IRA council the money lent to local fishermen (including Evan Jamison) for the purchase of limited entry permits. The rationale was convoluted. Because the fishing permits purchased with the loan monies were not legally foreclosable, the only assets held by the fishermen were their boats; but these had no value without the permits. This meant that the individual borrowers had, in effect, no assets. Because the IRA council had promised the supply of fish, and had encouraged the loans, the arbitrator found that they were on the hook, so to speak, for the defaults. In the end, the IRA council's only asset was the revamped fish-processing house and cannery building, and this was awarded in lieu of cash for the financial damages.

The result, though it took several years, was that the contractor owned the cannery it had formerly leased, and those who had made the lease on behalf of the community owned a number of valuable permits which they had bought with borrowed money, which now did not need to be repaid. Charges of corruption and cries of injustice followed, made worse by the subsequent decision of the new owner of the fish-plant to operate on only a limited basis—packing salmon roe for export to Japan. This was specialized work, done almost entirely by specialists from Japan who were brought in by the buyer's agent. Apart from one or two young women hired to assist the Japanese workers, the plant subsequently provided little local employment. Permit holders with the right to fish in other species, like Jamison, moved their primary operation to Ketchikan for most of the season, where markets for shrimp and halibut and other fisheries still existed.

Many of those in the village blame the then-current board for the loss of the cannery, and some hold the two leaders of the board—one of whom was Evan Jamison—personally responsible. Since that time, Evan Jamison has left politics and never again run for mayor or for the IRA council. His younger brother, Henry, had never been involved in formal politics. All of his influence is carried out informally, and this has diminished as the suspicions around his brother have grown. Thus, in effect, the older generation of Jamisons has been out of politics since the late 1980s.

In many villages, this might have meant the end of the Jamisons as a real family, especially because neither of these central members has any children. Nevertheless, despite past suspicions, a limited number of direct kin links, and a diminished role in the formal politics of the village, the Jamisons remain one of the most powerful families in the village.

Their influence comes from two places. First, two members of the most recent generation—a daughter and son of Clara Jamison's daughter (who had moved away from the village)—have been educated outside the village and have now returned. The daughter, Jean, has a college degree, and her brother, Tim, has a technical degree. Both have lived outside the village for extended periods of time, but they have used this time and their uncles' powerful connections to forge important links with regional political entities: the BIA, non-Native politicians, and T&H.

PHOTO 8: *One of the four canneries owned, for a time, by local IRA cooperative associations. During the 1950s and 60s, these canneries were an important part of the village economies, but coming at the end of the cannery period, none proved sustainable in the long run.*

Jean was once the village representative to the Tlingit and Haida Central Council, and thus she knows (and is well-known-to) the administration of that body. Tim worked for several of the logging contractors hired to log the village's ANCSA corporation land. This experience, and his family name, have allowed him to play a central role in several of the village ANCSA corporation board of director elections even when he was not a candidate. At present he holds a seat on that board. Jean has recently been part of an effort to revive the IRA council within the village, with the help of T&H, as discussed above.

Neither Jean nor Tim has a large household of her or his own, and neither is married to a member of another prominent family. In fact, both have married individuals from what might be called more marginal households within the village. However the size of the Jamison family is not limited to these links, and in a sense it might be enhanced by the lack of relatives with strong ties to these two new, central figures. The lack of immediate family members has prompted a number of marginal families to emphasize links that go back to the original generation of Jamisons (the schoolteacher and her husband), such as that of the son of the totem pole carver above who told me: "My dad's grandmother was a cousin of Clara Jamison, and she told me before she died that we were the same family before that." These sorts of links, in a village where many people marry and have children with more than one partner during the course of a lifetime, allow just about anyone to claim family ties like these. What makes the Jamisons likely candidates for such connection is both their powerful positions in the past and the fact that a lack of immediate family members makes the central core of relatives more dependent on what might be seen as voluntary—and thus potentially reciprocal—links and kinships.

The result of this situation is that the patronage expectations of these marginal kin on the current generation of Jamisons (neither of whom actually has the last name Jamison, since they are the children of a married daughter) are very high. This pressure is felt by both, though neither has been in a position of power long enough to have felt the loss of disgruntled members.

What remains clear is that the actual decision-making and organizing responsibilities of the family now lie with the current generation. The two uncles who remain in the village can and do lend support and advice on some issues, particularly when it comes to dealing with the leaders of other families—most of whom are a generation senior to the current Jamisons. But by and large they remain above most of the current machinations, leaving Jean and Tim to deal with the family politics. The power they wield as a result was recently made clear when both were elected by an ample margin in a village-wide election for a new tribal council.

*\*\**

**The Outs:** An example of a more marginal household comes from the other side of the struggle. This household is composed of a Native man, his wife, who is of Aleut descent, and their four children. Neither parent has close relatives in the village. His parents live in a nearby city, hers in the Aleutians. Siblings of both live in these places as well. Their two oldest children have left the village, the daughter to live with her maternal grandparents, a son to go fishing in a nearby, predominantly white town. The two younger boys still live at home. The older of these is in high school, the younger in grade school.

The father, Tom, is an occasional heavy-equipment operator, trained in the 1970s when he worked on the pipeline. The mother, Mary, primarily a housewife for the first decade of marriage, has recently gotten a job with the Head Start program and is now employed full-time. Tom now stays home with the younger son and is seldom employed full-time. When there is a log ship in the village he works as a longshorer. He wishes he could get a job driving a crane for the loading and unloading of these ships, but he has no formal training, and only those with family connections can get training, he says. Longshoreman work comes along about once every month or two in this village, though in the past it was more frequent. In a good day on the ship he can make one hundred dollars or more as a longshorer, and sometimes he will get three or four days in a row. For the most part the household lives on Mary's salary and what government assistance they can get. They live in a T&H-built house in constant need of repair, but they own a relatively new truck and are up to date on their bills.

To supplement their income, Mary makes cakes for special occasions such as birthdays and retirement parties as a side business. This brings in a little cash, perhaps as often as once every two weeks. Tom pursues subsistence activities, though perhaps not as regularly as some. He has a skiff and a net, and often he will lend these out to a friend for a share of the catch. He has a subsistence "partner," a childhood friend with whom he fishes during the peak salmon runs and hunts deer with on occasion. He also receives fish from commercial boat crews and skippers who give him by-catch king salmon (for which they have no limited entry permit) for a share of the smoked fish he will process from it. Though Tom uses fewer of the alternative subsistence species (shellfish, crabs, seals, seaweed), and despite the fact that he takes a sometimes casual approach to fishing and hunting, their household is among the highest users of fish and deer in the village, and is known for its large smokehouse and carefully smoked fish.

Tom grew up in a commercial fishing family. His father, now mostly retired, and elder brother are both fishermen. His brother inherited the family seine boat, and his father sold his seining permit years ago. Tom says that he does not feel excluded, though he wishes he had gotten some of the money from the sale of the license—based on the fact that he could have asked for it, he says, and they would probably have given it to him. But he does not like commercial fishing and is for the most part glad to be left out.

PHOTO 9: *A modern fish processing operation, much smaller in scale (and therefore local employment) than the canneries of the past. Throughout the region, jobs in the resource economy are now difficult to come by, with much employment shifting to public sector employment.*

Jobs for heavy-equipment operators were available when ANCSA corporations first began road-building plans back in the 1980s, but Tom failed to act right away and was too late for anything but a second-tier job on one of the older machines. Rather than do this, he stays at home. He talks about going back to work at times, but knows that the situation has not changed and that he lacks the connections to get the type of job he wants. "It's all connections," he states plainly.

The lack of immediate kin connections with anyone in the village has caused Tom and his family to be loosely affiliated with several families in the past several years. Tom claims a distant link (great-grandparent generation) to the most powerful family in the village, the Jamisons, and his middle son refers to a member of that family as his uncle. Most often in the past he has voted along with this family and been counted as a part of it by core members of the other families.

But these connections waned as that family gained considerable power in the village, including leadership of the tribal council and a seat on the village city-council. Tom had hoped that this might turn into a salaried job, but nothing came of it. Things came to a head when he was passed over for a village job about three years ago. The details are revealing of the expectations marginal households have of the families they join.

The story goes like this: in this village, few families have paid their trash bill at any time in the recent past; some because they cannot afford to, others because the village government has shown little will to collect the money owed. In response the village decided to let those who wanted to, and who owed more than one year's bill, to work on the trash truck for a week. Rather than receiving pay, these volunteer laborers would substitute one week's work for one year's trash fees. For reasons discussed below, Tom was eager to sign up, and we walked up to the village offices to do so on the first day we heard about the opportunity.

Problems arose for Tom, though, when many of the people in the village signed up to work on the truck rather than pay their bill—so many, in fact, that they had more weeklong volunteers than weeks in the year.

The reason for Tom's eagerness to volunteer was not the outstanding bill, but rather the prospect of full-time work. At the time of the opportunity, there remained only one permanent worker on the truck, the driver. The volunteers would replace the other permanent worker, who followed along behind the truck and emptied the barrels into the back. The person who had done that job had quit or been fired, no one was quite sure, and no one seemed all that concerned. Rather, many, like Tom, wanted to be put on the list of volunteers in order to advertise himself for the full-time job, should the village decide to replace the second worker on a permanent basis. When the senior member of the Jamisons—the family with which he was then affiliated and who held a seat on the village council—could not or would not place his name near the top of the list of volunteers, Tom became disillusioned with this family and more or less cut his ties.

A few years later, when the individuals who eventually became the radicals lobbied for local tribal government to replace T&H, Tom backed the reformers, hoping to earn a place in one of the two families marginally involved in the movement. When that failed and the radical tribal movement dissolved, Tom remained associated with one of these families. But this family, having lost its last struggle, is not in a position to help Tom or his family.

When queried, senior members of this family, the Wilsons, remarked that they have always considered Tom and his household members as part of their family, ever since he was a child eating dinner at their house. Tom reconciles his marginal place in the Wilsons by saying that he was not getting anywhere with the Jamisons anyway. For the time being he is willing to be counted (as much as anyone is counted when there is little political activity) among a different family despite the absence of any obvious or immediate rewards. The situation is fluid, though, and my suspicion is that he is just as likely to return to the Jamisons as he is to stay away.

*****

These stories are typical, and even a bit timeless. One would no doubt have heard similar stories at any time since the 1930s. Yet the family form swims in a delicate history, very much tied to the fact that villages exist at far remove from many of the engines of political and economic change. Indeed, were it not for two related political-economic changes that coincided with the limited-entry program, most Native villages might have been abandoned by the late 1970s, as many non-Native villages in Southeast Alaska were. Family power at this time reached an historic low, as the chief means for holding together large, extended family groups—family-owned and -crewed fishing boats—began to gradually disappear from most Native villages. As is clear in the examples above, rather than depend on family-owned boats and the jobs these provided, most family power (beginning in the early 1970s) derived from the ability to deliver patronage jobs in any of the many political structures discussed in Chapter 2.

An increase in the number of non-fishing, primarily public-sector jobs available and a growing ability of individuals in the village to control who got these jobs coincided with fishing's region-wide downturn to transform Native villages in ways that non-Native villages were not transformed. In the process, bureaucratization and patronage likely perhaps saved many Southeast Alaska's Native villages from abandonment, and in all likelihood, the flexibility of the family form saved Native villages. In the process, however, the types of ties necessary to become or remain a family were redefined.

The ultimate source of these changes was the discovery of large reserves of crude oil under Native lands on Alaska's North Slope. The discovery led to a statewide settlement of all Native land claims in order to transfer title to most of the oil-containing land to the state and federal government, and to facilitate the leasing of drilling rights on the remaining lands. This settlement led to the introduction of settlement-based Native corporations and sparked a dramatic increase in the size of local government throughout the state. For Native villages, the institutions that resulted brought with them a host of new jobs, virtually all of which were controlled locally (most especially, municipal government and village corporations). Families that had revolved around fishing either disappeared or turned their attention to these new opportunities. In many villages, new families emerged that were better able, or perhaps simply more willing, to lay claim to these sorts of jobs and the machinations necessary to control them.

After the 1970s, revenues from drilling leases on lands eventually taken by the state, and tax revenues from the exploitation of other reserves on Native or federal lands, rose dramatically. To this day, Alaska collects virtually no taxes beyond corporate taxes. There is no state income tax, and in fact the state pays out a yearly dividend to all state residents from an annual fund set up with money from the original oil leases. Since the 1970s, consistent budget surpluses have led to an expansion of public employment at all levels, including the local or village level, where state funding supports many village-based projects. Case in point: in 1965, 5,920 people in Southeast Alaska worked for state, local, and federal governments, 3,160 of them for state and local governments.[17] In 1990 the overall total was 11,860, of which 9,263 were state and local workers.

The differences are telling. During the two and one-half decades of oil revenue, federal employment in the region has actually dropped, while state and local governments tripled in size. The working population of the Southeast region as a whole went from 17,470 in the early 1970s to 32,670 in 1990, or an 87 percent increase in roughly twenty years. Much of the growth of administration has been in rural areas, while the majority of the population growth in the region has been confined to the large cities. In fact, many of the Native villages have retained a near constant population throughout this same period, while the size of local governments has tripled.

The result has been a transformation of village employment patterns. Even in the most industrialized Southeast villages, such as Kake, close to one-third of all workers are employed by the state, federal, or local governments. If contrasted with the number of those employed full-time and year-round, which most government employees are, and many other village occupations are not, the percentage would be much higher. In poorer villages with little local industry, such as Hydaburg, the ratio is staggering: 55 percent of all jobs are now in the public sector.

Beyond the statistical shift, other, more crucial changes have accompanied this trend. The most notable is that many of the new jobs, indeed most in some

---

[17] See Rogers, Listowski, Brakel (*ibid*), pp. 174 [table 79].

areas, are held by women. Women make up the majority of the employees at any of the federal health care clinics, run by Southeast Regional Health Corporation (SEARHC). Likewise, most of the new Head Start workers are women.

Within village governments, men still hold many of the more "public" positions of the public administration (mayor, city or village council member, magistrate), but numerically women often outnumber the men, holding almost all of the secretarial and mid-level administrative jobs. While the majority of the public school teachers in the villages continue to come from outside the villages (and often outside the state), the majority of the remaining school positions are filled by local women: the support staff, secretaries, monitors, cafeteria workers, and so on.

In small villages, like Klukwan, women are twice as likely to be employed as men. In larger villages, like Klawock, men's unemployment rates are twice as high as women's. Perhaps the best example is Angoon, where the numbers of men and women seeking jobs are closer than in some other villages. Here, among Natives especially, the differences are telling: of the 113 Native men in the labor force, 49 are employed; for Native women, 67 of the 87 are employed. Women hold 67 of the 116 jobs (58 percent), while comprising 44 percent of the labor force.[18]

For village families, these changes have far-reaching implications. When past family forms centered around family boats or family stores, they depended on the ability of a core group to mobilize capital (through connections to outside sources, like the BIA, as well as through their own ability to gather it through savings and work). New systems, in contrast, are contingent upon family leaders' ability to mobilize votes. Elected positions (e.g., mayor or city council member) are the key to patronage positions. These positions have become more valuable as alternative employment in most villages has diminished.

Also, gender relations seem to have shifted in families, with women now playing a more central role in the leadership of many families. While family boats had formerly been run and crewed by men only, the vast majority of the jobs available through the patronage networks are now held by women. This has raised the status of women, for quite often now the "spoils" of the family system must be realized through women. Thus, if we reflect back upon the vignette that opened this chapter, it should come as no shock that T&H chose two women to head the election committee. Nor should it be a surprise that a

---

[18] All figures for 1990, the midpoint of the period in question, and were taken from the 1990 U.S. Census.

well-educated, well-connected woman in a powerful family was able to turn an entire village.

As will be seen below, gender figures prominently in the identity issues raised in Chapter 5. It also plays a role in the recruitment for church membership, which, as discussed in Chapter 1, plays a role as *contratemps* to the culture movements that make up the backbone of the "new traditions" and identity projects that have emerged post-ANCSA. At the root of this is a question of economy, and the declining economy of subsistence production that confronts those on all village's economic margins. This decline set the stage for the rise of anti-cultural church groups, even while family economies and families themselves were being reoriented to what remains a surprisingly new Alaska.

CHAPTER 5

# Livelihood and Identity

*For the family I am staying with, food and livelihood during the summer months means salmon seining. Having grown up the son a commercial fisherman, it is a job I take to easily, and one in which I can keep up with the locals and (at least marginally) pull my weight. Salmon seining by hand requires three people and is most efficient with two powerboats and a skiff, though we almost always wind up fishing with one powerboat and a skiff, which means more sets, and thus more labor. Today I am fishing with Joe and his son Algie, who normally fish with one of Joe's subsistence partners.*

*It is a beautiful warm August day and we are fishing at Hetta Creek. The whole family is here. Joe's wife Anna and son Greg, who is too young to be on the skiff, are in the power boat, playing with the new puppy while they wait and hope for a good haul. We set the net right in the mouth of the creek, hoping to fully surround the school of sockeye before they see the net and swim out the open side.*

*Most of the labor involved in seining comes after the net has been set and the school of fish (hopefully) trapped inside. Then Algie and I pull the net while Joe "plunges" near the boat— using a stick or long-handled plunger to splash, and frightening the fish from swimming through the opening that is left where the net is pulled aboard. The work is backbreaking and long, longer and more backbreaking if the participants are inexperienced, as I am with purse seining, or shorthanded and unaccustomed to working together, as we are today. Individuals who have worked together in the past tend to be much faster, and thus far more efficient, making fewer sets and avoiding "water hauls"—that is, sets that return no fish. For this reason, most people go subsistence fishing with the same people every year. Still, today is a good day. Though we are new together, we have only one water haul, and we net three hundred sockeye in under twelve hours.*

*Unlike commercial fishing, subsistence fishing is done near the creek mouths where the salmon school to ascend and breed. Different species of salmon (in the North Pacific there are five, and they are quite distinct) use different types of streams for spawning, such that any particular stream is likely to have only one kind of salmon milling about its mouth at any given time. Sockeye breed in streams that feed freshwater lakes, and between late July and early August they can be found in schools at the mouths of creeks that empty from these lakes into the open ocean.*

*Fishermen will approach the creek mouth and wait, looking for "jumps" and trying to guess the location of a school. Salmon are fast swimmers, and contrary to many assertions, when near a creek mouth they will swim in any direction, with or against the tide. When a sufficiently large school is spotted and approached, an attempt is made to get ahead of it and to lay the seine in front of the fish (in the direction they are traveling at the time), and then to circle the school with the powerboat while laying out the seine from a skiff towed behind. It is the decision of the boat's driver, in this case Joe, when and how the seine will be set, and at least one person must stay in the seine skiff to cast over the end of the seine and make sure that the entire net feeds out smoothly. Today that is my job; Algie stays in the powerboat with his father.*

*The seine we use is not as long as commercial seines. It is only 100 to 120 fathoms (600 to 720 feet) long and 4 fathoms deep, but it is old and made of woven mesh that is heavy when wet. There is a row of floats across the top line, and "leads" (small, ring-shaped weights usually cast from lead) on the bottom or "lead line," so that the seine will hang vertically in the water like a curtain. Because the net is pulled by hand, efforts are made to keep it light and fewer leads are used than on commercial seines. Still, the seine weighs several hundred pounds. The use of this much lead is not uncommon because fishermen want the net to sink quickly and reliably. Seines that fish inefficiently—that let fish out under a net that too easily gets hung up on itself—cost more labor and time than they save by reduced weight.*

*When set well, the net encircles the fish, dropping to form a deep, circular curtain around the entire school. Once the loop is complete, Joe and Algie jump into the skiff with me. Algie and I begin pulling in the leaded line at the bottom of the net from the opposite directions, hoping to close off the only way out. Until this is done, Joe "plunges" beside the skiff, frightening the fish toward the back of the net and preventing them from escaping from the opening created where we are pulling the net aboard. If Joe can keep the fish from swimming under the boat, and if the leads can be brought aboard before the fish dive and swim under the net, then all of the fish caught in the circle will be trapped by the net.*

*Once the lead line is aboard and the fish more or less contained, we pull the remaining web and "corks" (the floating line at the top of the net), freeing any gilled fish who have forced themselves partly through the net and gotten caught by the gills as we go along. Those fish not caught by the gills continue to swim until there is no room left in the submerged portion of the web. These fish will then be pulled aboard with the bag formed by the remaining web or will be picked individually from the water. After the leads have been brought aboard, Joe stops plunging and returns to the powerboat to begin looking for the next place to set. Algie and I pull the seine from back to front—that is, beginning with the end attached to the skiff (which is also the last section laid out). This allows the seine to be pulled freely from the skiff when it is next set. If this is not done properly the seine will cross over or hang up, usually resulting in a water haul.*

*This entire process is referred to as a "set" and may net anywhere from zero to one hundred fish, depending on skill, season, and even time of day, for the fish tend to disperse into smaller schools as the day goes on. Much of the responsibility for the number of fish caught rests with the skipper of the powerboat, though obviously an inexperienced net man can ruin the very best set. Initially, success depends on the skipper's ability to guess correctly the size of a school and the direction in which it is heading. Once the net is set, though, the chance of success shifts to the group's ability to coordinate its work. Sockeye are exceptionally fast swimmers, and if the plunger misses his cue the entire school will swim out under the boat. Subsistence fishers may make as many as fifteen sets in a day, taking eight to ten total hours. Two powerboats (in place of one) can usually catch more fish—by towing the net in opposite directions they can close around a school more quickly—though inevitably it takes the same time to haul the net and clear the fish, and if anything, more coordination between partners. If fishers save time it is because their efficiency allows for fewer sets, not quicker ones, and this is not always the case.*

*By the end of the day we have made more than a dozen sets. My arms are swollen with the stings of jellyfish that come aboard with webbing. We have two good-sized barrels of fish, about a third of which will go to Joe's partner, who was not here today but whose net and skiff we used. We will, I know, spend much of the remainder of the evening and a good part of the night processing the fish we have caught—cutting them open and gutting them, removing the head and tail, cutting them into strips, and putting them on long, thin sticks to be hung in rows in the smokehouse. There is more work ahead, but it is made easier by the fact that most everyone we know is doing the same. The sockeye are at Hetta Creek for only two weeks, and everyone will take as many fish as possible while the supply lasts.*

During my early years in Southeast Alaska, between 1993 and 2000, food and livelihood for those still dependent on resources they obtained for themselves was in flux. This shift emerged following the large-scale clear-cutting of old-growth forests near Southeast Native villages in the preceding ten to fifteen years. The diminishing system of subsistence had functioned since the mid-1960s when the gradual collapse of the commercial cannery industry throughout the region put in place a more pronounced, community-wide dependence on locally obtained resources. That system lasted well into the late 1980s when the effects of clear-cut timber harvests and the distribution of ANCSA corporate proceeds initiated the dramatic transformation of most villages. Subsistence hunting and fishing did not disappear entirely, and many of these same practices continue today, reflecting a continuum from earlier in the 20th century or before. What has changed most recently is not so much the practices or resources involved, but their political context and symbolic value, and the long and even short term viability of the households involved in their harvest and consumption.

During nearly three decades of the 1960s through the early 1990s, subsistence practices of Alaska Natives were very diverse, in part a reflection of the richness of local ecosystems and the new technological means to exploit them, which in turn built on residents' deep historical familiarity with and dependency on local resources. Studies made during this time reflect this richness. During the 1980s, George and Bosworth list at least fourteen principal resources used by Angoon residents;[19] Ellanna and Sherrod list twenty-three resources used regularly by Klawock Natives[20]; and Gmelch and Gmelch list fourteen deep-water species, eight kinds of hunted animals, fifteen inter-tidal resources, ten kinds of berries, and hosts of other plant resources used for medicine, craft, and food preparation that were regularly pursued by Sitka Natives.[21] Reports for neighboring communities throughout the region confirm these claims.

The main categories of resources used by Southeast village residents were fish and marine invertebrates (crabs and shellfish), deer and other land mammals (including bear and moose), and plant resources (including many kinds of berries and regular use of several seaweeds). Harvest levels of heavy users included several hundred pounds annually in each of these categories. By far the most widely harvested resources, in terms of pounds harvested and time spent in collection, were fish (and in particular salmon) and deer.

The harvest seasons of these two resources complement one another, as salmon in Southeast Alaska were and are available in large numbers generally only in the summer and fall, when they return to local streams to spawn. Deer were most accessible in the winter when they must retreat from the higher elevations because of weather, and thus can be hunted from the water or, more recently, from logging roads. Both resources were generally pursued by small groups

---

[19] Gabriel D. George and Robert G. Bosworth. "The Use of Fish and Wildlife by Residents of Angoon, Admiralty Island, Alaska." Alaska Department of Fish and Game, Division of Subsistence, 1988.

[20] Linda J. Ellanna and George K. Sherrod. "Timber Management and Fish and Wildlife Use in Selected Southeastern Alaska Communities, Klawock, Prince of Wales Island, Alaska." Alaska Department of Fish and Game, Division of Subsistence, 1987.

[21] G. Gmelch and S. B. Gmelch. "Resource use in a small Alaskan city–Sitka. Alaska Department of Fish and Game Division of Subsistence Technical Paper No. 90, Juneau, 1985.

(discussed in more detail below) who shared the expenses of the hunting or fishing effort.

Salmon and deer were pursued primarily by men. Women participated significantly in the processing of salmon (discussed below), but less so for deer. Both were pursued with contemporary technology: pickup trucks and high-powered rifles were used to hunt deer; gasoline-powered skiffs and synthetic mesh nets or "seines" were used to fish for salmon.

In addition, almost all subsistence-using households (generally over half of the households in any village) collected berries and seaweed. These activities were performed by household groups rather than with subsistence partners, and were often organized by women rather than men, though both men and women usually participated. Berries were "jarred" or frozen for use throughout the year, while seaweed was considered always available. Seaweed was sometimes eaten alone, but more often cooked with boiled rice, which adds flavor and considerable nutrition. Berries were eaten alone or in cakes, and occasionally in "Eskimo ice cream" (in local parlance), i.e. stored in refrigerated seal grease and eaten as such. Other frequently used resources included seals, which were caught in the winter when they returned to the Southeast region in large numbers. Seals were hunted with high-powered rifles from open, gas-powered boats. In addition to the use of meat and blubber, skins were cured and sold to offset some of the cost of subsistence equipment and supplies.

Numerous other resources were pursued as well, including waterfowl and their eggs, moose and bear, mollusks and other marine invertebrates, and other species of fish, such as trout and halibut. A brief summary of statistics, in table form, drawn from research in 1984 in the village of Angoon (with a population of about 600, almost 80% of whom are Alaska Natives) will serve to finish this general profile of resource use and local participation.

From these data, it is clear that among heavy users, individuals devoted considerable time and effort, and reaped considerable reward (totaling hundreds of pounds of harvested resources among heavy users) from subsistence production.

In addition, as will be discussed in more detail below, the data presented by George and Bosworth also make clear the extent to which these resources were redistributed throughout the community. In fact, the household basis of their survey may actually miss some critical elements of redistribution that were less important for the amounts involved than they were for the relations they indicated and made possible, that is, the traditional, "Indian foods" given to individuals and extended families for distribution at village-wide celebrations and ceremonies.[22] In this case, virtually the entire village partakes in the harvest of a few individuals, not as households (and so, not revealed in the survey data, I suspect), but rather, as village residents and more importantly, as Native village residents.

***

This last point raises what is perhaps the most overlooked element of subsistence production during the period: the relationships among people that the work of producing one's own food entails and makes possible—relations which now, for the most part, bear a complex relationship with ANCSA and the changes the act has wrought.

Among those subsistence relations already mentioned above are "partners" and the informal subsistence-gathering party. Partnerships were maintained by nearly all heavy subsistence users. They were frequently long-term relationships through which partners shared the expense of subsistence harvests by contributing complementary pieces of equipment, and by coordinating harvest labor. Partnerships were not necessarily warm relationships, but they were necessary for effective and efficient harvests. Many tasks, like salmon fishing, required several persons (minimally two, but usually three in the case of hand-seining) if they were to be done at the scale necessary for large, multiple household consumption. Beyond this, familiarity between partners made for increased efficiency, as coordination of activities, even beyond individual fishing expertise and knowledge, leads to larger harvests. Deer hunting could be done individually, but most hunters chose to hunt with partners, sharing out the expense of the boat or truck used and gaining some insurance against a later unsuccessful hunt, as anyone along for the day received some share of what was obtained, even though a deer was assumed to belong to the person who shot it.

---

[22] It should be noted that all of the data in TABLE 1 are aggregate figures, obtained by researchers working for the Alaska Department of Fish and Game, an organization better known to village residents for its enforcement of hunting and fishing regulations than for its research. As noted below, my suspicion, grounded in conversations with heavy subsistence users from other villages, is that such figures represent a significant under-reporting in the size of harvests by heavy users and those most dependent on subsistence resources for resources which carry strict and frequently enforced limits. Thus, no household in George and Bosworth's (1988) sample reported harvesting more than twelve deer (the legal limit for a two adult household). Deer hunters in other villages reported to me that, in large subsistence-dependent households, they may take as many as thirty or forty deer each year, well above the legal limit, and I suspect, well above what they would be willing to reveal to state Fish and Game researchers.

PHOTO 10: *Out hunting with friends from Hydaburg. I remember these as among the happiest days I spent in Alaska. Native hunters talk frequently about a connection with "the land," and my feeling is that much of what they mean by this is captured in the relaxed sense of joy common to all on these days.*

As most subsistence hunting and fishing was done by men, most of those entering into partnerships were men. Women, almost invariably the wives of those doing the hunting or fishing, participated in the processing of resources—the gutting, cutting, drying and smoking of fish; the butchering of deer; the preparation of seal meat and fat—which took place after the harvest. Partners generally did not process fish or other resources together, and there was no extension of partnering relations to the wives of even long-term partners.

Relations between women did structure some harvests, however. In particular, berry picking and other plant harvests were often initiated by women, and involved groups linked by relations among women. Thus a woman may have coordinated a trip to the berrying grounds with her friends or close female kin. Men usually accompanied their wives on these trips, as did children of both sexes (which is not necessarily the case for hunting and fishing), and all participated in the harvest. Part of the purpose of bringing such a large party together, I was told, was safety—bears are likely to flee an area where there is a large group and, conversely, will potentially attack a small group or a person working alone. Yet the subsistence party, as one might call it, lacked the collectiveness of those tasks pursued by partners, especially fishing. Berry harvests were kept separate even during collection, with each household harvesting its own stores, rather than pooling the entire harvest and dividing the total into shares as was done in fishing.

Some subsistence resources were gathered by single individuals, such as mollusks and other inter-tidal resources (cockles, clams, gumboots, and seaweed, in the table above). Others were shared widely, usually along "family" lines. Yet the contrast between the relationships involved in hunting, fishing, gathering, and the accompanying sharing, processing, and storing, versus those upon which families were organized and maintained is strong. Family-based social relations were, structurally, the set of local relations most closely tied to the dynamics of the larger economy; subsistence relationships normally stood outside the formal economy.

*\*\*\**

The tension between these two realms of relationships is sometimes very obvious. One example: while families played a role in the sharing of subsistence resources, a man's partners were seldom drawn from within his current family. One likely reason for this is that heavy subsistence users were so because they were among the most marginal members of any village (or, conversely, they were among the most marginal because of their continued dependence on subsistence, which works out to mean the same thing in practice), and were thus among those most dependent on subsistence foods for their day-to-day survival. Indeed, among heavy users, even short-term shortages or complications meant dramatic changes in their ability to remain housed and fed within the village.

Partnerships drawn from within a single family worked against this sort of consistency in several ways. Family lines usually cut across economic lines—as the need for votes encouraged family leaders to cast their own political net as widely as possible. Thus choosing a partner from within a family meant either crossing lines of economic difference, or choosing among those with whom one was competing for jobs and patronage. For a straightforward set of reasons, neither strategy worked well. In order for partnerships to be effective, both partners must be equally committed to subsistence tasks. A man's partner must be available to go hunting or fishing when the weather and season permit. The opportunity costs of days missed fishing or berrying were enormous, for these, like many resources, were available only briefly. Differing obligations between partners impeded flexibility and coordination, and choosing a partner across economic divisions meant, inevitably, choosing someone whose availability and commitment to subsistence tasks for basic survival differed markedly from one's own. For this reason, no heavy subsistence user could afford a partner who was regularly employed; and no regularly employed, part-time subsistence user could meet the cooperative needs of a heavy user.

Conversely, by choosing a partner on a similar economic level within a family, one would be choosing as a partner someone with whom one was normally competing for patronage from family leaders—patronage that includes part-time cash employment, which all heavy users depended on to continue to pursue subsistence. For this reason, partnerships within a family that match individuals from a single economic stratum were seldom any more long-lasting than those that crossed strata. As a result, most lasting subsistence partnerships were made between marginal members of separate families within the same village.

Beyond partnerships and subsistence parties like those made of close female kin who go berrying together, other relations were directly involved in the processing of subsistence foods and other locally produced use-values as well. In villages like Hydaburg, where the prime resource processing sites within the village (smokehouses and areas along the beachfront) tended to be held by older residents, many of these residents exchanged use of processing equipment (like a smokehouse) and their own labor for a share of the final product. In these cases, elderly men and women would rise frequently in the night to tend the fire and at other times assist in the cutting and re-cutting of salmon, and perhaps even help in the canning or jarring of fish. In return they received several cases of salmon, or some well-dried "hard-smoke" for their own use.

As above, spouses were frequent participants in subsistence processing tasks. Indeed, smoking and canning salmon usually involved far more labor than the actual harvest. After collecting berries, these must be frozen or jarred (a process like canning that involves sealing and boiling at high temperatures for extended periods). Seal fat must be rendered (by boiling and skimming) and herring and salmon eggs smoked or boiled. Where job opportunities for women arose, this could conflict with spousal participation in subsistence production, often complicating the ability of even the most dedicated user to continue in a subsistence livelihood, despite a willingness to do so.

Beyond the relations entailed in the actual harvest and processing of resources, there were other relations as well that subsistence fostered or allowed. Harvesting households invariably shared some of what they produced, sometimes with expectations of exchange, such as when people gave gifts of deer meat or herring roe to a well-known seal hunter, fully expecting to receive some seal oil or "grease" the following winter. Exchange relations like these resulted from specialization among users, or, as in the last example, people's unwillingness or inability to participate in a particularly difficult harvest—few people regularly hunted seals because of the dangers involved, even in villages where seal meat was a popular food. In all of these cases, whether gifting reflected a desire for the products of other people's subsistence work or a desire for recognition and the continuation of friendly social relations, exchange of subsistence items created an obvious sort of village-wide interdependency.

As one can see from **TABLE 1**, many people shared food, particularly resources like deer and seal meat that were difficult to store, in effect pooling labor and redistributing harvests among several households. The webs of relations created by these exchanges were thus broad, sometimes blanketing an entire village. Some sharing was clearly "interested," as in those cases where gifting followed family lines and was designed to curry favor with powerful members of extended kin groups, with the hope of receiving or repaying other sorts of (often financial) favors. Other gifting was almost entirely altruistic, as when a successful hunter donated a large seal to a village elders' center, knowing that it would be appreciated but not repaid in anything more concrete than good will and local reputation.

In addition to all of the relations formed through subsistence work and exchange, there remained other relations—relations not formed directly by or for subsistence hunting, fishing, gathering, or processing of subsistence foods—which were nevertheless influenced and enhanced by these practices, especially among those most dependent on subsistence for day-to-day living. The most basic of these was the households of subsistence users themselves.

This point is often overlooked by those who focus overtly on the role of subsistence in shaping local identity. Among many of the heaviest users I encountered, subsistence was not simply a "lifestyle," it was also, at times, a "livelihood." For these individuals and the households they supported, it is clear that subsistence harvests allowed them to remain in the village without participating fully in the formal economy, and to do so during times when that economy would normally force them to leave. In this way, marginal households remained part of the extended kin groups (families) and participated in the community as a whole, its ceremonies and traditions, village and church groups, basketball rivalries, friendships of various intensity, and all of those born-of-continuous-familiarity relations that go with living in a small town. Such relations need not be idealized to be counted as significant in people's sense of self and sense of well-being.

## TABLE 1: Resource Use and Sharing in Angoon (1984)[i]

| RESOURCE | Percent of Households Using | Mean Harvest (lbs) / Household | Percent Households Receiving |
|---|---|---|---|
| KING SALMON | 36.8 | 83.7 | 15.8 |
| CHUM SALMON | 26.3 | 168.6 | 2.6 |
| PINK SALMON | 21.1 | 80.5 | 7.9 |
| SOCKEYE SALMON | 21.1 | 262.5 | 10.5 |
| COHO SALMON | 39.5 | 154.3 | 13.2 |
| CUTTHROAT TROUT | 15.8 | 18.3 | 7.9 |
| DOLLY VARDEN | 28.9 | 17.5 | 5.3 |
| HERRING | 36.8 | 32.2 | 7.9 |
| HERRING EGGS | 15.8 | 193.3 | 10.5 |
| HALIBUT | 81.6 | 139.3 | 26.3 |
| PACIFIC COD | 21.1 | 26.4 | 7.9 |
| SABLEFISH | 13.2 | 69.6 | 10.5 |
| RED SNAPPER | 26.3 | 34.5 | 13.2 |
| HEART COCKLES | 52.6 | 8.6 | 26.3 |
| CLAMS | 71.1 | 7.8 | 23.7 |
| DUNGENESS CRAB | 23.7 | 32.3 | 31.6 |
| BLACK GUMBOOT | 63.2 | 19 | 15.8 |
| OCTOPUS | 21.1 | 45 | 5.3 |
| BLACK SEAWEED | 21.1 | 106 | 34.2 |
| HARBOR SEAL | 15.8 | 450 | 23.7 |
| DEER | 60.5 | 396.7 | 44.7 |
| DUCKS | 7.9 | 26.3 | 7.9 |
| BERRIES | 63.2 | 17.7 | 23.7 |
| PLANTS | 13.2 | 1.8 | 5.3 |
| WOOD | 73.7 | N/A | N/A |

[i] Abridged from George and Bosworth 1988 (ibid): 55-6

By the mid-1990s, the gradual erosion of these relationships was felt by everyone who faced the prospect of having to leave the village. As it was explained to me by one village resident who had left and returned: "Down south [meaning the continental U.S.], we are just plain old Indians." Insofar as subsistence production and livelihood allowed individuals and marginal households to stay in the village and remain intact, it was inextricably bound to those types of relations that are generally glossed over with the simplistic terminology of "local community" or "close friends," phrases that too often defy their proper weight and significance, and of which do not exist away from the village itself.

In related form, by allowing marginal individuals to stay in the village, subsistence production allowed for a personal sense of belonging that is hard to explain clearly but which is, nonetheless, a powerful motivating force in Native communities. In this way, subsistence provided people with a sense of uniqueness and participation in a community, and though subject to ideological and political manipulation, it furnished a strong sense of belonging. This 'spiritual' side of local relations is seldom discussed, even by identity theorists, but it features prominently in village residents' own discussions of their lives. Subsistence contributed to these feelings in the same way that it contributed to the friendships and feelings of community discussed above, i.e. by allowing people to remain in the place where such feelings could and did take place.

\*\*\*

By the early 1980s, issues of identity began to figure strongly in public manifestations of the desire for subsistence resources in Southeast Alaska. Notably, this was especially true among light users and those who did not necessarily engage in the harvest of subsistence resources at all—often as much as half the population of Southeast Alaska Native villages. Not coincidentally, the latter category (non-producers) usually included those most central to village political and economic organization, and thus the leaders of most families.

Elite members of all Native villages derived prestige from being able to provide "Indian foods" at any of the social gatherings that they sponsored. Such gatherings were actually quite common, especially in the summer months when they coincide with the peak of the subsistence harvests. These include, and included "pay-off parties," where another family, or even one "side" of a village[23] is rewarded for help in the funeral arrangements of a deceased relative, a process akin to the historical Tlingit potlatch. And they include "giveaways" intended to mark some important social event, such as a fundraiser for the local Native dancing group; celebrations of local accomplishments such as college graduation parties or engagements; or political parties, as when a local sponsor threw a party to introduce a favored candidate. Events of this scale were often held in the school gymnasium and included virtually the entire village population. On these occasions, individuals known for their hunting, fishing, and gathering were recruited (often informally, usually along family lines) to obtain and process specialty foods for distribution at the party. Those who did were always formally acknowledged, and good hunters received much local prestige from their participation as providers of traditional subsistence foods at these events.

In turn, on these occasions subsistence foods were used by elite members of the community to forge relations across economic and political lines, both within the village and beyond. This was certainly the case when locally powerful village residents used an event simultaneously to broaden a family network, and to direct that network toward some specific goal, i.e. the election of a favored candidate to the state assembly, local ANCSA board of directors, or school superintendent position—often the subtext of any number of social or celebratory events. In this way, extensive family connections were assembled that allowed family leaders to bridge village boundaries with the outside world and place themselves in a nodal position in local and larger (regional, state or federal) patronage networks.

From the perspective of those attending such an event, inclusion in the celebrations and the common consumption of traditional foods encouraged more marginal members of the village to consider themselves part of the family of such a leader and thus, at least potentially, recipients of the sorts of patronage created. In dialogical fashion, this sort of optimism provided the family leader with the social support necessary for greater participation in larger-than-local (usually regional or statewide) politics—his means of acquiring resources such as jobs, contacts, and positions that were the source of his local power.

Native identity played a critical role in this process, and subsistence foods had

---

[23] The issue of "sides" or moieties in Southeast Alaska is complicated. Historical accounts speak of exogamous moieties designated as ravens and wolves, composed of exogamous, property holding clans (which in turn were composed of housegroups). Clans crosscut villages or "quans," and so did moieties. Moieties ceased to function as exogamous units in the early part of this century, and clans lost most of their corporateness at the same time, though in fact possession of clan-owned resource areas were remembered much longer.

a critical part in that performance. What allowed powerful individuals to occupy such a nodal position in a family or even village-wide hierarchy was the perceived (as well as the actual) separation between the village and the larger political economy of the region. By reinforcing the idea that villages were, first and foremost, "Indian" villages, local leaders in Southeast Alaska named and created a political bloc whose perceived collective interests outweighed any competing sense of local differentiation in needs and desires.

PHOTO 11: *The old and the new: a smokehouse by the waterfront, behind one of the older houses. Satellite dishes are increasing ubiquitous in even the smallest villages...making the isolation of rural Alaska increasingly a myth.*

Likewise, villages seen from the outside as essentially "closed" encouraged outside (regional, state, or federal) leaders to work through local intermediaries, furthering the isolation of non-elites in the villages. The manifest distance between local and larger—visible in the costumes, foods, limited-but-symbolically-significant Native language use—discouraged both outside interests and village residents from attempting to bridge the perceived gaps that separated the local from the larger. Local leaders who thus could effectively mobilize the key tokens of identity became both the intermediaries as well as the presumed protectors between the local and the larger.

On such occasions, "Indian foods" (as they are sometimes called) allowed Native identity to overwhelm and obfuscate well-known village-based social differentiation in residents' perception of their individual circumstance, intensifying the distance between village and its regional, state and federal surroundings. It did this while simultaneously strengthening a collectivity of belonging and community that submerged the actual differences in power, wealth, access, or political objective that separate those who oversaw the distribution of special foods and those who supplied them. Subsistence thus played a crucial role (especially in the absence of other signifiers) in making these events into "Native" functions, a role which was often enhanced by the presence of the local Native dance group. In this way, subsistence foods were fundamental to the reproduction of a specifically local form of power, one that was, for the most part, disconnected with the sorts of relations actually used to obtain and process the foods.[24]

ANCSA contributed significantly to the escalation of this discourse, and perhaps inadvertently helped place subsistence politics at the center of local-larger differences, by officially extinguishing Native hunting and fishing rights on the lands taken by the state and federal governments under the Act. In the early days of ANCSA, this more than any other aspect of the Act caused outrage and anger throughout the state.

The results were swift and among the few local victories that followed the settlement. The Alaska Federation of Natives, the original statewide Native voice in ANCSA negotiations, advocated against this portion of the Act immediately after it was passed, and was able to draw support from throughout the state in the effort to have it overturned. This work, and more like it throughout Alaska, eventually resulted in the creation of the *Alaska National Interest Land Conservation Act* (ANILCA)[25] which restored Native and rural subsistence rights, and made them a priority over sport and recreation uses of federal lands. To this day ANILCA is seen by many Natives as a political accomplishment on par with the original ANCSA settlement. Similarly, in Southeast Alaska, the Southeast Native

---

[24] For related reasons, subsistence production took a central place in discourses of regional Native identity as well, though the means and occasions of its mobilization were quite different. Thomas Berger, in his influential *Village Journey* (1985), made subsistence virtually synonymous with Native identity throughout Alaska. And Dauenhauer and Dauenhauer argued that subsistence practices (like other elements of individual life in Southeast villages) were intimately caught up with Tlingit collective self-understanding. Others, including Thomas Thornton, have demonstrated the role that research on subsistence practices played in securing the land claims of Southeast Natives in the U.S. Court of Claims, and in the eventual statewide settlement (ANCSA), further heightening the importance of the very idea of subsistence to those most active in regional land and sovereignty claims. Studies like that by Goldschmidt and Haas in the 1940s were used by Native advocates to demonstrate continuing use and occupancy based on past and contemporary reports of subsistence practices in areas around Native villages.

[25] Alaska National Interest Land Conservation Act, 94 stat. 2371.

Subsistence Commission was formed in 1990 to continue to advocate for Native subsistence rights, and it has become one of the more visible regional advocacy groups.

The reasons for this pride are subtle yet important. One reason that ANILCA was so important to Alaska Natives is that ANILCA laid the groundwork for the continuation of many of the relationships discussed above—of partnership, community, livelihood, and household. These are relationships that occur outside of the larger-than-local political economy of timber harvests, oil drilling rights, industrial mining and all those elements of the global economy that ANCSA brought to Alaska and indeed to the doorstep of most Southeast Native villages. It made no difference to Southeast Alaska Natives that their own region had been immersed in industrial relations for nearly a century. The radical ebb and flow of global capital, and the fact that many households had been thrown back into subsistence production with the collapse of the fisheries demonstrated to many households the need for a set of relationships independent of the juggernaut of global industry.[26] This point is crucial, as it underlies so many of the ways that ANCSA, even in its successes, became the point of such profound dissatisfaction. In spite of what will be said below about the manner in which the lives of subsistence users reflect the changes of the larger economy, subsistence relationships were shaped by an internal dynamic largely independent of wider political economic forces. That is, issues such as tribal membership, ANCSA corporation shareholder status, and even questions of the ownership of surrounding forests and waters, had little influence on the nature of the relations that went into, and came out of hunting, fishing, and eating foods caught by and for one's self and household.

Rather, subsistence relations drew their significance and their nature from local ideas and meanings. This last point is critical because it is equally clear that subsistence users on the whole were greatly affected by changes in outside political economic dynamics. Consider that, while partnering was a practice largely independent of ANCSA shareholder status, the issue of who had the opportunity to enter into a partnership was significantly influenced by such

---

[26] This in no way implies that subsistence users were not dependent on the larger economy—they were. All users had to have access to cash income (either their own or that of a spouse) for gas, bullets, equipment, and so on. Even the most autonomous subsistence user lived in a house with electricity and heating costs, and the majority had children and spouses who required clothes and basic necessities, all of which required some access to cash income. Some subsistence products were sold (otter skins could fetch upwards of $1000 or more), though these were rare. As a result, even the most autonomous subsistence user had to take on cash employment, on a temporary or intermittent basis, and nearly all counted on the income of a spouse.

factors as the ANCSA-shareholder status of those involved.

This inter-relatedness could be summed up by saying that while partnering was governed by a set of values and ideas independent of ANCSA, no one was free to live according to these values alone. The relations that sprang from subsistence ideas and values: partnering, cooperation, responsibility within households, intra-community links of sharing and exchange, recognition across economic divisions within a village; all reflected and were inflected with the shifting dynamics of the surrounding political economy, by virtue of the fact that those individuals and groups that form these relations were inextricably involved in the wider political economy. In this way, subsistence represents an incomplete alternative to the current political economy; one whose internal dynamics exists apart from issues such as ANCSA but whose overall shape was constantly influenced and buffeted by these same outside forces through the very people who sought out subsistence as an alternative.

***

By the early 1990s, ANCSA and the political economy it inspired had undermined the ability of individuals and households to enter into or maintain subsistence relations, and it had done so by endangering the viability of the resources themselves, and undermining the sustainability of subsistence relations by intensifying the stakes of local inequality.

The ecological implications of clear-cutting large segments of old growth temperate rainforest in the Pacific Northwest are by now fairly well known. Most ecologists agree that it will take more than 100 years to restore these areas to their pre-1980s condition. In the meantime, logged areas do not provide nearly the potential for subsistence harvests that unlogged areas do, and areas that have been clear-cut are generally known to local hunters and fishermen as barren.

The situation is intensified by the legal status of the lands involved. ANCSA corporation forests are, by law, privately held, and thus not subject to a host of recent laws aimed at ameliorating the environmental effects of industrial logging in U.S. National Forests. Stream buffers—the practice of leaving un-logged trees on either side of a stream—mandated under various federal harvest policies are unenforceable on village-corporation or Sealaska lands, as such laws apply mainly to public lands. While many ANCSA corporations do make some efforts to leave stream buffers, the economic incentive to do so, particularly for companies harvesting timber far from their own village (but perhaps near to someone else's) is minimal. In tours of several village corporation clear cuts, I seldom saw stream buffers more than 20-40 feet, despite ANILCA requirements of 50-100 foot buffers on private lands, and despite conservationist requests for buffers of up to 300 feet. Such minimal buffering practices are scarcely an improvement on total clear-cutting, as narrow buffers are quickly knocked down by harsh winter winds.[27] Yet the effect of wind-fallen timber in these narrow buffers is actually small compared to the effects of the roads built to access timberlands throughout the region.

Gravel logging roads now spider-web the areas around most Native villages, often amounting to hundreds of miles of road on any particular island. These are used by hunters, and have been a boon to deer hunting in some ways. But their effects on the streams they cross are marked. Logging roads are sources of silt for the streams that run by them or under them, and silt can greatly affect the carrying capacity of the streams involved.

The problems of clear-cutting do not end with road cuts, however. When clear-cut forests grow back, they raise another set of ecological problems. Normally, re-grown areas sprout so many new saplings that they become, in effect, impassable. This is true not just for humans, but for deer, bear, moose, and other forest creatures for whom the thick undergrowth is an impenetrable barrier. Without exaggeration, one can say that clear cuts become impassable for even mid-sized woodland creatures for at least the first fifty years of re-growth.

Conservation efforts to leave un-harvested segments of land, to enhance habitat maintenance, are also troubled by harvest patterns encouraged by ANCSA and its subsequent amendments. For while village corporations may be willing to leave unlogged less profitable areas (usually in exchange for nearby lots with better harvest potential), the cutting of large portions of neighboring land means that these become, in effect, forest islands, unable to sustain subsistence resource harvest levels that their combined island-wide size might indicate. In addition, many ANCSA corporation holdings border on one another. When thus combined, these areas greatly intensify this effect, creating clear-cuts and isolated patches of forest that resemble an archipelago of small treed plots stretched over tens of miles.

---

[27] Narrow stream buffers located in clear cuts are subject to being knocked down by winter winds, for the trees left standing grew originally in the shelter of the surrounding forest and many are unable to withstand winters once exposed on their own. Ironically, once blown over, they expose the streams they were guarding to heavy silting with soil washed from their own disturbed footprint. This effect is potentially quite large when a whole section of buffer is knocked over.

The situation is difficult for village residents throughout the region, primarily because ANCSA required village corporations to choose land from the area surrounding their homes. The regional corporation, Sealaska, was also required to choose lots for timber harvesting that were nearby or abutting village parcels, further intensifying the effects of village selections. Taken together, this means that, in addition to the area already cleared for town use, almost 50,000 acres (or roughly 80 square miles) of nearby forest has been clearcut around most villages, and so remains, in practical terms, permanently unusable for subsistence purposes. Yet in addition to this, villages located in areas deemed inappropriate for harvest by the framers of ANCSA (often because they were located in areas already designated for other uses – national wilderness areas or national parks, for example) were allowed to choose parcels far from their own villages. Most of these village corporations chose land on Prince of Wales Island or its smaller neighboring islands in the southern end of the Alaska panhandle, where potential commercial harvests were the largest. This area is already home to four Native villages, and thus four village corporations. When the land selected by these four corporations is combined with those parcels owned by villages located in areas deemed off limits by ANCSA, and combined with the adjoining areas selected by the regional corporation Sealaska, the result is that over 275,000 acres (roughly 460 square miles) of traditional subsistence land has been slated for harvest in the vicinity of Hydaburg, Klawock, Kasaan, and Craig. Together with the timber allotments granted to the large non-Native timber producers in the same area, the consequences are dramatic, especially for residents who are most dependent on a subsistence livelihood.

Some of the implications of this process are not immediately visible, but are, in the end, critical to understanding the impact of ecological devastation on those involved. One such result of the clearing of such large stretches of land immediately around villages is that individuals dependent on fish and deer harvest for household livelihood must now go further, at greater risk of accident and of encountering Fish and Game enforcement, to find foods formerly locally available. This increases the likelihood of equipment failures and the costs of those failures. It also increases the danger involved in many subsistence practices, where small boat travel over long distances increases risks due to weather and mishaps.

In a region where subsistence regulations virtually require heavy users to break the law if they are to actually pursue subsistence foods as a livelihood, long trips to diminishing areas radically increase the chances of being caught fishing or hunting illegally. Almost every heavy subsistence user I met had had some recent encounter with Fish and Game officials, and most recognized this as an immediate threat to their livelihood—as even suspicion of illegal fishing can be cause for the confiscation of equipment and harvest, pending a hearing. Cash fines and loss of equipment also present special and immediate problems to those without regular cash income who are dependent on hunting and fishing equipment for even short-term survival. It is no exaggeration to say that the loss of hunting and fishing equipment for even a short time can cause significant hardship for heavy users, often requiring that they depend more on partners, or are forced to leave the village to look for employment in the formal economy.

Decreasing harvest areas also means that hunters and fishermen face greater competition in the areas to which they must now go, as hunters from other villages and an increasing number of tourists react to problems of reduced habitat throughout the region. Indeed tourist competition has only begun to affect the situation. And as more and more Natives turn to "guiding," the local term for serving as a hunting or fishing guide, as a replacement for lost employment in the villages, the number of tourists hunting and fishing in these areas is likely to increase considerably. In fact, many Native villages and several tribal organizations have advocated tourism as a way to replace livelihoods lost to the decline of commercial fishing and logging, despite the pressure created by increased hunting and fishing on subsistence-based households. The effects of this, like other village-based development projects, are unevenly distributed among current village residents.

It is not difficult to see the ways in which habitat loss for subsistence resources directly impacts the relations involved in subsistence harvests, as well as those that stem from the consumption and trade in subsistence foods. Individuals who lose equipment to fines or confiscation risk losing partners as they are unable to fulfil reciprocal obligations. Those who leave the village in pursuit of even short-term cash employment leave behind partners whose ability to remain in the village is now compromised. Subsistence-based households face decreased harvests because of decreasing resources or the loss of efficiency when working with a new partner, and higher costs associated with more distant travel for subsistence resources, which together strain already limited cash incomes. For those hunters, gatherers, and fishers pushed out of their own villages but unwilling or unable to pursue wage-based cash employment outside of a small town, relatives in other villages can provide the opportunity for relocation to new subsistence areas. But such strategies further strain resources in those areas, intensifying the loss of sustainable subsistence resources there as well.

In all of these ways, the loss of a subsistence livelihood due to habitat loss creates a ripple effect. First the household, then the partners, and eventually an entire village can be affected by these processes. Village schools, funded by the state on a per capita basis, lose funding when households are forced to relocate away from the village, causing further losses (and further relocations) in what is normally considered "safe" employment in the school or other public sector jobs. Village stores are dependent on village residents for income. Losses in local population threaten the viability of ancillary businesses in any village. In the past, region-wide economic declines in Southeast Alaska forced the abandonment of virtually every non-Native village. What allowed many Native villages to survive this process (and the end of the cannery era in Southeast Alaska in general) was the willingness of some Native village residents to pursue a subsistence livelihood. As this livelihood is slowly but definitively diminished, Native villages face the renewed prospect of the earlier fate of their non-Native neighbors.

PHOTO 12: *Pulling a beach seine with Algie and Supe near one of the creeks on southern Prince of Wales Island. The rippled water in the net furthest from the boat indicates that this time, we will get some fish. Photograph by Anna Frisby.*

Critically, habitat loss has a less immediate negative impact on the ideological side of subsistence. That is, when "Indian foods" serve a mainly symbolic or ideological function, featured at large gatherings and them marking as a specifically "Native" event, the increased expense or decreased availability of these resources can diminish the amounts of those foods, but not their symbolic value. In fact, shortages may even serve to heighten the ideological power of these foods. For once "Indian" foods come to be seen as icons of Native lifeways, any threat to their viability becomes, by extension, a threat to the community. In this way Native foods and the subsistence practices that produce them become a sign not just of community, but of its potential dissolution, and hence the need for greater solidarity—even across the economic lines that separate those who supply the food from those who sponsor the events at which they are consumed.

As such, these foods also help mask the extent to which forms of inequality are produced locally, as ANCSA has increasingly become the engine driving the intensification of local inequality and the greatest threat to local habitat. While these ceremonies can be a source of considerable recognition and even limited fame for those who produce the special foods involved, it seems to make little difference in the economic viability of the households of those so recognized. I was often told that the hunters and fishermen I knew well (i.e. those most heavily dependent on a subsistence livelihood and thus those most knowledgeable and reliable in their subsistence harvests) were like "old time Indians." If such a reputation somehow compensated them for the loss of livelihood that ANCSA and its shareholders (many of whom are neighbors and are attending these same events, indeed perhaps even sponsoring them) bring about, then there might be some rough compensation in the personal and collective identities thereby created. But this is seldom the case, and most of the time, individuals held on a pedestal in this way fare no better than other marginal members of their communities in their attempts to remain in the village amid the destruction of their livelihood.

***

One could summarize the above by noting the extent to which ANCSA has intensified the need for alternative notions of what it means to "be Native" (especially for those on the bottom) while simultaneously undermining opportunities in the realm most connected to the livelihoods of these same individuals and households. ANCSA has impaired subsistence as a livelihood in several very different ways. The most obvious of these is the widespread ecological destruction encouraged (perhaps mandated) by the Act, effects felt first and mainly by those for whom subsistence practices remain fundamentally a form of livelihood. In addition, far-reaching changes in the village economy like the collapse of commercial fishing have destabilized village populations, making it increasingly difficult for individuals pursuing a subsistence livelihood to maintain the critical work relationships that make this livelihood possible (i.e. partners and exchange relations, but also households and other village-wide ties).

The results of this are easy to see. Hydaburg, located in the heart of the some of the most clearcutting, went from a population of nearly 500 during the NOL distribution to less than 350 people by the late 2000s, a drop of nearly 30%. Nearby by Kasaan dropped by nearly 50%. In Kake and Hoonah, the decline was nearly 20%. The predominantly non-Native communities of Sitka, Ketchikan, or Petersburg either remained steady or increased during this same period.

Less directly, but perhaps more importantly, because ANCSA has proceeded through the limited and qualified (though nonetheless significant) recognition of Native claims, it has placed issues of Native culture at the center of the ongoing transformation of the local economy. One immediate result of this, a result exacerbated by language in ANCSA eliminating Native subsistence rights on state and federal land, including most of Southeast Alaska, has been a dramatic increase in the symbolic importance of subsistence in Native identity. Subsistence use and consumption, more than any other local practice, has come to be seen by village residents as iconic with Nativeness in the region. Anything that imperils or even affects subsistence is seen as something that directly affects not just Native people, but their ability to live and reproduce their Nativeness.

One might expect that such a situation would help those most dependent on subsistence by safeguarding their livelihood, though here it is important to consider what the increased symbolic value of subsistence practices to notions of Nativeness has. What becomes obvious in the undermining of the role these practices play in sustaining households for their livelihood, is the shift in the discourse on subsistence to questions of lifestyle rather than livelihood. The nature of ANCSA-based development complicates this situation, for much of the ecological and social disruption in the lives of subsistence users has been caused by Natives themselves, acting through village corporations and the regional corporation, Sealaska.

This encourages people to separate the practical from the symbolic elements of subsistence practices. While ANCSA corporations do much to endanger the practical results of subsistence practices, they do nothing to prevent subsistence practices themselves. In fact, it is just the opposite. ANCSA corporate politics have become a significant social process in most villages, intensifying issues like sponsorship and patronage discussed above, and consequently, raise the symbolic importance of subsistence practices and products. As ANCSA corporations draw on Native claims for their origin and expansion, and beyond this, as they incorporate conventional Native iconography in their logos and self-representations, Nativeness itself has become, more than ever, a critical factor in local political processes.

Thus, as above, one result of ANCSA-based development is the need for an alternative set of distinctly Native relationships capable of answering the sorts of social and personal divisions created by the transformations wrought by ANCSA—some sense that there exists a viable alternative to the sorts of social and political processes that participation in ANCSA involves—on the part of those most marginal to the current political and cultural project.

Subsistence seems, ironically, to provide an alternative. Nevertheless the ecological and social devastation caused by ANCSA seems to denigrate the sustainability of subsistence as a possibility, in ecological terms. Thus, ironically, it is those most directly involved in subsistence livelihood that seem increasingly pushed to reject subsistence as an icon for Nativeness, in order to assert its place in the simple material reproduction of their households and persons. The results of this, for both individuals and communities, is taken up in the next chapter, but early hints can be found in the Flo Ellers incident that opened Chapter 1. As discussed briefly in the Introduction, one way to understand the anti-cultural response of many of the new Evangelical and Pentecostal churches is to see their actions as a reflection of the tensions around the social divisions wrought by ANCSA—tensions that have pushed more and more to the margins, while capturing and redefining the means by which they manage to stay in the community. But before turning to this, it seems important to look more closely at how these tensions are lived and understood, individually, and collectively.

CHAPTER 6

# Subsistence & the Cost of Culture

*It's winter 1996, and I am staying in Hoonah, a large village (by Alaska Native standards) of about twelve hundred people. Like most Southeast Alaska villages, it is built in a relatively sheltered area along the coast of one of the region's many large islands. The Alexander Archipelago, in which Hoonah is located, is actually a submerged mountain chain, and in most places the land rises abruptly from the ocean. In areas near productive resources, and somewhat out of the weather—areas where good winter hunting and forage were available, and good defensive positions against occasional raids from neighbors or more distant travelers—people have built villages along the steep shores for at least the last ten thousand years. When the salmon canning industry came to the area in the late nineteenth century, companies built their industrial canning plants near existing villages to take advantage of Native labor. Other villages relocated to be near the canneries in order to take advantage of opportunities for cash income and access to novel Western goods. Hoonah is something of both. Originally a camping and work area for one of the several clans that later came to be known as the Hunakwan, or "Hoonah people," the village itself was formed shortly after the building of a cannery in the late 1800s when the Hunakwan moved to the present location.*

*The village itself is rather compact, with houses built up the hill that rises behind the village rather than out from the town center. One can walk from one end of the village (by the airport and the school) to the other (by the grocery store and the road to the cannery) in about fifteen minutes. Despite Hoonah's compact size, most residents have automobiles and about half of the roads are paved.*

*Outside Hoonah there is a logging camp at Whitehorse about twenty miles to the south, and a religious settlement referred to as "the camp" beyond that. Travel on the roads outside* town is limited to vehicles that can withstand the rough surface built for logging trucks, and no roads lead off the island. People coming and going from Hoonah travel by ferry, or, more recently, by one of the small airplanes that link many of the out-island villages throughout the region. The ferry and air service connect Hoonah to all of the ten or so Native villages in the area and to the region's three large (by Alaska standards) cities: Juneau, Ketchikan, and Sitka. The ferry arrives and departs several times each week, carrying most of the village's material needs.

On this trip to Hoonah I am staying with Owen, a friend I met when he was running a "culture camp" in Kake in 1993, the village he is originally from. He now lives in Hoonah with his wife and six children in a small, five-room house along the waterfront. Owen is a subsistence hunter and fishermen; subsistence is his "livelihood," as he puts it. He also works on logging ships, work that people call "longshoring," when one is in town. This wage work allows him to earn the money he needs for hunting and fishing supplies, and staples like rice and coffee, as well as for the "light bill" and things for his family. Altogether his income seldom exceeds three or four hundred dollars per month during the summer, and less during the winter. Quite often his wife goes to the store to buy on credit, a deal she renegotiates each and every time with the store manager. In the past, when everyone in the town was involved in some form or another with commercial fishing and cannery work, winter credit was a regular part of people's lives. Now, with commercial fishing all but gone from Hoonah, credit is scarce for those like Owen who are known to lack regular employment.

The day after I arrive, Owen invites me to go seal hunting with him and Mike, his subsistence "partner." Owen and I fished together frequently during a summer several years before, and he knows I'm interested in the sorts of daily activities subsistence workers participate in. This is my first time seal hunting, here or anywhere, and both Owen and Mike tell me it is illegal for whites. "You're not even supposed to be in the boat if we're seal hunting," they tell me, laughing, though they take me along anyway. I try to reassure them by saying that if we get caught, I will tell them that this is anthropology research. Neither actually seems very concerned, nor are they any more relaxed by my assurances. Fish and Game wardens do not patrol the winter hunters. Southeast Alaska's winters are too cold and dangerous for any but those most dependent on hunting for their basic food needs, and wardens are reluctant to halt this sort of harvest, legal or illegal.

Winter conditions in Alaska, even in the more mild Southeast panhandle, are difficult. Around Hoonah, the ice and water are particularly dangerous, for Hoonah is located in the northern end of the region, across an open and broad bay from Glacier Bay and the permanently frozen Saint Elias Mountains. We leave the village at about six in the morning. The sun won't be up for another four and a half hours, and then it will only stay up for three hours. By two-thirty in the afternoon it will be dark again. We will stay out *hunting until six in the evening. The temperature is five degrees Fahrenheit when we leave, and it remains below five degrees for the rest of the day, dipping down into the negative numbers in the evening. The wind is worse in the morning, when it blows about twenty-five miles per hour from the northeast, the coldest direction. The wind chill is about thirty-five below zero; we picked what turns out to be perhaps the coldest day of the year.*

*We take Owen's boat, a sixteen-foot aluminum skiff with a twenty-horsepower outboard motor, to travel down into the bay south of Hoonah where the seals shelter themselves from the weather and lounge about on patches of ice along the shore. Mike and I sit in the bow while Owen operates the motor from the stern. We face backward, he faces forward, taking the oncoming wind and freezing spray directly on his face. Altogether we say very little to each other. Mike and Owen seem to know implicitly where we are going before we set out, and there is no discussion of any plan once we are in the boat.*

*When we get to the head of the bay that morning, or at least as close as we can before the frozen ocean forbids the boat to go any further, it's about seven-thirty. Owen directs the skiff in to the beach. The first hunting we will do is on land, hoping to catch seals still resting on top of the ice, but the wind was at our backs as we approached in the skiff and the noise of the motor has scared the seals off the ice. Mike explains that it is difficult to hit a seal in the water because they seldom surface and can travel great distances underwater, staying down for up to twenty minutes. With no prospects in the bay, we return to the boat and travel up another inlet. On the way Owen shoots at one seal bobbing in the water beyond the ice, but he misses and it disappears below the surface.*

*In the next inlet, however, there are two seals, both in the water. Owen fires at one and misses, and both disappear. Shortly after, one reappears closer to the boat. Owen and Mike both laugh, and Owen shoots the seal quickly and easily. We move up on it with haste, for a dead seal in the water will occasionally sink. Mike puts a gaff hook through the eye of the seal, and we tow it into the beach. At the beach, Owen and Mike leave the skiff to work on the seal while I stand and watch. They cut out the internal organs, saving most, which they clean in salt water. They strip the remains from inside the intestines as well, and wash and save these. Mike removes the long bones from the seal, leaving the skin intact except for the first cut up the belly and neck. Even the skull is removed without cutting the outer skin covering the face. The organs are then placed back in the chest cavity and the seal is placed in the bow of the boat. In all, the operation takes less than ten minutes.*

*We've brought no food along, only a thermos of black coffee that by ten in the morning is ice cold. By eleven the java has turned to frozen slush and we pour it out. I've done little work beyond simply holding the boat at the beach so it doesn't drift away. The climate is so frigid that even my camera won't work. I watch what I can, thinking of what I'll write in my journal this evening, but at the same time I can't help but think about how cold my feet are, as I stand in amazement and witness Owen strip off his jacket and gloves and work in knee-deep water dressing the seals we catch.*

*Several times, Owen drops Mike and me off at a point near the entrance to one or another of the many inlets south of Hoonah. We wait while he runs the outboard around the bay, scaring the seals into the water. The hope is that they will try to escape the inlet (and the motor) underwater and resurface where the inlet opens into the bay. If they do, Mike will try to shoot them from the point where we are standing. When Owen hears a shot, he returns to see if we hit something. We try this in a few places, but the seals never surface within range of where we are standing. "It's a lot of luck," Mike explains.*

*While we are waiting, Mike tells me stories about hunting with Owen. Mike and Owen are about the same age—late forties—but Mike states plainly that Owen taught him how to hunt. "Owen's like an old-time Indian," he explains. Owen's family is originally from a village south of here called Kake; he came to Hoonah when he was married, and his wife's family is still in Hoonah. Owen's father, who still lives in Kake, is among the last of the traditional Tlingit orators. He had many children, of which Owen was among the youngest.*

*By the end of the day we have taken three seals. Two of them are quite large at over two hundred pounds. Each was killed in the same way, by a long-distance rifle shot from a moving boat when the seal was momentarily at the surface. Though Owen killed all three, Mike will take one of the larger seals and Owen will take the other two. This distribution is made with no discussion. At the beach back in Hoonah, Mike simply says, "I'll take this one?"—half question, half statement. Owen doesn't say anything, and like that, it's settled. In all the two partners speak very little at any point in the day, perhaps a dozen sentences over twelve hours of hunting.*

*Owen and I carry his two seals up the beach and into his house, where we place them on a tarp on the floor in the kitchen. Owen's son Lyle then begins the work of carving up the seals and separating the skin from the meat and fat. Lyle is about fourteen and already a good hunter—he would have gone today, but I was lent his Mustang suit and other gear. He begins by running a knife between the skin and the seal meat and then stripping the fat from inside the skin, all the while being careful not to puncture or thin the skin in any one place. Such a slip would reduce its value, and the money from the skin is counted on to offset the costs of hunting. Lyle puts the fat he scrapes from the inside of the skin into a large pot, and when the pot is full he gets another. From a two-hundred-pound seal, people will sometimes recover thirty or more pounds of fat, and at the height of winter, such as it is now, perhaps fifty or more pounds.*

*The fat will be rendered to produce oil, which is considered a valuable specialty food. People dip dried salmon and halibut in seal oil (or "seal grease," as it is referred to when it is refrigerated and becomes a semi-solid), much as some people put butter on bread. It is also used in a number of homemade remedies. A tablespoon of seal oil is said to cure digestion troubles.*

*The organs of the seals are used more immediately. The heart and liver are sometimes used together to make a stew, as are deer heart and liver during the summer months. The remainder of the meat will be placed in a smokehouse, locked to keep the dogs from getting in, and used when necessary. People in Hoonah eat seal meat in stews, and they barbecue the ribs. They will deep-fry the intestines, cut into short pieces, similar to the deep-fried pig intestines eaten in the American South.*

*A large portion will be distributed to friends and to older people. Owen talks about giving the entire smaller seal to the Salvation Army in town. Around town, Owen is known as a good hunter and a generous man, and he is well liked as a result. The oil that is rendered from the fat will be distributed too, usually in pint mason jars, to people who like it or "need it," as Owen says. When someone in town is planning an event, Owen can be counted on to donate "Indian foods," which raises the prestige of the occasion.*

*While Lyle works on the seals, Owen and I sit and watch television. We drink black coffee and eat cake made from a boxed mix with sugar and lard frosting. There is rice mixed with seaweed on the stove, and when Lyle is finished working on the seals he will make a dinner of seal meat stew.*

*Owen and I talk a little about the day, mostly at my prompting, which he considered a successful hunt, though he had expected to get more than three seals. I ask about the danger, and whether he thinks the risk involved in winter hunting is worth it. On our return, as the temperature dropped and the wind died down, the entire southern section of the bay began to freeze, and at times our small boat had trouble breaking through the ice. In the end we went out further in the bay in order to loop around and come in from a direction the remaining wind had kept clear, but there the waves were higher and more dangerous. To me, the chance of being overturned or trapped in the ice overnight seems a high price to pay for three seals.*

*To my surprise, Owen does not justify the risks with reasons drawn from the obvious economic necessity in which he is trying to raise a family, though he might well have, for he is very conscious of it in other ways and at other times. I knew there was nothing else to eat in Owen's house that day, and that, as was often the case during my summer visits, the fruits of our hunting or fishing were for immediate consumption. Instead, Owen justifies what he has done by saying that this is his life, his "culture."*

*Thomas Berger, in his survey of Alaska villages in the mid-1980s, found this to be a common sentiment throughout the state, and referred to it as the "subsistence way of life" (Berger 1985). By "way of life" Berger meant more than just livelihood in the sense we normally understand the term—more than simply a way of earning the necessities of life. He meant that it was a way of being in the world that created meaning—more than just survival. Had Owen read Berger's book, he would likely have agreed, and would just as likely have used the term "culture" to describe what Berger referred to as "way of life." Many of the Alaska Natives to whom Berger spoke did, in fact, use the term "culture" in this way.*

*Owen would add: "I like hunting." He would later tell me that he wouldn't know what to do if he didn't hunt or fish: it is what he does with most of his days. "It's who he is," Mike would explain.*

For reasons that have as much to do with laws passed in the last three decades as they do with the long-term changes in village economies, subsistence—the fundamental place of hunting and gathering in Native lives and families—has emerged as the key issue for village residents seeking to resist larger-than-local forces. In particular, Native advocates have used subsistence to counter external political manipulation in two ways: first, and mostly employed in the past, by demonstrating de facto possession of lands and resources sought for expropriation and development by outside interests; and second, by making use of the social relations and sentiments spawned by subsistence work that lie outside the relations of the current political economy, around which ties within and between communities can be mobilized.

Much of the history of the former, the use of subsistence to demonstrate past occupation of disputed lands during the late 1950s and early 1960s, has been published recently by the Sealaska Cultural Heritage Foundation in *Haa Aani, Our Land: Tlingit and Haida Land Rights and Use.* In fact, the form of the final statewide land settlement, ANCSA, was in large part prompted by lawsuits won in the U.S. Court of Claims on the basis of continuing de facto possession of subsistence areas in the Southeast region. This and other small victories did much to demonstrate to Natives that their claims could be used to pose serious, time-consuming roadblocks to unsatisfactory land settlements, and hence used to delay government and industry access to Alaska's natural resources, especially oil.

In these cases, and principally the land claims case brought by the Tlingit and Haida Central Council in the 1950s and 1960s, subsistence and traditional-use practices played a large role in both mobilizing support among village residents, usually by counter-posing development with people's continued reliance on certain areas, and establishing a historical record of land and resource use.

More recently, however, some Natives have wanted to turn the issue of subsistence away from any direct historical connection to land claims, seeking instead to contrast subsistence practices with the sorts of relations that emerge through and from ANCSA. This change has been critical in reshaping the regional political landscape, but it has also, perhaps inadvertently, brought about deep changes in subsistence hunting, fishing, and gathering in every

Southeast Alaska community.

In one way, the opposition between subsistence and ANCSA was determined by ANCSA itself. One provision in the original Act eliminated any special rights to subsistence use or harvest by Natives on lands taken by the state of Alaska and the federal government.[28] This meant no special access to roughly four-fifths of the territory within Alaska's borders, including virtually all of those areas that Natives had previously considered crucial to subsistence and traditional-use practices. A host of litigation followed, and in 1980 the Alaska National Interest Land Conservation Act (ANILCA) was signed into law as a partial remedy to these problems. Even now, however, the implementation of ANILCA has remained partial, and the disputes generated by ANCSA's subsistence-ending provisions are far from over.

Beyond this, however, subsistence has always been an issue with strong emotional resonance throughout Alaska. In his travels across the state, advocate and Canadian federal judge, Thomas Berger, noted the central place subsistence played in Native reactions to the Act. He was told: "Subsistence to us is...our spiritual way of life, our culture," and, "This land is part of...our identity. The land is very important. It is part of the religion, it's part of the heritage, and to put a dollar value on it would be something that would [only] come from Congress." One Southeast Alaska Native noted: "Us Natives, we should have the right to live out our culture, something that cannot die...to take away our culture would be to take away our lives, everything we knew, everything our parents knew, everything our children should know...What is that billion dollars? I'd rather have my fishing and hunting rights."[29]

The irony of this last statement, that culture is something that cannot—in the sense of "must not"—die if people are to live, and which the speaker clearly feels to be imperiled by ANCSA, seems to capture the central yet ambiguous place of subsistence and the culture that surrounds it in the post-ANCSA period. Over and over again, Berger was told (as was I) that subsistence and Native culture are so closely knit that it is impossible to have one without the other.

The uneasy predicament for most Natives is that while ANCSA empowers some ways of being Native, that is, by recognizing historic claims and empowering cultural economies, it simultaneously undermines what most

---

[28]See Thomas R Berger, *Village Journey: The Report of the Alaska Native Review Commission*. New York: Hill and Wang (1985), pp. 60-65.

[29]*Ibid*: photo captions.

Natives consider the material and spiritual basis for a distinctive Native culture: subsistence hunting, fishing, and gathering. For this reason, subsistence rights and traditional-use practices have emerged as key elements in Native identity struggles in the post-ANCSA period.

The complexity of the situation is most apparent to those dependent on subsistence foods for daily survival. Many of the regular subsistence users I knew in Alaska—Joe, or Mike, or Owen, or Tom, for example—would agree that subsistence means more to them than simply a way to make a living or having enough to eat. They would agree with Berger's conclusions, that subsistence is a way of life that informs and shapes almost every part of their lives and the lives of those they are closest to. But they also insisted that subsistence is a livelihood, and that as such, it was something far beyond an identity. For most heavy subsistence users, subsistence is not something they could choose to leave, or that they had chosen to take up. More importantly, for them, anything that limited or put an end to subsistence work meant not simply the loss of identity, but far more immediate, the loss of family, home, and the sum of their entire lives.

Yet these same people—Owen, Tom, or the ten or so households like theirs in every village (out of, say, thirty to fifty)—are also among the more marginal individuals in their communities for reasons that are closely related to their subsistence livelihood. It is impossible to say whether they turned to subsistence because of their marginality or whether their marginality stems from their opting out of much of the local economy. Although, the end result is the same: those who are most dependent on subsistence for their livelihood are also those least likely to have a say in how subsistence, as a political issue and central aspect of Native identity, is manipulated, assessed, or even asserted in the higher political realms where things like ANCSA or ANILCA are decided.

***

Subsistence has become a rallying point in resisting ANCSA for several reasons. The first, is that the ecological decimation caused by ANCSA corporation harvests is the most visible, and visibly disturbing, impact on the physical landscape that surrounds most Southeast Alaska villages. Around virtually every village, 25,000 to 50,000-acre patches of clear-cut forest constantly remind residents of the source and costs of their very limited political-economic success. This contrasts strongly with an equally widespread notion of the historic importance that subsistence work and subsistence relationships played in the past. People attach great value to Indian foods, to the extent that there is occasionally an informal cash market for rare products (e.g., oolichan, or "hooligan" oil). Beyond the actual relations of subsistence production developed between partners, many of the village's poorer families derive significant local prestige from their ability to provide traditional foods to those who spend little time hunting or fishing, but who nonetheless choose to use these foods to demonstrate to the community their identity and Native values. Thus a household known to take good care when processing fish will be given "by-catch" (i.e., fish that cannot be sold commercially because of out-of-season restrictions or lack of permits) by better-off commercial fishermen, which they will then process and keep a share of. This was the case for Tom, discussed in Chapter 4. When such foods are used for a party or social gathering, those who prepared them are always recognized.

The utility of the relations, sentiments, and identities produced in this way can be seen in one example from the village of Hydaburg. One summer in the early 1990s, an airplane used by Alaska Fish and Game enforcement officials spotted several subsistence fishermen fishing illegally. The fishermen saw the plane as well and knew that this meant an immediate visit from state enforcement officials. Realizing also that in addition to the illegal fishing, they already had an illegal number of fish, the crews returned quickly to Hydaburg, taking with them their entire catch, and radioing ahead to the village to explain their predicament. When they arrived in Hydaburg, shortly ahead of the game officers' boat, they were met at the dock by much of the town's adult population, altogether perhaps one hundred or more men and women. The boat's crew gave all of the fish to those gathered at the dock and then joined the crowd, waiting for the enforcement officials who would arrive by boat from the nearby non-Native town of Craig.

When the officials did arrive, the gathered crowd prevented them from landing their boat, taunting and mocking them. Eventually the officials gave up trying to land their boat or identify the individuals involved. Later, when several state policemen arrived by automobile, the crowd reassembled to once again stand together for "Native rights." In the end, no one was arrested and none of the fish taken. Many people, in speaking later of the incident, pointed out with pride: "We stood up for our culture."

Disputes like these between enforcement officials and subsistence users often mystify officials from the Department of Fish and Game. Most point out that the harvest levels are determined only after careful research on the levels of use common to particular villages and according to their best estimates of the ecological health of particular resources. As many Natives are known to share these same concerns, Fish and Game administrators thus see the problem as deriving from a small group of overly stubborn individuals who flout the rules out of spite or ecological foolishness. Situations like the one in Hydaburg, where entire villages seem to fall into the latter category, then seem strange and incomprehensible, feeding the stereotype that is common throughout the region: "Oh, that's just the Haidas. That's how they are."

PHOTO 13: *Eating "Indian foods," in this case herring eggs captured on spruce boughs that are placed in fish breeding areas. Such foods mark the events or "doins" at which they are served as special, Native-community events.*

However, all of these issues point to a fact seldom discussed by advocates like Berger, and one that is especially absent among those who advocate subsistence as an alternative to ANCSA: subsistence use, and the time devoted to subsistence practices, tend to vary considerably within any community. Such a notion is similarly obscured by official statistics on subsistence harvests, which have been used to direct policy throughout the region. Because these studies use only village-based aggregate figures, they seldom provide information on the variability of individual use. Thus Native subsistence users are allowed six deer per year, based on the fact that most community-based studies show that the average household uses far less. Yet poor families, that is, those most likely to use subsistence resources for basic survival, who hunt and fish frequently and are thus most likely to confront the enforcement personnel in charge of maintaining those limits, have told me that they need to harvest as many as forty deer per year. Taking such a large harvest reflects a need for more than they themselves will eat. While much of this harvest will be used within the household, some will be used to create and maintain social relations between subsistence partners and their kin and allies, and with the elite members of their own communities as well, or to forge links with a new family, or intensify links with the family in which they are already members.

All of these activities are critical in allowing more marginal households to remain in the village. This is what makes hunting more than simply hunting. It is also more than what Berger meant by "subsistence lifestyle." Importantly, the basis of this lifestyle, particularly for those who have no choice but to live within it, is more than an emotional attachment to particular practices and the sentiments they provoke. The fears aroused by practices as fraught with possible failure as subsistence hunting, fishing, and gathering, are heightened by laws contrary to what regular users consider minimum necessary harvest levels. When, early on, I asked Owen if he liked to hunt his expression registered confusion and frustration. It was clear he had never considered it, and even more apparent that he was entirely unwilling to frame his work in such simplistic terms.

Similar issues of law and use apply to the harvest of salmon. Subsistence regulations in Southeast Alaska allow an individual to take six sockeye salmon on any given day. Issues of efficiency aside (for salmon are most easily caught when entire schools can be captured in a hand-pulled beach seine, and are otherwise seldom caught), many large households that are heavily dependent on subsistence require 450 to 500 fish annually. At six fish per day, this number would require more than seventy days of fishing. Given the fact that sockeye tend to school in places where they can be harvested for only two to three weeks, subsistence users dependent on a large number of fish must break the law and risk fine and imprisonment to do so. Likewise, the cost of fishing for six fish is not very different from the cost of fishing for one hundred or more, for one must still own and maintain a boat and seine and pay for the gasoline necessary to go to the fishing grounds. The opportunity cost on seventy days of fishing as opposed to five or ten days—opportunity costs assessed in the loss of occasional, temporary cash employment or work on other, also briefly available subsistence resources like berries or other kinds of fish—is immense.

PHOTO 14: *Cutting fish for hanging in the smokehouse. This part of the subsistence process is just as time consuming and labor intensive as the actual hunting or fishing.*

Throughout Alaska, those most dependent on subsistence as a livelihood are thus often forced to put themselves in serious legal jeopardy. Of those I knew in Southeast Alaska for whom subsistence was a livelihood, virtually all had been to court, and many had been to jail. Some had their boats or hunting equipment confiscated when they could not pay the cash fines levied for violations. Likewise, many of these same individuals live in houses that reflect the heavy toll that subsistence use extracts; houses that look more like workshops than like the other homes in the villages. Indeed, this has long been a necessity of large-scale subsistence production, and many older village residents point out that for this reason, most food processing in the distant past took place in camps built near resources.

In addition, full-time subsistence users that I met were dependent on the income of a spouse for the supplies necessary to hunt and fish: gasoline for boats, bullets for guns, heavy clothing for Alaska winters. In addition, they need their spouses to contribute labor to subsistence production, either through help in processing resources or in allowing them flexibility in other home responsibilities to take advantage of briefly available resources or advantageous weather. Many relationships reflect this strain.

Changes in village economy have further heightened these strains. In Southeast Alaska today, women are more likely to hold regular, year-round jobs than their husbands, meaning that they are better able to provide cash assistance to their husbands' hunting and fishing endeavors, but less able to provide the sorts of support that many women provided in the past—help in processing fish, for example, or in providing child care while a spouse goes hunting or fishing. These things cut into productivity of a regular hunter, and impact his relationship with, and productivity levels of, his partners as well. Tensions like these tend to further marginalize those men who see their subsistence production as a livelihood, revealing a potentially hidden dimension of the dependence of subsistence work on the formal economy.

In fact, many women face the exceptional challenge of having to provide the material support as well as the complementary labor for their husbands' subsistence work. At the same time, their new role in the workplace further removes them, in the eyes of some, from the contemporary basis of traditional Native culture and identity, i.e. subsistence. Once thought of as critical for their role in conserving Native identity and tradition, women now seem further removed from those roles. In response, perhaps, women now make up a majority of both dance group members and church members, activities that reflect how tensions surrounding culture and cultural production are intensified by gender lines.

In general, households that take and consume more subsistence resources than others are those with the lowest or least-regular cash income. Underemployment contributes in two ways to increased subsistence. First, families with lower cash income can save considerable money by using subsistence resources. A single deer frequently provides over fifty pounds of meat, enough to feed even a very large family for two weeks. Seal meat is similar in quantity (and usually greater), though because it is hunted by fewer individuals, it tends to be shared more widely. Fish provides constant summertime food, either fresh or half-smoked, cooked with potatoes or rice. Berries, seaweed, and grease or oil all provide vitamins and flavor. For poor families the importance of these resources is magnified by the high cost of groceries due to the remoteness of most Native villages, which increases transportation costs and, more commonly, allows a single supplier to set high prices.

A second way that unemployment and underemployment intersect with subsistence use is the time that most subsistence tasks require for any measure of efficiency. It makes little sense to drive all the way to the far end of the island (across, say, forty or fifty miles of gravel logging roads) to hunt one deer. Normally two or three men, "partners" if they do it on a regular basis, will make the trip together. If each takes a single deer, this cuts the expense of the trip (per person) by tripling the return. But this means waiting for all three men to take a deer, which frequently requires an entire, and often very long, day. Regular partners avoid this by sharing out the catch, regardless of who actually "took" the deer in question.

Seining salmon works similarly. Individuals who cannot commit to an entire day—and sometimes more than one, due to unforeseeable factors such as weather, mechanical factors such as boats or trucks breaking down, or trouble with enforcement officials—cannot participate on the same level as someone whose time is largely his own. Thus the households that make the greatest use of subsistence materials are frequently not those employed in logging, or by the municipality, schools, or health clinic, or in one of the few full-time occupations in each village: checkout clerk at the grocery store, waitress or cook at the coffee shop, or administrative employee for the village ANCSA corporation.

Commercial fishing might once have appeared on this list of full-time occupations as well, though the nature of the enterprise has always provided some resources for household consumption. More recently, however, commercial fishing has been subject to rigid, frequently spread-out, official openings and closings such that commercial fishermen now spend far more time tied up at the dock than they have in the past. Altogether, it is not uncommon for seining crews to spend three, four, or even five days at home between the end of one fishing period and the beginning of another. Reduced commercial fishing time has cut overall income for fishing families as well, further contributing to the dependence of many on subsistence resources.

As a result, commercial fishermen participate much more in day-to-day subsistence production than they did in the past. Yet subsistence regulations require that no fishing equipment used in commercial harvest be used for subsistence purposes. Commercial fishermen who wish to participate in subsistence must thus maintain two complete sets of equipment. This means, of course, more time and money spent in the purchase and upkeep of equipment, further adding to overall cost.

*** 

When ANCSA corporations elect to cut timber on land adjacent to their own or to another village, it has a significant impact on the "livelihood" side of subsistence use. Despite timber industry resistance to the idea, logging greatly affects the ability of an ecosystem to support and recover from human use. Timber harvests of 50,000 to 100,000 acres around some villages mean, in effect, the elimination of vast stretches of forest from subsistence production until the forest can return to the ecologically sound old-growth status.

Despite this, there is seldom open conflict between those who view subsistence as a key element of Native identity and those for whom subsistence is a livelihood. Individuals and households dependent on subsistence may view ANCSA as a threat to their ability to remain in the village or to endure as a household, but they are unlikely to blame those around them for the deprivations that ANCSA has inspired. This may be because they continue to rely on patronage for part-time work and support, or perhaps for their spouse's job. Or it may be because they too feel some pride in the fact that Natives are now, at least, significant players in the local political economy.

One case where tensions did come to the surface involved an attempt to establish in more formal political terms elements of the identity argument that has been growing since the mid-1980s. The event took place in September 1994 and centered initially on a 1993 robbery by two young men, living in Seattle, of a pizza delivery person, during which they beat the delivery person badly. Both boys had kinship links to the village of Klawock, in Southeast Alaska, and it was at the urging of some of the boys' Alaska relatives that events unfolded the way they did.

Originally, charges in the case were brought by the state of Washington, though eventually an unusual plea bargain was reached. Both boys pleaded guilty to the robbery, but they were turned over to a "tribal judge" from Klawock for punishment. In addition, the judge and his panel assured the court that the "tribe" would absorb the responsibility for the $25,000 damages awarded by the court to the injured delivery person as a part of the settlement.

The main advocate for the plea bargain was Rudy James, of Klawock, who claimed to be a "tribal judge" of the "Kuiu Kwan" or Kuiu Tribe of Alaska. In August 1994 the boys were released by a Washington State Court into James's custody, and they traveled to Klawock for a punishment hearing. During the hearing, James and eleven other "tribal judges" from around the region heard testimony from the boys, their victim, and the boys' families. After deliberations, the judges sentenced the two boys to banishment on one of the more remote islands in the region, separately, for one year. They would be provided with the equipment necessary to subsist for the year by the tribe, but they would have to survive without outside help or contact with family and friends. For this reason, the location of their banishment was kept secret. Following this sentencing, the boys were taken to the Klawock dock and from there by fishing boat to the punishment locations.

Reaction among other Native leaders was predominantly outrage. The local IRA council president resigned, noting that the recognized tribal entity in Klawock, the Klawock Cooperative Association, did not recognize the court or any status claimed by James. Tlingit and Haida Central Council president Edward Thomas sent an affidavit to the Washington State Court noting that neither Rudy James nor any other member of the court was recognized as "tribal judge" by the Central Council; nor was James or anyone else empowered to pledge T&H tribal assets for the compensation awarded in the case. One Native leader working for the Bureau of Indian Affairs agreed, saying: "This is theatrics. It has everything to do with Hollywood and nothing to do with truth and Tlingit culture."

Indeed, the tribal judges seemed very sensitive to the numerous television cameras and magazine reporters that arrived to cover the trial. For the most part, the punishment had been decided before the hearing, but that didn't stop the proceedings from lasting an entire day. The panel had spent the week prior deciding how long the banishment would be, what sort of supplies the boys would be allowed to take with them, and what would be forbidden. Finally, the panel made arrangements for the boys' removal to the island. Despite this, the hearing was held and testimony taken as though the decision was still pending.

At the hearing itself, all of the judges wore ceremonial regalia. The boys also wore regalia, but it was worn inside out as "a sign of shame." The hearing was preceded by a cleansing ritual, in which a special plant was used to strike the walls of the local Alaska Native Brotherhood hall while invocations were made in Tlingit. The court panel entered in procession to the beat of a traditional drum, and rather than taking an oath, the boys were instructed to testify while holding sacred feathers, raven feathers for one boy, eagle for the other.

The gathering itself was given a Native title, the "Kuye'di Kuiu Kwaan Tribal Court," although some pointed out that the Kuiu Kwan, or Kuiu people, were dispersed in the so-called Kake bombings by the U.S. Navy in the late nineteenth century. Indeed, the traditional tribal name for the village of Klawock is the Henya Kwan, and there is no current village whose residents are known as the Kuiu Kwan.

Many people in Klawock understood the events in local terms. By far the majority at the time saw the trial as the effort of one family, centered around James and his brothers, to move outside the traditional power politics of the village, controlled mainly by two other families. Embert James acknowledged as much, saying, "This town is divided…there are some people here who are used to being the kingpins of this town, but this is not their show."

Outside Klawock, where the particulars of family politics were less well known, the reaction was different. People pointed out that over the next year, the boys' families knew where they were and helped them out with supplies and visits. There were popular rumors that one of the boys had been seen around the nearby town of Craig prior to the end of his banishment. At one point, one of the boys was rumored to have been moved to another location after friends had found out where he was and the information became common knowledge. Few, if any beyond the court participants, considered the effort a success.

For young people, however, the formation of the court was a welcome step toward tribal autonomy—one that the current bureaucracy had never undertaken. In addition, many appreciated the power of a "culture" that could cause a U.S. court to defer to its jurisdiction.

Among those most dependent on subsistence, the reaction was uniform and quite different. I was told: "If they're serious, it's a death sentence. And if they're not, there's no point in it." Others pointed out that none of the twelve court judges could possibly survive a year's banishment on an island. Still others noted that the boys, who were raised in the suburbs of Seattle, knew little of what it would take to survive alone in Alaska's forest. The most dramatic comment came from Owen, who is perhaps among the most skilled hunters and outdoorsmen in all of Southeast Alaska. He said plainly: "I feel like they are making a mockery of my whole life."

In such stories it becomes immediately obvious that issues of subsistence are deeply caught up with cultural difference, as issues of culture are caught up with power, and issues of power are, at present, caught up with resource development. In addition, resource development, especially in its current form, greatly affects subsistence. At every turn, all of these struggles intensify, like waves in ever more shallow water, when they cross gender lines. As one of the judges in the Kuiu Kwan trial explained, no women served on the court because, "In our culture, we never let a woman tell the men folks what to do." In each case, subsistence, gender, power, culture, and development nest inequality in overlapping, overdetermining ways.

*** 

This is, plainly, one of the reasons why subsistence issues have been so regularly a part of the effort to halt development, and, in equal measure, so sensitive to the shifting landscape of power that has emerged under ANCSA. It is also why the issue of Native culture quickly becomes part of these same debates even after issues of land claims have been, in the eyes of most village residents, settled.

However, each of these connections, between subsistence, culture, power, gender, and development, rests on an assumption held by many, and introduced to me by Owen in the story that began this chapter: that by "culture," ordinary people like Owen mean something more than the sides that have evolved in the current political struggle, and also more than the plainly political notions of "tradition," whether new or old. In a way that Owen has never articulated to me, and which I can only estimate on the basis of our friendship, what he means by "culture" is a sort of connectedness to a particular set of meanings and practices, notwithstanding their political import, or even their practicality, and probably regardless of their being shared by others around him (which, in increasing fashion, they are not). This, I think, is what he meant when he said, despite all the other reasons he might have given, that he went seal hunting that day because it was his culture.

Beyond the sociality of the event, however, the process of hunting and fishing for a living ensures that subsistence is seldom a solitary task. In fact, it is practically impossible when acting alone. Yet it is work that is done primarily in silence, as was the seal hunting of Owen and Mike. Beyond this, the fact that subsistence is, for many of those involved, an issue of survival, the silence is heightened by the fact that the issues, skills, and practices—in short, the meaning—of every element and stage of the process are deeply, personally, existentially important. Critically, it is this domain of meaning, and not (simply) the sorts of meanings assembled at Kuiu court, that Owen and others like him refer to when they speak of culture. It is this domain that allows culture to be mobilized with such suddenness and such gravity to some kinds of political processes, as it was in Hydaburg in confronting the state enforcement officials.

It is also what makes these processes seem intensely risky to those whose culture is at stake, for meaning as such is not easily made, and thus the cost of its unmaking is very high. All of this points to culture as a domain of "feeling," as Raymond Williams (1977) proposed, but one whose stakes and vulnerabilities are not adequately captured by that term, or by the terms anthropologists usually use (like "meaning," used here).

***

Returning the issues raised in the first chapter of this book, it seems to me now, looking back on it after so many years, that it is the bound up value and vulnerability of culture that marks it as something people can never wholly embrace, and only ever accept with great caution, even while it is something they take great pride in making and continuing, and which they value immensely. In the introduction I raised the idea that culture is something people find themselves "within and against" in the words of anthropologist Gerald Sider. At this point it is possible to look at this proposition more closely in the concrete details of the case described thus far.

Without exaggeration, one can say that those subsistence users more dependent on subsistence for their livelihood potentially pay a disproportionate part of the cost of Native participation in ANCSA, for they are most often the first to be forced to leave their villages when ANCSA corporations make subsistence livelihoods impossible. For them, the money from ANCSA, even during the heyday of the NOL windfalls, can scarcely compensate for the gradual diminution of any chance of remaining in the village, and as such, of remaining part of these same individuals mean when they say "my culture." As one Southeast village resident explained to me, when speaking of moving out of the village: "Down south [meaning in the contiguous forty-eight states] we're just plain-old Indians."

Native identities that center on subsistence practices lend prestige to well-known hunters like Owen, or careful elders like Ester Nix of Hydaburg, who, at more than eighty years old, still tended a smokehouse fire for those who will give her fish to process. In this way, both Ester and Owen, and many others like them, feel as though they have a stake in the culture that underlies their identity. Even so, neither can be sure, regardless of how very much their "own" this culture seems, that it can help them stay in the village. Along these lines, it is worth noting that all of the leading individuals involved in the Hydaburg confrontation with Alaska Fish and Game enforcement officials in 1992 have since had to move away from Hydaburg in search of jobs or new livelihoods. All were part of the mass exodus that ANCSA and its associated clear cutting prompted. Ironically, they were forced to move by circumstances that far outweighed the power of local law enforcement to accomplish this same end.

One result of this predicament, of being within and against culture, is that people often find themselves at odds with those around them over what will be included in culture and what will not: whether, for example, it is more consistent with "Native culture" to conserve the environment or to use it to exist as a community; or whether it is better to spend some of the money gained in NOL sales for recovering cultural heirlooms lost to theft or sale earlier in the century or, instead, to encourage better schooling. Outsiders, including members of Alaska's U.S. Senate delegation, and especially those who find themselves confronted by Natives on issues like development, are fond of pointing out the contradictions in Native culture—meaning opposing sides within the Native communities on these and other issues. Such a predicament is not specific to Natives, though. Many communities find the question of culture to be a contest of meanings rather than a consensus.

Struggles such as these are capable of splitting communities. For some Native communities—the Lumbees, Lakotas, Utes, and others—splits of this sort have formed lasting divides, sometimes so permanent that the resulting sides can come to see themselves as two different groups or even two different tribes. More often, however, the issues are not lasting enough to render their sides so different. Instead, sides change and new sides form as the issues upon which the community is focused themselves change and are changed by forces well beyond local control. The result of all this is a community that appears to outsiders as one rife with factionalism and discord, yet which appears to insiders to be a single community in search of itself.

In looking ahead, I want to propose that these sorts of divisions and conflicts—both community-forming and community-splitting divisions over issues of what is to be culture and what is not—have much to do with the struggles between Pentecostal church members and others in their communities. In seeing the conflict this way, we go beyond the idea that conversion and church membership is just another phase of colonial domination, or that people have been brainwashed by all the messages they hear from missionaries and government officials. The church in which the Flo Ellers incident took place was the only all-Native, Native-led church in the community. And following the burnings, it was the missionary churches, those who had brought Christianity to the region, that were the first to disown the message of the burnings, and the first to tell anyone who would listen that they fully supported Native culture.

When attempting to understand conversion under difficult times, anthropologists usually point to the "integrative" aspects of culture, and of religion for that matter—that religion (or culture) does what it does by pulling together the chaos of life into a readable story where things make sense. Interpretive approaches stress that culture works in this way like a code book: life's events, changes, messages and mixed messages get assigned a code that tells the believer how any particular thing relates to all the others. What seems missing, in this view of culture, is how life's chaos gets distributed. The ins and outs of places like Kake or Hydaburg or any of the other Native towns in Southeast Alaska, are not apportioned equal amounts of chaos. Not everyone gets their fair share of things that need explaining. As such, not everyone's current explanations are asked to do the same amount of work. Those on the bottom, with the least ability to take advantage of the new political dynamics that come with ANCSA—the Native corporations and federal Tribal representation and the whole torrent of changes that swept through these communities in the late 20th century—lack the connections and personal social capital to turn these events into opportunities.

The emergence of "tradition" is one of those changes. To those on the top, it looks a lot like an opportunity. To those on the bottom, tradition is largely unaffordable, and most are left with simple continuity. And while both tradition and continuity point backwards in their attempts to direct us forward, they do so in very different ways.

This contrast was never more clear to me than one day returning to Hydaburg with Joe from a 100 mile round trip grocery run up to Craig. One of the young men from the village was posting a sign on a tree just outside of town. It read:

"Now Entering Indian Country." This is the hopefulness of new traditions. We gave him a ride back into town when he was done, and I couldn't help but notice the contrasting message he wore across his bright orange tee-shirt. It read: "SSDD: Same Shit, Different Day."

CHAPTER 7

# The Spirit in Alaska

*On the night the Juneau prayer group comes to town, I too have just arrived. Owen picks me up at the ferry, but rather than go immediately to his house, we gather eight others and arrange rides for them. Owen's brother-in-law is there in his Salvation Army uniform, and many of the prayer group visitors are staying with him. Other people—Hoonah residents I had not met before, many of them women—are talking, visiting, waiting, and helping as well. Indeed, I've never met most of the people gathered to greet the ferry this night, though I have lived here for several months over the last two years. There is, it seems, a whole other Hoonah.*

*The Juneau-based pastor and his wife are staying at Owen's house. Owen knows them well, though the relationship is not exactly close. Owen is polite. Betsy, Owen's wife, an active member of the Hoonah prayer group, is talking with the pastor, saying how glad she is that everyone made it in okay, by the grace of God. Travel in January in Alaska can be harrowing, and is generally unreliable. The prayer group is in town for just a weekend, to hold a prayer revival and services. Hoonah is near enough to Juneau that a weekend revival is possible, and the visit by the Juneau prayer group is a special occasion that is certain to liven up the village for quite a few days.*

*For most of the prayer group, and for those receiving them, like Betsy, the safe journey is a sign that the planned revival is blessed. Other signs will reinforce this conclusion. By the time services are held, there will be close to one hundred people in attendance, even though the largest congregation in Hoonah is only one-quarter this size.*

*From the ferry landing we drop off the bags of the pastor and his wife at Owen's house and go from there to the house of one of the leaders of the Hoonah prayer group, the official hosts for the revival. The house is brightly painted on the inside, one room in a sunny yellow, the other in a resplendent blue, with several wall hangings depicting romantic images of*

*Native Americans on horseback, sometimes with a ghostly looking figure of Jesus in the background. Other hangings are more plainly religious and lack any specific Native American theme: large tapestries with prayers and biblical images on them. There are also "dream catchers" and elements of Native religious decoration displayed: a carved silver cross, a crucified Jesus with accompanying American eagle carved from wood.*

*Before dinner, we pray. After this, the women vacate the table very quickly—so quickly, in fact, that I am uncertain whether they have eaten or not. They gather in the kitchen where a small TV broadcasts "Christian television." The dinner is deer meat, perhaps meant as a treat for the "city" guests from Juneau.*

*After dinner the group gathers for prayer, this time standing in the living room and holding hands. The preacher for the Juneau prayer group leads the prayer. He shakes as he speaks, modulating his tone for emphasis. Several in the group weep. Many speak aloud their own prayers while he prays, and several from the Juneau prayer group leave the circle to be seated or to kneel and continue their own prayers while the rest remain standing. Owen prays with the others, and knows the songs quite well. We sing several songs, in fact, though it is difficult for me to distinguish when one song ends and the next begins, or sometimes to distinguish singing from chanted prayers.*

*Overall, my impression is that people in the prayer groups talk a lot. They talk all the time, in fact. Sitting in the room as an outsider and non-Christian, I am surrounded by a barrage of words. And the speech acts are not random. By and large they stick to a single theme: recognizing the many acts of the Holy Spirit in the life of the person talking…this event was a crisis, but I recognized that this other way of understanding it would allow me to see it as an act of the Spirit….and so on. For me it is like being dunked in a semiotic soup. For the speakers it is taking one step at a time in a long walk toward Christ, as they would put it. But in my mind, I can't help contrast it with the silence that seems such a part of the hunting and fishing that Owen and I have done together in the past.*

*After the prayer meeting, Owen and I drive the members of the prayer group who are staying at his house back there and drop them off. It is well past midnight now, but we return to the car and drive around Hoonah, just the two of us. I have been given many tours of Hoonah in the past. This is the first tour during winter and late at night, though, and both the appearance of the town and the content of the tour change as a result.*

*The entire town is buried beneath a three foot deep quilt of snow, which cloaks the town in silence and dims the lights, giving everything we see an ethereal glow. As we drive, Owen points out a different set of supernatural landmarks. There was a "witch" who lived here in this house who used to jump from roof to roof across the town. Over there lived a "witch doctor" who could change his shape into a bear. One time, when pursued by people from Hoonah, he ran straight up that cliff over there. Actually, it took him two tries to run up it, he explains.*

There are perhaps twenty or twenty-five Evangelical churches, Pentecostal churches, and affiliated prayer groups in the villages and larger towns of Southeast Alaska. Beyond this there are likely just as many mission churches without a significant following, but attended by one or two households nonetheless. There is usually more than one new church in each of the predominantly Native villages. Some are affiliated with national or international organizations—Southern Baptist, Assembly of God, Church of God, United Pentecostal, and Four Square. Others are unaffiliated or marginally affiliated. Those with national affiliations tend to be run by pastors from outside the region. Some of these are missionary churches as well, meaning that they are not self-supporting, and as a result cannot choose their own pastors. Independent churches are not missions, of course, and these are the churches most likely to be led by a Native preacher.

Few of these newer churches were established before the early 1970s, when the Assembly of God began a number of missions in Southeast Alaska. Some of these missions were more successful than others, but their general success led other church organizations to begin mission programs of their own, mostly beginning in the mid to late 1980s. Part of the reason for their popularity was that the long-standing churches in the region—Presbyterian, Russian Orthodox, and Salvation Army—had difficulty maintaining regular church services in many villages. Despite their success in the early twentieth century, these older organizations weren't able to achieve the sort of independent and self-sustaining congregations that early missionaries had hoped for, even after sixty or more years. The economic woes of the 70s and 80s likely played a role in this as well, and in the early 1990s, the majority of the more established churches remained or had reverted to the status of missions.

One result of this was that both the Presbyterians and the Salvation Army were finding it increasingly difficult to fill vacating pastors' positions and maintain regular services for many Southeast congregations. It was in this vacuum that the Assembly of God began its mission program, and though progress was slow, the greater missionary support received by the new churches allowed them to hold regular services where some of the others could not.

Members of the newly arrived churches explain their early interest in many of these same terms. Most were members of either the Salvation Army or Presbyterian churches when the new mission churches arrived. And many felt frustrated and abandoned when their Presbyterian or Salvation Army churches were closed for long periods of time, or when pastors came and went quickly, displaying little commitment to the community.

The result was that former Presbyterians or Salvation Army members began attending Assembly of God services when they were the only services regularly available in the village. Once a few people began going, others, many of whom had been away from any church for a time, attended out of curiosity. And surprisingly, especially to those long-standing mission programs in Alaska, many of the new churches quickly attained financial independence, and many lost their official "missionary" status by the mid- to late-1980s. In part this was aided by the original strength of the missionary programs—most operated out of new buildings, stocked with expensive amplification systems and well-decorated rooms, rather than churches built in the 1910s and 1920s. Another factor was the tithing practiced by some groups, where church members are expected to turn over a portion of their income (often 10 percent) to support the pastor and the facilities—a practice not employed by either the Presbyterian or Salvation Army organizations for rear of losing even more members. For this reason, some of the most financially successful churches by the mid-1990s were the newest ones, despite the fact that these churches most often draw their membership from the more marginal portions of the community. This rapid financial success has caused them to be viewed with even greater suspicion by nonmembers, and with some envy by other pastors.

The success of the Evangelical churches of the early 1980s brought three consequences. The first was the arrival of a number of even newer, and sometimes even more dramatic or dynamic, Evangelical and Pentecostal groups. The second was the increased participation of Alaska Natives in pastoral training programs, and from this the creation of a number of village prayer groups and Bible study groups, run by church members rather than formally trained church pastors. The third result was that many of the older Presbyterian and Salvation Army churches have since taken on a more Pentecostal air, so much so that one Presbyterian pastor in a popular village church now has a reputation of being "more Pentecostal than the Pentecostal preacher" in the same village. This tactic, he explained, was to help draw people to the message, though the message itself, he maintained, remained in keeping with traditional Presbyterian ideals. Indeed, almost all churches have been pulled toward the more dramatic type of services (and practices) that mark the new arrivals.

Still, memberships are far from solid. In most villages there tends to be considerable movement between Pentecostal churches by attendees. Some go to other churches only for special events—guest preachers or revivals that tend to break the monotony of regular services. Others will go to one church for a year or so and then change congregations, perhaps at some future time ending up back at their original starting point. In all churches, revivals and special services, usually during the fall or winter and which may involve guest preachers from out of town, attract members of all of the Pentecostal and Evangelical congregations in a village, and from nearby villages as well if the host village is accessible to its neighbors. They also, increasingly, attract regular members of the Presbyterian and Salvation Army congregations who live in these same villages. As a result, these meetings can be quite large, with seventy or more people in attendance. They are, however, not held very often—maybe once per year, maybe less.

Similarly, all congregations in the Native villages are characterized by seasonal fluctuations. During the summer months church attendance is low, since many people are more concerned with summer activities like subsistence food harvests, travel, and seasonal employment. Participation begins again during the fall, and winter is the high point of attendance in every church. Additionally, in many villages there is a prayer group that meets most often during the winter. In the summer, when there is seldom enough interest to support a regular meeting of a prayer group in any but the largest towns, most groups fade, only to be rejoined with enthusiasm in October or November.

Altogether, village congregations are not large by suburban standards. A popular church will have twenty to thirty attendees—six to eight households, or one or more "families." A few congregations are larger, of course, but just as many are smaller. Much of this has to do with the isolation of the villages and the competition from other churches. Kake, for example, has six active churches in a village of less than a thousand people. Two of these are quite small (one or two households), and each of the others is attended by fifteen to thirty people weekly.

\*\*\*

Regular Sunday service at most Pentecostal churches follows a similar pattern. It begins with a song service—songs sung from a hymnal, or from sheets handed around if the songs are new. Some are old Protestant hymns, others are quite new, and it is not uncommon to sing songs written by the preacher or his or her spouse. Christian television also has had an impact on the content of services, for many church members watch one of the several national Christian channels that are broadcast in most villages. Songs from these programs are very popular even for regular Sunday services. Quite often members of the congregation will play instruments to accompany the singing. Indeed, successful churches often have expensive amplification systems that support electric guitars and microphones, even though the church buildings do not seem large enough to require them.

During the song service there is usually no preset number of songs to be sung. The pastor will have picked out several that support or introduce the subject of the day's sermon. In addition, members of the congregation are invited to—and often do—propose songs that they would like to hear, or even that they would like to perform. These can come out of the hymn book, or might be "specials." In the latter case the church member proposing the song will go to the dais or front of the congregation and sing, perhaps accompanied by instruments. This is more common at a revival, but it also happens occasionally during regular Sunday services. When it does, it marks these services with a special air.

Most of those at the service participate in the singing enthusiastically. Some have instruments of their own, tambourines or shakers that they bring along. Many people in the village point out that this sort of participation was common for early church membership throughout the region, and that early-twentieth-century Salvation Army bands in various villages were always well supported and very popular, though this is not the case today. Indeed, many older Southeast Natives, even those who do not now attend church, can sing traditional hymns from memory.

Song service usually takes up about thirty minutes, or half of the regular service, and is followed by prayer, readings, and a sermon. The prayer is usually begun with a request by the pastor, who begins by announcing his or her own prayers, generally pertaining to issues that affect the congregation as a whole, or for ill relatives of members who are away and cannot request prayers themselves, or, in those churches with a national affiliation, for national church issues such as mission work. The pastor will then solicit prayers from the congregation. These are generally volunteered in large numbers, prayers for sick or troubled relatives, home lives, absent friends, and some are left unspoken when a topic might seem too personal or controversial to mention. The preacher will generally make a list of these prayers, and this list will be repeated when he or she and the group pray.

PHOTO 15: *One of the new, more radical Evangelical/Pentecostal churches. This Assembly of God congregation was among the first to be built in the region. Its popularity was small until the mid-1980s when the popularity of this church and others like it grew dramatically.*

Overall, prayers for help are more common than prayers for guidance, and prayers for success are the least common. When a congregation in any of the more Pentecostal churches prays, the members stand, bow their heads, close their eyes, and either join hands with a neighbor or raise their own hands over their head. The prayer leader, usually the pastor, will recite all of the requested prayers, including those with which he or she began. When given by the preacher, the prayer is usually done in a dramatic voice, with the volume modulated to accent certain words or phrases in a way that can be described as penetrating. While the congregation members' heads are bowed, the prayer leader's head begins bowed but normally rises, like the volume of the voice used in prayer, and at times he or she speaks directly at the roof of the church.

While the pastor is praying, the members of Pentecostal and many Evangelical congregations will say their own prayers aloud, though their heads normally remain bowed and their voices lower. The modulation in people's voices draws attention to their own emphases in their prayers as they follow along with the prayer leader. Thus it might sound like this:

*Prayer leader: [gaining volume and pitch, until the final syllables] ... and we ASK you Lord, praise Jesus, to remember the Dear FRIEND of Anita, as she enters the hospital,*

*this coming Tuesday . . .*
*Church member: [quietly, timed to coincide with "as she enters"] . . . yes Lord, for Anita's*
*friend . . .*

The style of prayer practiced by most non-pastor prayer leaders is similar, and drawn, one might guess based simply on cadence, word choice, and even assumed accents, on the Southern Baptist style of prayer of the mid-twentieth century that has become the emblem of the evangelizing preachers on Christian television. Not all prayer leaders assume this style, of course, and some preachers do come to Alaska from the southern United States, and as such their accents are clearly not affectation. Yet, by far, this style pervades most prayer and prayer leaders, even those born and raised in Alaska who do not otherwise speak in that fashion.

Prayer is generally followed by readings from one or another Protestant Bible. Annotated Bibles are especially popular among church members (for reasons discussed below), but the King James Version is usually preferred by pastors and used for readings in church services. The latter may reflect a preference for the archaism of the language used in the King James Version, which sometimes reappear in the wording of individual prayers or sermons. Among some groups, the King James Version is also given special status as a "divine" translation. For these groups, the language of the King James Version is itself inspired, with a status equal to that of the original texts from which it and the other translations are drawn. For these groups especially—though to some extent it is true of all of the radical Christian churches I attended—the words do not just represent power; they themselves have power. This is most apparent when used in healing and casting out demons, but a sense of this power pervades most services, and underlies, one might guess, the patterns of emphasis so clear in the cadence of people's prayers.

Quite often, in regularly attended churches where things can be arranged beforehand, readings will be done by members of the audience, at times standing where they are, and at other times going up to the altar. Most people bring their own Bibles to church, and some bring more than one version. In most Pentecostal churches time is usually taken to allow the congregation to find the passage and read along in their own Bible, making use of what notes or other aids to interpretation they might have. The readings and sermon are sometimes done together, with the pastor or the day's speaker reading the passages and then giving the accompanying sermon. In virtually all cases, readings are selected to introduce or underline certain elements of the sermon that follows. This establishes a clear emphasis on Bible reading and interpretation.

The function of the sermon is generally to interpret the read passages—yet by "interpret" I do not mean "explain." Stories or passages are seldom contextualized either historically or in terms of their place in the Bible, nor is there often an emphasis on justice or correctness or causality. Rather, interpretation consists of the recognition of patterns of signs within stories. That is, interpretation is foremost the isolation or recognition of significant elements and the attempt to link them to other significant elements within the story and beyond, to events and concerns of a church member's daily life.

For example, the following passage was read at a revival service at the Assembly of God church in Kake in 1995:

*And I saw when the Lamb opened one of the seals, and I heard, as it were the noise of thunder, one of the four beasts saying, Come and see. And I saw, and behold a white horse; and he that sat on him had a bow; and a crown was given unto him; and he went forth conquering, and to conquer* (Revelation 6:1—2).

Following this reading, the interpretation focused on the significance of the crown, and what it would mean to be a conqueror should Christ arrive (again) today. "Who of you will receive a crown?" the preacher asked several times.

This sort of interpretation allows Evangelical and Pentecostal church pastors to establish biblical language as a verbal texture evoked in the sermon. Readings become, in a sense, sources of potent, usually unfamiliar signs that can be manipulated and applied to lend significance to current events, or at the very least, lend contemporary events an alternative, often emotionally charged significance.

This may be why church members prefer the annotated version of the Bible for their own use. These versions are often valued because they provide expanded versions of the text itself, rather than adding historical background. Church members spend considerable time in Bible study and interpretation, and the textuality of the Bible is significant in their relationship with church practice and membership. While it is common for many Pentecostal churches to insist on a literal translation for points of doctrine, much of the emphasis that church members place on biblical understanding is based on the significance of the Bible in their daily lives. Annotated versions, in expanding the text, multiply the potential number of signs contained in any particular passage.

During normal services, sermons usually follow immediately after Bible readings. Topics vary, and they are generally less than twenty minutes. In contrast to members' prayers and testimonials (discussed below), seldom is village business or local happenings breached by the preacher from the pulpit. The majority of sermon topics remain clearly pointed in the direction of traditional theology—notions of salvation, judgment, and sin—rather than local news. In this way sermons contrast strongly with the prayers that precede them and the interpretation and discussion of Bible reading that takes place outside church services.

People react to the sermons as they do to Bible study, where they weigh images and interpretations against events and issues in their everyday lives, so that sermons on traditional theological issues tend to be treated as multiplications of the text. Devout church members ordinarily deal with a greatly expanded "text"—one that includes actual text, annotations, and powerful interpretations. The components of the expanded text are not necessarily differentiated, instead, they are treated as capable of revealing divine activity in people's ordinary lives.

And finally, there is a definite sense among church members that this practice is something they engage in personally. Many find it crucially important that sermon topics avoid any reference to the personal lives of the individuals in the congregation, even while nearly all attendees will frame their own attendance with reference to personal needs and benefits. People, however, react negatively to any overt reference or obvious connection between the sermon topic and the life of one or another person in the congregation. Incidents such as these have split some churches and caused longtime members to leave for other congregations. This fact has led many non-churchgoers to assert that church members do not really go to church to live a better life, but rather to be told glowing stories of an afterlife. Critics note: "Anytime anyone says anything to them they change churches."

***

Revivals are infrequent occurrences, happening once per year or once every few years in most villages. Quite often they are associated with a sponsoring local church, although the visiting preachers as well as much of the audience will be drawn from many separate churches and denominations. Crowds for a revival can be large, and some people will travel several days by ferry to attend revivals held in more distant villages. Quite often as much as half of the audience at a revival will be from outside the host village.

Many revivals are themselves traveling groups, going from village to village throughout the Southeast region and into other regions, holding revival meetings along the way. They are organized by the revival preachers with the support of the host churches at each stop. Some participants will travel with the revival, at times spending several weeks traveling and attending services in many different towns. Such services can take place during the day or at night, but the most active revival sessions usually happen in the evening and continue past midnight and into the early hours of the morning. In some villages the meetings go on for several days, with one or two long services each day.

Revival services follow a pattern similar to regular Sunday services. They begin with the song service, although the production is generally larger and more polished. As many as six or seven musicians and singers will take a place by the altar and perform. The audience generally knows the songs, as some are taken from a hymnal. Many are the more popular songs from Christian television or radio, or from Christian music tapes and CDs that are popular in many villages.

Local musicians of the host church may be asked to join in, but the lead is generally taken by the revival preacher. The preacher selects the songs and singles out audience members for song requests, calling those he or she knows by their first name, preceded by "Brother" or "Sister": "Sister Mary" or "Brother Tim." Those making requests are often invited to the altar to lead the singing. Likewise, several "specials" are usually performed, which are carefully rehearsed. People singing specials that are not standard hymns will sometimes carry portable stereos up to the altar to help in the accompaniment with recorded music.

Song service is the first of several opportunities for individual expression at a revival. People will frequently preface a selected hymn or special with some words about why they chose it or what its particular significance means to them. In such cases, unlike in the sermons, singling out other audience members is common, as are expressions of personal feelings or happenings. Many will bring someone with them to the altar to support them and help lead in the singing—a friend, sibling, parent, or spouse—sometimes holding hands or joking together. If the sound system has more than one microphone, the preacher retains one, ready to offer additional support or humor, and the other is left for those who come up to the altar.

Throughout, the song service is lively, not least because the musicians will break into an up-tempo, tambourine-shaking song if things appear to be slowing down. It is also during the song service that the first interaction with the supernatural may take place. Like Pentecostals in other areas, those in Southeast Alaska practice "gifts of faith" (also called "gifts of the Spirit") and acknowledge two forms of spirit possession—possession by the Holy Spirit or, conversely, by demons that seek to undo the work of the Holy Spirit. It should be noted that both of these are far less common during the song service than later in the service. Thus some may speak in tongues momentarily when discussing the choice of a song, or may get carried away by the Holy Spirit in the passion of dancing and begin to jump or move much more vigorously and uncontrollably around the aisles. These are usually brief incidents, however, and do not generally affect the musicians or the preacher. The preacher will often use these opportunities to interject (between songs) that the Holy Spirit has seemingly entered the congregation and is "with us tonight."

Song service at a revival can last anywhere from one to two or more hours, and usually ends with the preacher taking back control of the proceedings. The musicians will acknowledge this by putting down their instruments, though they most often remain on the dais with the preacher. As in regular service, song service is followed by prayer and by the request for prayers from the congregation. When given from the congregation, these prayers are generally very similar to those offered on most Sundays, though more impassioned. Prayers are given for those in the community who have left the church—that they may return—and for those who have returned only recently or are attending a revival for the first time, that they be "born again" in Christ, and thus become a regular member of this or another congregation. The request for prayers can also be joined with or take the form of altar testimonies. Here people take the dais to address the audience, make a confession, announce their intentions to be reborn in Jesus, or tell the stories of their rebirth.

Testimonies are always to some extent stories about the village, the people in it, and the speaker's relation to them. In ways that reemphasize much of what has already been noted above, testimonies are opportunities for people to discuss their own conclusions about the significance and signification of local events, happenings, and relations—often in relation to specific Bible passages. Throughout it is a process of drawing the lessons of salvation from daily life and from other individuals (most of whom, if they have had an impact on a person's salvation, are likely themselves to have been reborn and so are just as likely to be in the audience)—in all, a matching process between the signs of biblical salvation and the events of ordinary life.

These are always very personal statements, revealing of both the speaker and many of those listening. Old personal feuds or antagonisms are revisited, sometimes to announce forgiveness, sometimes as testimony to forgiveness already made and now kept: "Two years ago I stood up here and said that I would never again…and since that time I have not. And I have Sister — to thank, especially for the times when I wanted to… and she said…"

While testimonies are ostensibly about a person's own faith and discoveries, almost every speaker raises issues of contemporary social relations and processes. Divisions and relations between important families are frequent topics, as are divisions within families. Indeed, very few personal and interpersonal issues seem inappropriate when the speakers are members of the community. People will speak of former marriages or affairs that they or their spouses and ex-spouses have had, fallings-out with siblings or children, or bad blood between neighbors.

Perhaps the most common theme, though, is alcohol. Drinking problems are common in many villages, as are problems with drugs. Few villages have bars or even liquor stores, and many are ostensibly dry. But all have bootleggers who buy alcohol outside the village and resell it locally at greatly inflated prices. Most testimonies involve a confession of being a former hard drinker and of having hurt spouses, children, friends, and neighbors as a result. Altar testimonies seldom involve announcing the intention to stop drinking; more often they take place after the drinking has stopped, and are thus used to announce that it has been some number of months or years since the speaker last had a drink.

People exhibit a great deal of emotion when giving testimonies, but very few are overcome by their emotions while speaking. This is surprising in that such topics are not common in conversations outside church, and the emotional pitch of a revival is very high. Some have practiced by giving multiple testimonies over the years, but others, giving their testimony for the first time, seem surprisingly calm even when discussing very difficult subjects. At times the stories and examples are as long as five or more minutes. Most end with a request for prayer (which is the ostensible purpose for an open microphone).

When the preacher does eventually take back control of the service and pray, he or she replicates the cadence and intonation for prayer discussed above, though the level and volume of audience participation is much greater at a revival than at a normal Sunday service. People yell and shriek during prayer at a revival, and in a spontaneous fashion, less in time with the prayer leader. Gifts of faith are more common at this time as well. Revival preachers will frequently speak in tongues while praying, and audience members will weep, speak in tongues, or move erratically, sometimes shaking or falling down.

Most people pray aloud, often loudly, while the prayer leader is praying, such that the collective volume is constant and rising gradually throughout the prayer to a crescendo after several minutes. The body movements of those in prayer are initially quite similar to what occurs in regular service. Most begin to pray with their eyes lowered and hands held with those nearby. But often at a revival people will raise one or both hands when praying and look directly at the ceiling while saying their prayer aloud. Many of those experiencing the Holy Spirit will sway, and most seem to punctuate their prayer with jerking body movements. Even those who do not move so dramatically seem "moved" by prayer. They flinch and bob and sometimes shake softly while speaking their own quiet, but still audible, prayer.

During and following the prayer, many in the audience will exhibit gifts of faith or manifestations of spiritual struggle. This can include the preacher. On one occasion I witnessed a preacher was overcome by a "demon" upon finishing his prayer and prior to the start of his sermon. The manifestation of the possession was a loss of strength and pain in the side. A member of his regular congregation (this was a traveling revival and part of the preacher's own congregation had joined him) called out to the others, "Come on, prayer group, your minister needs your help." All of the members of his own congregation then went up to the dais, gathered around the preacher, and laid hands upon him, and the leader of the assembled group prayed aloud several times: "Lord, cast the demon out of this man" and "And he cast out the spirits with his words" (Matthew 8:16). The group prayed in a loud murmur, with very little else said that was comprehensible. The preacher recovered after a minute or two. During the time he was lying on the floor, most of the revival audience remained seated. They did not pray, or at least not uniformly, and only a few seemed to have any idea what else they might do. It was my impression that this was not necessarily a normal part of a revival service in this village, though afterward few seemed distracted, nor did anyone comment that the event seemed out of place or suspicious. It was, perhaps, unusual but not out of the ordinary.

All revival preachers in Pentecostal churches that I visited spoke in tongues while praying. This will come quite suddenly, interrupting the prayer briefly, and can be spaced sporadically throughout. It universally accorded a sign of possession by the Holy Spirit. Generally, the "words" spoken during these times are strings of monosyllables that contain no recognizable words. Church members believe that these acts represent the recitation of extinct biblical languages. Many treat speaking in tongues as proof of the authenticity of their beliefs.

As with normal Sunday service, readings and sermons tend to follow prayer. Sermon topics at revivals tend to focus on salvation. Many speakers draw on apocalyptic imagery, joined to a discussion of rewards and salvation, to impress upon their audience the importance of immediate conversion. Thus at the revival discussed above, the sermon topic that followed the passage from Revelations joined these two themes—crowns and conquering—to implore listeners to prepare for the immediate return of Christ. For those not already a member of a "born again" church, this preparation meant conversion.

Many of those not attending Pentecostal services tend to see this theme as emblematic of church strategies as a whole; the somewhat frenzied atmosphere joined with apocalyptic imagery and promises of salvation and reward. However, there is much more to conversion than this. Most of those "reborn" at a revival have been actively involved with other church members for a time. Indeed, anyone who attends a revival is viewed as a prospect and will be contacted by church members. Church members' hope is to prepare the prospect to receive Christ at a later revival. "Instantaneous" conversion, it turns out, is often a long process. Along these same lines, audience members at many revivals seem to exhibit as much patience as enthusiasm when listening to revival sermons. Thus many village residents are likely to sit and nod and say "Amen" when asked to respond by the preacher, but few I have spoken with worried deeply about either the pressure exerted in such speeches or their internal consistency.

After the sermon, the preacher or another of the guest preachers may have an altar call, this one for special, individual prayers made by the preacher, often involving requests for healing. Here the revival preacher will normally exhibit speaking in tongues, the band will play their songs, and people in the audience will pray, dance, or move to the front to be healed. Most often a line forms for those who seek to be healed, or for a special prayer, and people will approach the altar one at a time. The preacher will anoint the petitioner's forehead with holy oil or water, lay hands on the petitioner's head (unless some specific body part is to be healed), and pray quietly, seldom understandably. After such prayers, the petitioners return to their seats and continue to pray, or if in the course of prayer they are overcome by the Holy Spirit, they will faint and be caught by two of the preacher's helpers. Those "lying with the Spirit" are carried to the back of the church and laid in aisles or in empty pews. Those whose unconscious actions are more erratic and dramatic may be watched over to make sure they do not harm themselves.

Other gifts of the Spirit are common at this time. Among the healed are some who are overcome by tears, wailing, joy, and fits of hysterical laughter. Many dance and sing erratically as the musicians play continuously and the remaining congregation sings, dances, and sways rhythmically in their seats. Virtually all of the conscious audience stays standing and praying in one way or another for the entire altar call. The scene can become very chaotic, and most of the responsibility for maintaining a working situation falls on the close associates of the preacher, who are more accustomed to these circumstances. They help clear the aisles of those "lying with the Spirit" and aid those whom the Holy Spirit has overcome.

Note that not everyone at a revival practices the gifts of faith. In a revival of one hundred people, perhaps thirty or forty will respond to an altar call for prayer and healing, and of these perhaps twenty or twenty-five will be overcome by the Holy Spirit and lose consciousness or become affected in some dramatic way. Many simply stay in place and remain standing, praying and singing. The preacher may also call out to some in the audience who do not volunteer to come up to the altar for prayer and healing. These might be individuals who have given testimony previously or who the preacher feels are close to being born again. Here the preacher must exercise careful judgment. I have not seen anyone called up who did not go, but those I spoke with uniformly expressed the idea that untimely, unwanted attention would likely result in the loss of the person singled out as a potential new member.

When the altar call has ended and the preacher has called up all of those he or she intends to, the music slows and the congregation is allowed to settle. Those who had been moved to the rear of the church have usually regained consciousness and have retaken their seats. All of the dancing has subsided as well, and the weeping and laughing are either finished or muted. Then the preacher will ask the whole congregation to join him or her in prayer. All stand at this point and once again join hands. Like the opening prayer, this one tends to be loud and performed with the same cadence and intonation.

Often this prayer will reiterate themes from testimonies and from the previous prayer, and it will be one of the few times the preacher is able to single out individuals in the audience. This is often heavily coded so as to be less obvious, and prayer of this sort always lacks the personal issues and references of testimonies, song requests, or prayer requests. This prayer, often closing the revival, is generally lengthy, sometimes between five and ten minutes. During it, gifts of faith will again be exhibited by some, including speaking in tongues by the audience and the preacher. Few here will wail or laugh as they did during the altar call, but many sway and sometimes move spasmodically while in prayer. As before, the prayer of the audience is loud and less synchronized to the patterns of prayer used by the pastor than at a regular church service.

While gifts of faith are seen by church members as signifying the attainment of a certain spiritual communion (with others in the church as well as with God), they are seen by non-church members as emblematic of the Pentecostal movement as a whole. The term "holy rollers," used in derogatory fashion in Alaska as elsewhere, is a comment on the fact that those who "lie with the Spirit" will sometimes roll around the aisles of the church. No doubt the architectural privacy that accompanies most worship (no windows, limited information on meeting times and places) represents something of an attempt to limit the public face of such practices. As a result, and unlike the Native dancing they condemn, the only acceptable audience for church members practicing gifts of faith is the other participants.

This is an important point, and one that helps us understand not only the excessively private nature of Pentecostal churches in Alaska, but one of the hidden functions of the practice of gifts of faith. Stated simply, gifts of faith cement the community relationships among church members in ways that other church functions do not. They do so in part through what might be deemed very outrageous and strange practices by those who are not members. To understand this, one need only imagine the position of a new attendee at a revival, or even at an ordinary Pentecostal service. There, the sight of a church member engaged in speaking in tongues, lying with the spirit, or even rushing to the front of the church to help cast a demon out of a possessed church member, is a sight so unusual and discontinuous with other forms of behavior and relationship of these same individuals outside of church, that the viewer is left with only two choices. One must decide, on the spot, whether the individual demonstrating the gifts is engaged in some kind of personal/social deception, or on the contrary, that the explanations offered by church members (of visitation by the Holy Spirit) are true. There is no room for middle ground in such a situation.

Many choose the former, of course, hence the stigmatization of church membership in many communities. But others do not. Instead, when given the choice to either mock the practice as chicanery or even "temporary insanity" as I have heard it called, they choose to engage in the co-production of the practice as a gift of faith, tying their own performance to that of the person in the throes of the Spirit. In so doing, when the new attendee agrees to play along, he or she becomes part of a community in a way that is very difficult to describe, but for which there are numerous examples. Among the closest that I can think of is the casual use of the term "nigger" among young black men in the United States. This practice actually began in the late 1970s, at a time when the pejorative sense of the term was at its height and the political implications for its use were at a maximum. For a young black man under such conditions, being called "the n-word" was about the worst thing anyone could say to you.

Yet this is entirely the point, because upon hearing it, the subject has two, and only two, choices: he may define the relationship between himself and the speaker as entirely over, or he may define the relationship as one so strong that no amount of humiliation or denigration will affect it. There is no middle ground, the word is too extreme. In essence, when the hearer is confronted with "Hey n*…" and replies with no response except a friendly "What's up?" the initial speaker is assured of a kind of solidarity, a kind of connection or bond that has already withstood severe testing.

In this way, the speech act and its response are ordinary, day-to-day versions of what linguist J. L. Austin calls "performatives"—speech acts that transform the relationship between the two speakers. Other performatives are more well-known—marriage vows and the saying of "I do" mark an agreement between two people to act and be seen, from that moment on, as though they are married. What that means in practice is often still up in the air, but from the moment the words are spoken, the relationship is transformed. The same is true when the speech act of "n*" is passively accepted. From that point forward, the bond is sealed, though it may remain unclear to both people exactly what that bond means or implies.

Much the same, I would argue, happens in the performance of gifts of faith. When the potential convert "agrees" to act as though the practices of gifts of faith are indeed a visit from the Holy Spirit, and to play along and subject oneself to the very same ridicule and isolation that comes with church membership, she or he becomes part of the community of church members in a way that no amount of verbal confirmation could accomplish. By the willingness to practice the same stigmatized acts, church members become joined to one another by relationships that have already been tested and found to be strong in the acceptance of acts that are both strange and ordinary disapproved. It is in the constant co-production of mutually stigmatizing acts that the solidarity of the radical Christian movement is made. It is here, in this same solidarity, that many marginal members of Native communities find an alternative to the social relationships of identity, new traditions, and ANCSA-based economic development that have pushed them further to the edge.

\*\*\*

Beyond the regular services and revivals, some Pentecostal church members form prayer groups or Bible study groups. Usually specific to a particular village, these gatherings may draw individuals from several different congregations. Both kinds of groups practice prayer of the sort common to revivals and Sunday service alike, with a single individual or leader taking the role normally assumed by the pastor, collecting and noting the prayers, introducing one or more themes for prayer, and so on. Groups also tend to spend considerable time discussing biblical passages, forming and discussing their own interpretations. Unlike formal services, discussions of this sort will often involve taking direct examples from village happenings or from the daily life of the speaker. In this way individual members allow themselves considerably more liberty in introducing personal issues than is allowed the preachers during either normal or revival services. As with testimonies, these sorts of discussions often raise very personal issues involving others in the group.

Prayer groups tend to be more heavily attended by women than by men. On the other hand, prayer group leaders are usually men. This does not necessarily mean that the topics tend to be dominated by men, quite often women take the lead in introducing and maintaining discussions.

This last point rejoins issues raised above. Churches in Alaska parallel both the culture movements in their own villages, which are often weighted toward women in the number of participants, and radical churches outside Alaska, in which women frequently represent a majority of church membership. Yet there are important differences in how gender differences are integrated into each group's ideology. In contrast to the example of the Kuiu Court, the larger number of women participating in Bible study and prayer groups seldom receives comment, even when it is questioned directly. When addressing participation, people tend to point to issues in their personal lives and to their personal relationship with Christ rather than to any ideology of difference (gender or otherwise). All people note that female church members tend to try to get their husbands more involved, while the husbands seldom face the same sorts of struggles in recruiting their wives. This difference within the church stems from differences in the ideology of gender in the society that affects church dynamics and is thus reproduced there, but is not intrinsic to church practice or organization. In the context of rapidly changing gender roles, this difference is significant.

The members of prayer and Bible study groups are well known to one another, and the groups are usually small, drawing between five and ten people. Most convene weekly in the home of a member. They are at once insular (in that their activities are not usually discussed outside the meetings) and expansive (in that they will actively seek new members and make a considerable effort to see that current members continue to attend).

This inward-looking/expansive pattern is perhaps true of the more radical churches as a whole, and it is even replicated at times in church architecture. By way of example, one church, the host of the Flo Ellers revival, reflects church insularity in dramatic form. From the outside there is very little to indicate that the building is a church; no sign, no steeple, no list of times for Sunday services. Made of corrugated aluminum, the building resembles a large storage barn for a public works department. There are no windows, and no panes or openings in the doors; from the outside there is no indication of what might be going on inside. For someone wishing to attend services, the only option is to be invited, otherwise one would not even know when a service was in progress. At the same time, it is among the larger church buildings in the village, large enough to hold most of the village's churchgoing population. And for a while it was the most popular church in the village, with fifty or more regular attendees.

At another level, this inward-looking orientation is both individual (in the sense of spiritual introspection) and collective (meaning that there are clearly defined boundaries between members and nonmembers, and little concern shown to those outside the group). Service schedules at many churches are arranged in advance but changed with little notice other than word of mouth, thus those who are not already part of the church will have little luck in gaining access, unless, that is, they are actively sought out by the group itself. At the same time, virtually all of these churches are known for their tendency to constantly recruit new members, mainly through inviting individuals to church functions.

These two features arouse much suspicion among nonmembers. Many have commented on the insular nature of church groups, and of prayer groups in particular. Nonmembers voice resentment at the active recruiting, noting that once someone expresses an interest in a church or prayer group, there will be someone from that congregation at that person's house all the time until he or she actually joins (at which point the newcomer is expected to help do the same for other prospective members). Most of these accusations are true to an extent, although the suspicion they arouse is, I suspect, less a sign of concern for those targeted, who are often among any village's most marginal individuals or households, than a realization of a social dynamic quite apart from that of the non-church community.

Members of prayer and Bible study groups occasionally encourage this perception by marking themselves from the remainder of the village. Black T-shirts similar to the popular black rock concert T-shirts or Harley-Davidson motorcycle T-shirts, but emblazoned with religious and often radical statements, are popular among members. At one revival I saw a shirt with a picture of a crucified Christ figure on the front along with a mock Harley-Davidson logo with the slogan "Jesus Christ Lord of Heaven." On the back it had more iconography and symbols on a cartoon-like landscape with a slogan underneath: "Worship the best or burn with the rest." Of course, not all, and probably not even most, church members would feel comfortable with such a statement, but the evocation of the insularity of the church groups was very visible.

***

In all, church services provide both an opportunity, a language, and a set of practices for a very different set of social relations from those discussed in the previous chapters. There is no notion of shareholder versus non-shareholder status, or even questions of Native versus non-Native status. If such thoughts are still present among church members, they hold no place in the language of church services. Yet services do present many opportunities for the making and remaking of local social relationships, through prayers offered and asked, and through altar testimonies. Here, people can and do, single out others in ways that nonmembers and the preacher are forbidden to.

In addition, the overall otherworldly focus also keeps references to ordinary issues of local political economy to a minimum. One seldom hears prayers for financial help, job help, or related issues. I never heard discussions of village or regional politics at church or after-church functions.

Perhaps the biggest way church membership affects local relations, though, is that people are able to become members of just about any Evangelical church and be assured of an intimate and warm welcome. Because all of these churches are constantly seeking new members and are immediate in their use of members to evangelize nonmembers, people who join a church find themselves part of a group quite different from "families" or other local social forms. Drawn mainly from the more marginal members of the village, churches often provide for their new members their first sense of "community," that is, a group of people engaged in a common life task. In this new community, people are encouraged to speak about their past lives, in order both to reinterpret them in the language of church practice, and to move beyond them, to make new friends and relations out of people they may have known their entire lives.

Prayer group leaders are particularly aware of this issue. They frequently express their position or role as involving the creation of a community, meaning both a sense of group bondedness and a common purpose. Perhaps even more than preachers (who often come from outside the village), prayer group leaders take up the task of reinventing individuals, of helping people change their relations to others in the group and thus their image of themselves.

CHAPTER 8

# Jesus Loves You

*She began by telling me that her life with alcohol had begun after she got married. Her husband had been a drinker, even before she married him. But he was drunk more and more as the fishing got worse, and she used to drink to defend herself—or so she thought at the time—because she was a lot braver when she was drunk. She was often drunk in order to live with her kids as well, she said. There were a lot of them, and they always seemed to be asking more from her than she could give. So she would drink to be brave enough to tell them no. Usually when she drank she became so scary, she said, that she didn't have to say no. They would just leave her alone. Her husband as well, even when he was drunk, knew better than to start in on her.*

*When she was living in Wrangell, she came to know Jesus through a friend who explained to her that there was more to her drinking than this. She had lost control, and that was what the drinking was all about, but she didn't know how she had lost control. Her friend explained that drinking, like all sin, was a demon that got inside of you and didn't leave. Even when you weren't drinking, the demon was there, and it would take over again at some other time.*

*As we speak, she is sitting in a soft chair that makes her look small. Her hair is white and short, and my best guess is that she is about sixty-five, maybe a little more. Pictures of family and friends adorn the wall. There is a set of freestanding shelves with bric-a-brac accumulated over time, little of it is religious, and the house is very neat. The chair she sits in has lace covers over the armrests that she made herself. Her demeanor is entirely passive on the outside, but she appears amazingly steadfast. As I sit I think, "Should a terrible wind strike the house, she would not have the power to run and seek shelter, but if she did not move, no wind could dislodge her."*

*She doesn't know how the demon came to take control over her. Probably through jealousy or anger with her husband... some sin that let it in and stayed. Without Jesus, no one is strong enough to get a demon out of his or her body. So people who drink continue to drink, and those who sin in other ways, "like abuse," she says, will continue. They don't have the power to "evict" those demons. Only by praying to Jesus and accepting him as your savior, she says, can demons be banished from a person's life. Though even then, you have to have great faith, because by trusting Jesus you give up on trying to do anything about it yourself. You put yourself in his hands.*

*Part of the reason she had such trouble, she says, is that demons have always been around this area. Ever since the old days, when the Devil had his hand on this land, demons have been in and out of people. What people don't realize, she says as she sits up, is that by bringing demons into the village, even from their own greed, they make it dangerous for everyone.*

*We eat lunch: home-cured-canned salmon on pilot bread, and black coffee. It is summer, so she has plenty of fish around. "How do you like our Alaska salmon?" she asks me. "When people get old like me," she says smiling, "it's all that we eat. White people say it's good for you, and I think we've known this all along. But I eat it because it's all I really like to eat. If I could just have fish, I could be happy all the time." I smile when I catch the allusion, and she smiles back, laughing a little at the test she gives me.*

The description of services in the previous chapter might easily represent Pentecostal worship in other parts of the United States, or even in other areas of the world where Pentecostal missions have grown popular. Yet here, in Alaska, and I suspect elsewhere as well, the movement itself and the practices associated with it are far more revealing of the immediate social and personal dynamics of particular churches and church members than of the theological appeal of the mission message.

By way of example, Alaskan Pentecostal churches, like most Pentecostal churches "down south," practice a form of expression of faith called a "testimony." A testimony is simply the story of how one came to be saved. When given at the altar, the act is referred to as "testifying." When addressed to a non-church member, outside of church, it is called "witnessing." For most Evangelical Christians, witnessing is considered a quasi-sacramental act, one through which people deepen their relationship with Christ. For while testimonies are usually formal and often rehearsed, they are never finished. As people come to be conscious of the day-to-day manifestations of their salvation, their testimony grows and is multiplied, and hence so is their relationship with Christ. At each step, a person's consciousness of the supernatural significance of his or her life grows and new understandings are gained. In this way, people come to "know Christ" through talking about their lives. When individuals sit down and formalize their testimony, and then relate it to a listener, they mark and manifest a deepening relationship with Jesus.

Testimony stories often involve supernatural interventions in the life of the speaker—hence the idea that following these encounters the individual then acts as a "witness" for Christ, relating supernatural events he or she saw and experienced firsthand. When encouraging others to speak of their salvation, people will say, "Go ahead, give him (the person listening) your testimony."

Testimony stories often appear as a paradox. They are highly personal, even intimate stories, yet they follow predictable sorts of patterned, narrative development. On the personal side they involve elements that can only be described as local, and often these elements are critical to the conversion/salvation process. In the accounts that follow, several elements— the Bureau of Indian Affairs, the local tribal council, and even particular (and for most of those listening, identifiable) neighbors—are named and arranged or rearranged vis-à-vis the narrative. Yet for most testimonies, this narrative draws its form from an even deeper structure, the simple understanding that "Jesus loves you."

\*\*\*

Tom, now in his late sixties, is a retired fisherman, partly disabled as the result of a stroke. He has been a member of the local Assembly of God church since the mid-1970s. In fact, he was among the first local converts after the Assembly opened this church several years prior. Up to that time the church had served mainly itinerant white workers working on Sealaska's first logging projects and children from the village in an after-school program. Tom was among the first Natives to join, beginning a process that eventually led to the development of the Assembly of God church as a self-supporting congregation of primarily Native membership. His wife, Kate, joined after he did. Most often she defers to his testimony, saying that her inspiration came mainly from seeing the changes that salvation had brought to her husband.

Both were saved while members of the Salvation Army, moving over to the Assembly of God church only later. They moved because they had felt there was "something missing" at the Salvation Army church. Kate noted that she had never seen people at the Salvation Army church pray with a hand above their head, something she interpreted to signify a different approach to communion with the Holy Spirit.

Underlying this is the different level of participation offered by the Assembly of God church, in which they detailed their salvation by describing church and the frequent meeting- or service-based practices. They were led to the Assembly of God church by a Native-led revival featuring a visiting Makah pastor from Washington State. At that revival, they noted, many people from the village's other congregations attended, and perhaps thirty or forty people were saved. This was, in effect, the start of the Assembly of God church as a congregation and was perhaps an initial turning point for Pentecostalism in Southeast Alaska at a time when the collapse of the local economy seemed all but certain.

One other point is worth noting before moving on to the testimony itself. Though Tom and his wife are Native and both would once have been considered central figures in their "family," the family itself is now relatively small and somewhat torn by his and his wife's salvation. Several of their children still drink heavily, and this has caused some tension. One son lost a seine boat in an accident, which his father blames on the son's drinking and the Devil, who is ultimately responsible for his son's drinking. In addition, their public affiliation with several of the more radical Christians seems to have limited the number of extended family members who might otherwise have made this family a larger and more important group.

Altogether this makes their family one of the more dispersed and least politically powerful in the village, though Kate's role in one of the village government positions counters this a little. In all, the family holds no power on the village corporation board or in any of the corporation hirings. All this is true at the present time despite the fact that Tom and Kate have what might be considered among the larger kin networks in the village.

When Tom graduated from High School at Sheldon Jackson, the all-Native boarding school in Sitka, he came back to the village to fish. His father had been a fisherman, and Tom had grown up on the boats, along with his father and brothers. This was in 1948. His brothers were all in the service, and his father had died in a shooting in the village while they were away. His mother had died when he was young, and so the loss of his father left Tom relatively alone at twenty years old. At the time he drank, he notes, but not so much as he did later. He had plans to avenge his father's death, but he was waiting for the return of his brothers and looking for a fishing job.

Shortly after returning to the village he was approached by several members of the Juneau Area Office of the BIA and the village tribal council. The BIA had initiated a series of loans through the Indian Reorganization Act, which did not really reach Alaska until after World War II. The tribal council was going to use money loaned through the BIA to buy the cannery in the village, and to loan some of the money to individuals who could then buy seine boats and fish for the cannery. They wanted Tom to take on a loan and to become a seine-boat skipper. He was nervous at the time but felt like he couldn't say no to the council, and he had always wanted his own boat. The BIA representatives were all whites: "Caucasians, like you," he says to me.

By the time he got his boat it was the mid-1950s. They had a few good seasons, especially after the fish traps were outlawed. But by the early 1960s the cannery was closed and they were sent by the BIA to fish all over. Fishing was bad at this time, and lots of canneries were closing. This was when he began to drink heavily. With no family, he had to settle for what crew he could find, and these were usually hard drinkers as well. The more people that left the village, the less choice he had in who he could take on. His own drinking became so heavy that he had trouble keeping a crew, and his wife began to drink as well.

By the late 1960s Tom could not afford to keep fishing. The boat had deteriorated, and he could not maintain a good crew. Technology was improving the seining fleet across the region, and especially the new boats from Seattle and Washington State, but for those who could not afford improvements things got worse. At the time, he says, he blamed God for his troubles and for the loss of both parents he was very bitter.

One day Tom was sitting in his living room considering suicide, and he asked God for a sign or some miracle to give him faith and spare his life. Just as he was asking, there was a knock at his door. It was one of the local ministers who said that he was just walking by but had a feeling that he should go in and pray with Tom. As he stood at the door he just kept saying, "Jesus loves you, Jesus loves you." This Tom took to be the sign he was looking for, and he started to feel better. The next day was Sunday, and the pastor asked Tom and his wife to come to church that day.

They went to church together for the first time that Sunday. During services the preacher asked Tom to come up and pray. He said that he didn't know how, but the preacher said that he would lead him through it. When they had first come into the church, a man had come in behind them—a "Caucasian" who had sat in the pew at the back. When Tom did go up to the altar to pray, the Caucasian followed and kneeled behind him and prayed: "He was talking to God while I prayed." After the service the preacher invited everyone to stay for cake and coffee, but the Caucasian left. When they sent someone to look for him, he was gone. No one knew who he was, nor had anyone seen him before. After much conversation over the next couple of days, people decided that he was an angel. Tom said that he knew it to be so because after that day he never had the desire for another drink. Since that day, he has been a "good witness" for Christ in the village.

\*\*\*

Pentecostal churches have been most successful in those villages hardest hit by the economic collapse of the 1960s and 1970s. Within these villages and wherever these churches have proved successful, they have drawn new members from those most marginalized by the vast economic changes of the past fifty years. Sometimes this might include half or more of the Native population. In villages with high unemployment and consequent poverty, two or more radical churches have sometimes found success. This has not always been at the expense of the other established churches. Indeed, doctrinal differences and even differences in practice are not always the cause of an individual choice of church, at least not at first. Rather, both the Salvation Army and Presbyterian churches have often become the province of one or two powerful families in each village. These families dominate church orientation (often to the open dismay of resident preachers), and the salvationist mission of the church is subordinated to other causes or dynamics. One active Salvation Army pastor told me that his initial successes in bringing people into the church (especially those who, like Tom, had never been to church) are frequently countered by his inability to retain them. The new prospects are easily dismayed by family politics within the church—which recent converts perhaps more than old members see as a contradiction of church purpose. As a result, new members often leave to seek out the more radical, and more institutionally independent, Pentecostal churches.

The marginality that drives membership in Pentecostal churches also plays a role in determining the content of many testimonies. Drinking and abuse (sexual, physical, emotional) are consistent themes in church testimonies, and are topics used to hook new members or to relate to new members the signification of church practice. "I used to be a real hard drinker, but Jesus turned me away from all that," a new prospect will be told. Irene, a more recent convert to a well-established Pentecostal church, notes this as a crucial part of her own conversion.

Irene takes the podium at the revival. She is wearing a green sequined jacket and blue stretch pants and her hair is dyed red. She wears glasses with thick frames and speaks in a gravelly voice. She is about thirty-five, though at first glance she looks considerably older. She knows the pastor from their youth, even though he now lives in another village and preaches to a congregation there. He has said throughout the evening that he had once been a hard drinker, and it is apparent that she knew him as such, and that he knew her as one also. When she speaks, he remains behind her on the dais, and she speaks into the microphone facing the congregation. But her testimony, at least at first, is directed to him. Later she names several in the room in particular incidents, but not before her younger sister joins her at the podium in a show of support.

*Every time you [to the preacher] would come to town you would see me but I would try not to see you. Sometimes I'd go down to the bar in the village, (one of the few villages to have a bar) just because I knew you wouldn't come in there. And then if I saw you, you'd say, "Irene, I'm prayin' for you." That used to make me so mad, because I would think, what's he got to pray for me about? I do what I want and if I want someone to pray for me then I would do it. And there was one time when I was just standing by the store when you come in and then you were waiting for me outside when I come out and you said, "Lets pray together, but the whole time we were standing there prayin' I was just wishing that you would stop and go away. Now it's been about two years since I've had a drink, but I still think about it every day but I know that's not me talking, it's the Devil.*

Here she pauses because she is near tears, but surprisingly her voice is unwavering. Her sister joins her on the dais. They look nothing alike at the podium. Her sister is younger and heavier, and she is a regular church member in the congregation hosting this meeting. After she comes up, Irene starts again:

*Now I never thought I was a very good person and I still don't know how Jesus could find it in his heart to love someone like me. I been known around this town for the things I've done. And I know that I have said some terrible things about some of the people here in this room. And I know some of you have said some bad things about me. But it was always because I was real hateful towards people who thought I was no good. And I knew that some people, like when Sister M., a few years ago said what she said about me to the whole town, that made me real mad, so I would get drunk and then cuss and holler and make myself look real sorry. But I know that was the booze, and that the Devil, once he gets a hold of you, will do things that make you want to keep on drinking and being hateful towards your fellow man. And like I said, I ain't a good person, but Jesus loves me and he is stronger than any demon that could come around here. And I know that all I got to do is stay by him and he will help me. But like I say, there ain't a day that goes by that I don't want another drink and so I know I'm still fightin' but that Jesus is right there fighting for me too.*

Later, in the same revival, Sister M. goes to the podium and gives a speech in the form of a testimony about how hard it was to forgive Irene for something she had said to a member of her family prior (apparently) to the incident referred to in Irene's testimony. It is obvious she feels wounded and wrongfully accused, and she cries while at the podium. By the time she is speaking, the emotional pitch of the revival is at full swing and many people's feelings are right at the surface. The pastor gets her to move on by suggesting that she lead in a song, apparently knowing that she prides herself on her singing. Irene continues speaking, now again to the preacher.

*When you came to town a couple of years ago and you saw me I had been off booze for about two weeks and I was trying to quit but I was having withdrawal and not knowing if I was gonna be able to make it or if I was gonna die or what [she laughs, as do many of those in the church]. And then you said, if you are gonna die, you should accept Jesus as your savior and pray to him so when you die he can find it in his heart to stand up for you when sins are counted. And so that was when I started thinking about Jesus and how he could love someone like me and I still don't know how he could, but I'm countin' on it. And I didn't die [laughs again, congregation laughs as well], and it's been two years since I had a drink and I just wanted to say thanks 'cause otherwise I don't know where I'd be right now.*

The two testimonies together, Irene's and Tom's, present examples of several institutions mentioned above. The local elements of the story—the BIA and tribal council; the collapsing fishing economy; the death of Tom's parents and his family's participation in World War II; Irene's reference to local talk and a shared history with the preacher—are all resignified by their respective positions in narratives that, like many other conversion narratives, follow a pattern. Thus, there is often a progression where life prior to being "born again" follows a general spiral of loss and self-destruction coupled with the denial of one's own involvement in the problem. Following rebirth, both of these factors reverse themselves: life is made good again and is seen as getting progressively better, and the denial of responsibility is overturned, though at the same time control is relinquished yet again. In the latter instance, control is seen to rest with Jesus and not with worldly circumstances, and those things that had formerly been blamed on others are taken to be one's own fault.

The patterning of the story helps resignify its elements for other church members, who can see the significance of any particular element by its placement in the narrative. So when someone begins a testimony, "When I was younger I used to like to go to Juneau on the weekend and go to the movies," those hearing the testimony know right away what sort of role "Juneau" and "the movies" will take in the story that follows, and in the path to rebirth.

The elements of religious resignification include many different kinds of relations and institutions: ANCSA corporations, local family politics, even very personal relationships. Some will testify that they are up there to ask that the congregation help their spouse (often husband) find Jesus and join the church so that he or she can find the strength to stop drinking and be a better person. Indeed, the extent to which the spouse is not already a "better person" (and just what this term is meant to relate) is likely known by most of the audience. What becomes important, then, is that testimony signifies things according to its own ties and meanings. Narrative relations rewrite personal relations, at least for the extent of the service. This is what theorists of religion mean when they say that religion rationalizes people's experiences. Although it must be remembered that many forces outside religion do this as well, often in equally cosmo-historical terms. Thus it might be better to regard this as a resignifying practice, and more importantly, to note that all such practices have as their implicit backdrop another system of signifying practice which they stand against or in contrast to.

This process is captured for many people in the phrase "Jesus loves you." Most Pentecostal church members will state plainly that understanding the significance of this phrase is the first step in living "a new life," or being "reborn." The phrase itself hints at two understandings, both of which are central to the process of resignification. First, is that to understand who Jesus is and what this love means, one must read Scripture, which is itself the source of the majority of the signification involved. This is the new reality that church membership promotes. Thus, in addition to referring to local events in a new narrative form, the testimonies also invoke a host of supernatural entities that become tied to these events in almost seamless fashion.

The second critical observation that follows from the importance of the statement, "Jesus loves you," is that it comes as a revelation to a majority of those who discover it. This is significant because it reveals the marked contrast between the reality proposed by Pentecostal practice and people's prior notions of signification, in which they obviously feel unvalued and insignificant. This is

Irene's point in stating and repeating her own disbelief at the prospect of salvation, for the nature of her experience prior to being reborn was entirely the opposite. She reiterates several times that she still does not know how Jesus could love someone like her, but has accepted that he does. The power of such a statement, then, is its implicit contrast to the present—the present reality of family and regional political economy that results in poverty and desperation, abuse and alcoholism. To say to oneself, "Jesus loves me," is to undertake both of these two processes. It is at once an effort to invoke a host of new significations and to note these in contrast to those of one's current conceptions.

***

Testimonies like these make plain the involvement of supernatural entities (for lack of a better term) in ordinary people's daily lives. This is very clear in the testimonies above. When people say that drinking is a demon or caused by the Devil, they do not speak metaphorically. Though invisible, such spirits are real, with an object-like-ness unhindered by the fact that they are, most of the time, invisible. The same holds true for those spirits whose work is to help in the process of salvation. These include the Holy Spirit, who is the most important of these entities, and who is God himself in the form of an active presence in "this world." Alongside the Holy Spirit there are also angels, and guardian angels in particular.

Guardian angels are like devils and demons insofar as they are active in the world regardless of human knowledge. An individual need not be saved to have a guardian angel. One church member noted: "When I get to heaven I'll know my guardian angel by the way he's beaten up and full of holes. He saved my life several times that I'm sure of. I was checking a saw when I worked at the mill when the blade caught a spike that somebody missed. When I looked up, there was holes in the walls on both sides of me and all around in the ceiling and sticking out of the log, but I didn't even have a scratch. So I'll know my guardian angel by all the holes he took for me that day." Stories of guardian angels frequently invoke work circumstances. Quite often, they center on industrial accidents, whether in logging or fishing or mill work or even mining, mainly because many Pentecostal church members have held jobs in these industries.

Like guardian angels, demons are also active without people's direct understanding or acknowledgment. They are considered potentially active in anyone's life, believer or nonbeliever, saved or unsaved. Unlike guardian angels, who are ever present but whose ways are unknown, demons and the Devil are not always present (though they are always potentially present); instead they must be invoked. Once invoked, however, their manifestation is not limited to any individual. Made present by even just one person, they will affect an entire village. Although, unlike guardian angels, their ways are known. They work through "sin," and frequent and unremorseful sin is both an invocation and evidence of their manifestation. Such sins are often discussed in church meetings, where they are frequently and directly associated with demons:

*There was a time when the Devil had me in his hand. I would drink and cuss and swear and be a real embarrassment to my parents. Those were my hard-livin' days and before I found Jesus and that was when I didn't have no knowledge of the Devil, but he had me. And every time I would be drinking I'd get this feeling like I wanted to fight or holler at people, and I had a real foul mouth. And now I know that this was the Devil talkin' through me, and that I had brought the Devil down on my family cause my parents had been real God-fearin' people when I grew up, and it really pained them to see me like I was. And I sometimes think that it was his [the Devil's] way of getting back at them. 'Cause when I was drinking I was a miserable person, and I made them all miserable and caused them a lot of pain and hurt.*

Another stated:

*People who [practice "Indian dancing"] don't know that by bringing spirits into the town like they do that it affects the whole town and that even good people will get caught up with it and lose their way. Once the Devil gets a hold of a town, then it's very difficult to get him to let go, 'cause he holds on tight to what he's got.*

The Holy Spirit, however, is unlike either angels or demons or the Devil. The Holy Spirit is seen to be the active presence of God (creator) and Jesus (God in human form) in the world. During worship he comes into the bodies of Pentecostal church members, and gifts of faith are seen as evidence of his presence. While anthropologists might see this as a form of spirit possession, church members do not view this as in any way an equivalent to the type of spirit possession that they accuse Native dance group members of practicing, or the type of demonic possession that is manifest in drinking or sin. The two, visits by the Holy Spirit versus spirit or demonic possession, are said to be entirely different states, accomplished in different ways and with unrelated manifestations.

Gifts of faith were discussed in the previous chapter, and little need be added except to note that unlike stories about guardian angels, which are often told only to other church members, stories about demons or the Devil and visits by the Holy Spirit have as their implicit backdrop relations with non-church members in the community. That is, while both of these notions engage people outside the church—for people will occasionally share with others their stories about guardian angels—gifts of faith are emblematic of Pentecostal church membership and are thus much more tightly guarded.

Indeed, relations between church members and others in their communities are frequently mediated by notions of the supernatural. While those on the outside identify church membership with speaking in tongues, church members view outsiders as a constant potential source of demonic danger. This is easy to see in the Devil stories discussed above, where the actions of anyone in the community can endanger the salvation of all those in the community. By bringing demons into the community through drinking or other kinds of indulgence, or even through traditional dancing, non-church members are thought by church members to be capable of threatening the life and salvation of those who have already been saved. For this reason, the potential danger of invoking spirits or demons becomes the collective concern of those who know about such things, regardless of the intentions or beliefs of those whose practices are being questioned or opposed.

Apart from the immediate, often physical distance that comments by both sides have created, the accusations and counter-accusations point to a critical dynamic in relations between church members and culture-group members over how this division will be understood. Culture-group members point out that dancing allows them the same sort of communion with fellow participants and the spirits of past ancestors that church members claim for their own gifts of faith. In so doing, they invoke a language of cultural equivalence that is very familiar to anthropologists—known since the early part of the twentieth century as the idea of cultural relativism. In rejecting these claims, church members reject not just the "relative" conclusions, but the entire possibility of comparison and equivalence. They will state quite plainly that the differences are based entirely on the fact that they are possessed by the Holy Spirit, and there is only one Holy Spirit, and no equivalent. Likewise, Jesus is, for church members, not a symbol of God, similar in ways to other symbols; rather, Jesus is God.

This dispute, then, containing as it does both an implicit assumption about the preeminence of symbolic representation on the one side and an absolute denial of this on the other, is critical, for it shows that the dispute between culture-group members and church members is not simply over the theological standing of Native culture. What is at stake in this dispute is the place of *Culture* in general. This point was raised earlier in Chapter 1; but it is worth exploring further here, for it shows up in testimony and, for church members, completes the understanding of the phrase: "Jesus loves you." This point (of being against Culture, in its widest anthropological sense of recognizing symbolic form rather than content as preeminent) is complicated, but evidence of ideas about Culture, and not just Native culture, is available in church testimonies. Much of this comes through in statements about what it means to be Native in a Christian church.

*** 

Martha is an active member of one of the more radical churches in the region. She doesn't usually vote in village elections and has little to do with most of the village meetings, for her soul is "Christ's," she says. She grew up in the village and worked in Juneau for a few years. Also at another time she tried working in Anchorage at a hotel, but found the work repetitious and returned to the village to be with her family. Her father and mother were both Native, but of "mixed blood," and she says that she has "some Filipino and some white in [her]."

Martha started going to church when she was little. Her mother worked during the summer, and Jean D. took care of her and her brother. She would take them to church during the summer for Bible school and to the Wednesday and other services. Jean D. was white, and the preacher at the church was white. That was before the church got popular. After she returned to the village a Native preacher originally from her village came to speak at a revival. He had worked down south [in Washington State] in an airplane factory and had become involved in the ministry down there. He gave good sermons and told people about how Jesus was coming and it didn't make a difference if you were ready or not, he was going to come and save the good, "his people," and punish the others. Most people weren't sure whether they were going to be saved, Martha said, because not many of them had had much to do with church or "with Jesus as their personal savior." But for most of the people there, she said, because they were the kind of people who hadn't done a whole lot that "counted against themselves," they thought that they could be saved by being born again. None of the real bigwigs in the village were there and for her it was obvious why. They couldn't be saved unless they were willing to give up what they had in this world, and for them that was a lot more than for some others. She concluded that people thought more about it when there was Native preaching because he knew about their lives, and he knew that most of the people there needed to be saved. When she had heard white preachers talk about these things in the past, she said, it had always been "like a speech." But she felt that the Native preacher really wanted to save souls.

It is significant that the Native preacher had worked down south in an industrial job, a prospect that is common to many in the village without strong family patronage ties to the ANCSA corporation or village bureaucracy—those made marginal by these structures who are, simultaneously, the most likely prospects for Pentecostal participation. The implied point is that this minister would, as a result, know about people's souls and want to save them in a way that a white minister could not.

Such a notion stands in marked contrast to the way "Native" is understood or made useful to the culture movement, the BIA, or ANCSA corporate boards, for the commonalities drawn upon by church members invoke both the wider political-economic context and the lines of differentiation within that political economy.

This is a common theme in testimonials, and it is a critical point in the testimony narrative. Most people's lives, before receiving Christ, are disappointing, painful, and depressing. After being born again, however, these same lives, and everything in them, including what most Natives would think of as what it meant for them to "be Native," can be viewed as lessons on the path to salvation. Viewed in this way, growing up "Native" does not define the present life of the speaker. Rather, it simply becomes one among many elements left behind by salvation, something that has significance as it is lived against. It is a marker that shows where people have come from, but it says little about where they are going.

This is the essence of the "you" in "Jesus loves you." It is a "you" that is absolutely individual and solitary. It is not "Jesus loves everyone," or "Jesus loves the poor," or "Jesus loves Indians"—all of which, church members would say, are quite true but not theologically important. Jesus loves "you," church members say, apart from, in spite of, regardless of, whether you are poor or Indian or both of these things.

\*\*\*

In reading over conversion testimonies, it is clear that many church members have had immediate, firsthand experience with alcohol, and many root their own church experience in an escape from alcohol addiction. Alcohol also played a role in the divisions within the community that came to the surface in the Flo Ellers incident discussed in the introduction. In the year prior to the Flo Ellers revival a less obvious but equally revealing conflict had split the same village along similar lines. This conflict centered on a radical drug and alcohol treatment program, whose methods were thought to be very dangerous by the more radical Christians. Run by the Alkalai Lake organization, the treatment involved a program of spiritual reflection and rebirth and incorporated several very general "spiritual" practices modeled after traditional sorts of Native American ceremonies. Pentecostals, with their ideas about spirits, thought these practices were dangerously close to demonism.

At first, the program was enthusiastically received. The perceived need for some dramatic intervention was rooted in an earlier set of problems within the same village, for in the year prior to the intervention the village had the highest suicide rate in the United States and among the highest accidental death rates as well. The accidental deaths very often bordered on passive suicide, as in the case of deaths due to exposure or accident when the deceased was heavily intoxicated. Beyond this, most of the deaths or suicides had involved alcohol abuse.

Though it is difficult to say why the suicides happened in such large numbers, and so suddenly, changes in the local economy had done much to alter patterns of alcohol use and abuse, here and elsewhere in Southeast Alaska. Alcohol problems had been widespread in this village since the early 1960s. In some ways, past drinking, though fairly widespread and at times heavy, was not so different here from other working-class villages. To someone who had grown up in an East Coast fishing community in the 1970s, as I had, explanations of the patterns of alcohol use and abuse sounded, if anything, only too familiar. And as in other places, drinking problems were kept in check by the same forces that created them—individuals who drank to relieve the drudgery of a life of difficult work and minimal rewards could not stay drunk for too long, and had to sober up and go to work to keep their jobs. Fishing communities in particular seem subject to these sorts of patterns, prompted by a work schedule where boats and their crews fish for several days, pay out the shares owed the crew in one lump sum, and then tie up at the dock for several days, until the next quota opening or until the boat can be refitted and the crew made ready for new sorts of fishing. With money and time, drinking among boat crews is common, and some remain drunk for days, many right up until the boat is about to leave the dock. Yet once they are at work, alcohol is forbidden on almost all fishing boats, and many of the most severe drinkers are among the best and most valuable workers. This was true of every fishing town I had known in my youth.

The above pattern does not apply to everyone who fishes, of course, although it is true of most fishing communities, and is common enough to be well known to those around fishing in Alaska and elsewhere. By the 1980s, however, two factors had altered the pattern in Southeast Alaska and created a host of new, larger problems. The first was that the gradual decline of the fishing industry in most Southeast villages meant fewer boats (and hence fewer jobs) and more lengthy layoffs between trips. This had left many village residents with increased financial problems, more time on their hands, and fewer immediate incentives to stop drinking. While new sources of money lessened the financial side of the problem—welfare, Net Operating Loss (NOL) money, and related programs grew steadily to help mask the steady decline of the village fishery— they did little to remedy the impact of the decline, or to force people to stop their drinking once they had started.

In the past, drinking and the destruction it caused had been accepted (if not entirely approved of) in part because it remained within certain boundaries provided by the pattern of work itself. This is true for many of the village working poor, for whom alcohol is a regular and predictable part of their lives. Yet the changes in the pattern and boundaries of drinking that arrived in the 1980s were thought by many to be at the heart of the soon-to-follow suicides and deaths. Unchecked drinking was often the cause of drastic and damaging sorts of conflicts or abuse within households. ANCSA cash payments had actually exaggerated these effects in several villages. It was shortly after the large NOL payments began to flood the village in which the Flo Ellers incident took place that the suicides and accidental deaths grew to disproportionate numbers. Teenage suicides at the time compounded the sense of crisis that pervaded the village. Several of these were in homes with chronic alcohol and abuse problems. In all eight suicides occurred in a single calendar year—in a village with a population of around seven hundred. This is more than 1 percent of the total population, and accounting for the fact that the deaths were primarily among young people, these tragedies were the equivalent of losing two entire high school grades.

The state reacted by sending counselors and aid workers who targeted young people in the effort to stop what seemed an epidemic. The root causes were left for the time being, however, for it was assumed that they would require much more local participation, and some sense of what role culture and Native community life played in both the alcohol abuse and the suicides themselves.

Into this opening stepped the Bahai church, already established in the village but with few active followers. The Bahai organization is a syncretic missionary movement aimed mainly at indigenous peoples in colonized areas of the world, and especially Native Americans. Mission dogma is fluid, an amalgam of spiritual beliefs and practices drawn from many indigenous traditions, including Native American ceremonies. Following the deaths and suicides, the local Bahai church proposed a radical alcohol intervention, run by Native Americans from the continental United States. A dozen people were invited to attend what would have been a two-week program of spiritual and personal revitalization.

The program aroused suspicions among the Pentecostals within the village immediately. Part of the problem was that participants were not allowed to discuss its nature with those not in attendance. The secrecy heightened fears, and rumors were rampant in the village, though in fact the program quite clearly mirrored similar tactics used by many Pentecostal churches. In addition, there were well-publicized elements of Native American spiritualism that accompanied the program.

For many church members this hinted at the invocation of demonic forces. Church members' fears were enhanced by an individual who left the program after only brief participation and who, according to some, told exaggerated stories about the tactics of the intervention and the beliefs of its directors. The result was a rapid groundswell of protest from the Pentecostal members of the community.

Before the end of the program's first week, a village-wide meeting was held and pressure was brought to bear on the tribal government, which had sanctioned and unofficially cosponsored the program, to withdraw its support and force the program leaders and sponsors out of the village. Informal pressure was brought to bear on participants as well, and before the end of the second week the organizers were isolated and most of the participants had withdrawn. Plans for a follow-up program were canceled.

The recriminations that followed were even more exaggerated and unreliable (though also considerably more local) than those that would later follow the Flo Ellers incident. Many at the town meeting actually blamed the new churches for the suicides, for one particularly painful double teenage suicide happened in a home where the parents had recently been "reborn." It was said by culture-group members that the children had been made to feel ashamed of their Indianness and had been taught that their traditional values were wrong. Some felt that the parents of the children had become so convinced of the need for their own salvation that they had lost sight of their children's needs, feelings, or understanding of the situation.

On the other side, church members blamed the tribal government and the culture movement for long ignoring the smoldering alcohol and related abuse problems in the village. Rather than addressing and redressing "sin," they noted, the culture movement had invited outsiders and their demons, temptations, and distractions, which pulled people away from what they felt to be the only possible answer to such overwhelming sorrow and pain—salvation. Most Pentecostals in the villages remained leery of those in the tribal government who were affiliated with the Bahai intervention, and they often continue to speak with great suspicion of the tribe's sponsoring people to "write grants" to bring in outsiders or state psychologists.

In many ways this confrontation set the stage for the Flo Ellers incident. As it turned out, long before the revival began or Flo Ellers arrived in the village, the lines were clearly drawn; Pentecostals on one side and the culture movement, tribal government, and ANCSA corporations on the other.

After the Flo Ellers incident (while "all hell was breaking loose" in the village, in the words of one culture-group member), the host church and its members tried to maintain a low profile. Realizing that the burnings were more likely to draw the ire of people outside the village, though in fact they turned out be less divisive within the village than the Bahai intervention, church members closed ranks. The church that hosted the revival continued to be the most well attended in the village, but the congregation's normal inward-looking tendency became even more pronounced, and active evangelizing of new prospects came to a halt.

That summer, church members stuck together while pursuing subsistence resources, and prayer group meetings were reportedly very low-key. Few were willing to discuss the incident, even though many agreed strongly with what had been done. The church pastor, locally born and himself an Alaska Native, left for a time to pursue work in Seattle, but returned in the fall as the church season was beginning.

Sermons the following winter tended to focus on the usual issues. Dancing regalia and relations with the culture group were not mentioned, though the long-standing church rule that church members would not remain at social functions where the village dance group was appearing remained in effect. By the following spring, one could attend services and not know that the Flo Ellers incident had even taken place. Things remained the same for nearly three years after the incident, so much so that when I asked church members about the incident I would be told that it was "old news."

In the winter of 1995-96, however, similar issues were raised. And this time it split the congregation and, in the end, caused the church's pastor to retire and the congregation to, for the most part, dissolve. It was a sudden and surprising end to what had been, from the outside, a strong, cohesive, and radical group.

The start of the troubles was a sermon given by the pastor about the issue of Native culture and congregation members' responsibility to distance themselves from any Native cultural activity. It was, for the most part, simply a renewal of ideas and prescriptions that many in the church had heard before, and with which most had seemed to agree. While it is difficult to know for certain why the issue was raised anew, the church had again begun recruiting new members by this time and it is very likely that the question of relations with the culture group had arisen in that context. Perhaps, it was the several years of quietude that caused the message to seem so surprising and to be so negatively received; or it may have been the general feeling among Evangelical congregations that no pastor should single out members of the congregation, even new members, for criticism during services.

Either way, the congregation split, with one side remaining with the pastor and the other returning to the local Assembly of God congregation, from which the original independent church had sprung. The financial strain this placed on the church forced the pastor to leave in search of work elsewhere, and while a group of church members (mainly the members of the prayer group) attempted to hold regular services, church attendance and membership gradually declined. By the summer of 1997, the few remaining members opted to affiliate with a national Pentecostal church, with the hope of bringing in an outside pastor and outside support. Forgoing independent status, the church was forced to receive a non-Native pastor, and its appeal as an all-Native congregation declined instantly.

Many outside the congregation saw this as a fitting end. Culture-group members, while reluctant to appear victorious, noted with some pleasure that the same issues that originally divided the town had eventually divided and ruined the church.

Today, core members of the congregation remain somewhat isolated within the village, partly by choice. The Assembly of God church in the village welcomed the return of a number of former members. Fortuitously, this coincided with the hiring of a new, non-Native pastor for the Assembly church who was, because of his distance from the history of the congregations and the village, able to form a single congregation out of those who had left and returned and those who had remained with the Assembly church all along.

The former minister of the church that hosted the Flo Ellers revival, the individual whom many saw as responsible for the divisions, remains in the village today and is an occasional visitor and guest preacher at the Assembly church. The congregation of the host church itself has declined from being the most well attended in the village to being among the most marginal. With an Assembly of God church already established in the same town, it is unlikely that missionary support for this congregation will last very long.

Notably, most of the former members of the radical church still refuse to attend events where the dance group will perform. The new missionary minister of the church told me that he felt pressure to do the same, especially given that his few remaining church members had sided with the original pastor in his condemnation of the cultural events and items. Even many of those who left to rejoin the Assembly church remain suspicious of, and even openly opposed to, the activities of the culture group, though the former Assembly minister did not view this as a necessary conflict. Issues of culture are seldom mentioned among the Assembly congregation though, but past events have shown that this can change very quickly.

CHAPTER 9

# Culture Politics

*The man I will call "Billy" stopped by while Joe and I were working on fish in the yard.*
*He had heard we had some king salmon, and he was hoping for a ride to Craig, if we were*
*going. He was a little drunk though it was only ten o'clock in the morning. It was the first*
*time I had met Billy though I had seen him around Hydaburg, and he was very friendly,*
*which is not always the case for me when I am here, particularly in the Native villages*
*located on the outside of the archipelago. Joe asked him if he had been working. He said he*
*hadn't for a few weeks, but that he was going back now and that was the reason he was*
*going to town, to see if there was any work around. Joe seemed to think he would have no*
*trouble finding work and said so, more as a known fact than a compliment. Billy did not*
*respond. Joe said that we would come get him if we were going to town and gave him some*
*fish.*

*After he left I asked about the work. Billy is a choker-setter with one Alaskan logging*
*outfit or another, which means that after a tree has been taken down, he climbs up the side*
*of the mountain, over the other felled trees, with a thirty foot long, three-quarter-inch-thick*
*steel cable that he puts around the tree and cinches up tight by passing the cable through a*
*"choker." The cable is then attached to a hook from a tower crane and the tree is hoisted up*
*and maneuvered to the road. There it is put on a truck and taken down the mountain to a*
*sort yard, from where it will be eventually sent to Korea or Japan.*

*Joe, like Billy, is an Alaska Native, and he also once worked in timber. He is now well*
*past forty, the father of several children and a family man. He worked as a heavy*
*equipment driver in the past, a skill he learned in the boom days of labor back in the*
*1970s, working on the pipeline. He did "road work" for a while, after his return from*
*Fairbanks, but he doesn't any more. He set chokers only briefly, when he was young, and*
*took advantage of work available outside the region to get out of choker setting and get*

*trained. Now, when there is little work even for someone with his skills, he prefers to go fishing or hunting and depend on the income of his spouse rather than go back to timber work. This is not entirely his choice. Very few logging outfits would hire someone his age for a laboring job in the woods anyway. Even if he wanted to (which he says he does not), it is unlikely that he could get a job as a choker setter.*

*Choker setting is the lowest rung on the logging production hierarchy. It is physically grueling and few can or do stay at it past their late twenties. Billy is in his mid-to-late-twenties, I would guess, and getting toward the point where he will not be able to do the work anymore. The cable that the choker setters work with weighs about forty pounds. The ground they move over is a recently logged, often chaotic collection of felled trees up to six feet in diameter and over a hundred feet long, interspersed with the limbs of previously felled trees, bushes and small trees not worth cutting. The real ground is often ten or more feet below this timber-topped surface on which people work, and the cracks and holes between the logs are just as deep, and even more dangerous with the constant rain that makes the logs slick.*

*In Southeast Alaska, choker setting is a job commonly worked by Indians, like Billy, and it is often the only job that Indians hold in an Alaskan logging outfit. "You have to be part animal to do that job," Joe said.*

*Embedded in this phrase—to be part animal—is a dense mixture of admiration and denigration, pride of self (for having once been able to the do the job), and ethnic pride, coupled with the realization that such work is debilitating and thankless and brings with it a host of prejudices that mock the very attributes required. For Joe, older and more in touch with the sorts of politics that make possible jobs like choker setting and simultaneously the Indians needed to fill them, this ambivalent compliment is made alongside the realization that, even the difficult life offered to Natives by labor in the logging industry is itself coming to an end, undermined by cheaper and more compliant labor from "Mexico" and the ecological devastation of years of clear cutting. Perhaps more so, coming at the end of the NOL days, its end is underwritten by the politics of making and unmaking Native claims in Alaska, coupled with the gradual diminution of subsistence hunting and fishing as an alternative to the industrial labor prescribed by development experts.*

It goes without saying that anthropological writing has of late created widespread concern among Native communities. Understandably so, as this anxiety is rooted in a growing awareness on the part of Native communities of how they have been portrayed over the last 50 years—awareness of what sorts of things anthropologists have written about Indian lives and communities. Beyond this, though, there is growing awareness of the potential practical consequences that these writings can have on the lives of communities actively engaged in legal struggles. Here the possession of valuable resources, or even the minimal amounts of social support owed Native peoples under U.S. law, can hinge on questions of historical continuity and past ethnographic portrayals.

This message has been registered within anthropological circles, and few anthropologists would now dispute that questions of "collaboration" are a central criterion for responsible anthropological fieldwork with Native communities. This ethos, perhaps more than any other element of current ethnographic practice, sets anthropologists off from their social science peers.

The context of potential collaboration is important, though, and without intending to minimize the importance of calls for "collaborative" and "contractual" fieldwork, one notes that the rising awareness of anthropology among Native communities has accompanied a number of other changes.

After all, the greatest change in Native communities since the 1950s has not simply been the recognition of anthropological writing, but also the dramatic increase in the level of participation that Native American communities have come to play as specifically "Native" communities in the larger U.S. and Canadian political economies. From legalized gambling to timber production; from oil drilling to "offshore" banks located in very-far-from-the-shore Oklahoma; from mineral development in the Arctic to the warehousing of hazardous waste materials in the Arizona desert; Native communities today play a more active role *as Native communities* in the economic life of North America than at any time in perhaps the last 500 years.

It is entirely possible, from this perspective, that the politicization of anthropological research and writing reflects not simply greater awareness on the part of Natives of that writing, but an anxiety prompted by an awareness of the potential consequences, both positive and negative, that this writing might have on the political-economic participation of these same Native communities.

In this view, the need for collaboration is simply one element in a much larger set of changes that has politicized Native life, changes rooted in the re-emergence of Native communities within national and global political economies. In the previous chapters, I have argued that these same industrial changes have placed questions of Native culture at the center of many local and not-so-local political processes, complicating the way that anthropologists go about studying Native American culture and representing it to the outside world. They have also complicated the ways that Native American communities have come to think and feel about the things that have come to be called their culture and its representation. As is clear to anthropologists and Native communities alike, none of these questions of representation is ever far removed from very present, often pressing, questions of political and economic survival for the communities involved.

To tie this back to the previous chapters, we could restate the same observation by noting that, while ANCSA has seriously rewritten the meaning and significance of Native culture in Alaska, without ANCSA, it is very likely that many Native communities in Alaska would have gone the way of non-Native communities and simply disappeared during the economically troubled 1980s and 90s. In this way, it is the conjoined and complex nature of these two elements, culture and politics and their constantly renewed involution that challenges anthropology and Native communities alike, and does so in ways that notions of "collaboration" find difficult to accommodate fully.

To make this argument more specific, I want to use this concluding chapter to argue that three particular, somewhat separate, issues link Native American culture to larger questions of politics. In my mind, all three of these issues need to be addressed if anthropology and Native American communities are to have a meaningful future together, or apart:

- *Indigenous Claims.* Native peoples in North America have come, through the actions of outsiders and by their own actions, to be seen as distinct from other racial or ethnic minorities in the United States, both in the eyes of power and in their own eyes, for reasons that have largely to do with claims on specific pieces of property based on aboriginal ownership.

- *The Normalization and Naturalization of Native Marginality.* While claims to resources were once enforceable by Native groups themselves, much of the history of U.S./Native American relations over the last 200 years has been aimed at forcing Natives' claims into the bureaucratic structure of the U.S. Government, meaning that Native communities have become increasingly dependent on the very institutions that pushed aside their claims for the future of those claims.

- *Having Culture.* From the beginning, Native peoples have organized control over the resources they claim largely within the realm that anthropologists have come to call "culture"—the realm of custom and the symbolic and practical organization of local, community social life.

This has served to keep some elements of Native life and collective autonomy beyond the reach of non-Native institutions, but it has also further politicized community social life and its reproduction. Subsistence is a primary example here, but so is Pentecostalism.

***

***Indigenous claims.*** To understand the significance of indigenous claims we must start with why indigeneity has always been maintained as something quite different from simply another form of race or ethnic identity and segregation. This is, on the surface, somewhat surprising. After all, the creation and maintenance of racial and ethnic divisions within the U.S. has always been part of an attempt by the powerful to reduce the value of the labor of some communities by separating them from others, and by diminishing their sense of entitlement to the things they produce. In so doing, those in power reduce the cost of the social reproduction of society at large, making the goods and services made by those on the bottom worth less than the goods and services produced by those on the top. Given this history, one might ask why Native American did not become just another kind of "colored"?

The answer is that for a time they were, especially during those times when Native American communities still themselves produced important products for the market. Thus, during those times when Native American communities interacted with mercantile Euro-Americans primarily via trading deer skins, buffalo skins, otter skins or beaver pelts for the proverbial glass beads (and more often firearms), they were understood as little different from the black slaves that propped up the agricultural side of the early American dream, and many were themselves enslaved as a result.

Since the early 20th century, this has ceased to be the case, however, perhaps because by that time Native Americans remains so few in number—too few to count as a potential labor pool in any serious way, and because they no longer produced anything by the means of their own labors that Euro-Americans had any interest in. From this point on, the attitude of the surrounding society has been that Native Americans were to be a managed population, sustained in only the most marginal terms until destiny saw fit to finally remove them from any place in the country. That Indians and Indian communities held on through all this is amazing, and a testament to the stubborn refusal to simply go away. But this has been a rear-guard struggle, with victory defined as simple survival.

In the process, however, something perhaps unexpected happened. By simply hanging on and refusing to go away, Native Americans stayed around long enough for the antiquated rules in which they had initially been incorporated into the Euro-American economy to go beyond uselessness and into the realm of potentially creative fiction. Put plainly, government-to-government relationships developed to regulate exchanges between distinct nations roughly equal in power could, by the late 20th century, but understood in radically different ways.

The results of this process are clear. Few laws that govern the relationship between Native Americans and the surrounding U.S. society (including those still sought by Native communities) are aimed at questions of Native labor or at establishing a place for Natives in the ordinary political system of voting and representation. In this way, Native Americans are simply not, despite years of attempted "assimilation," viewed by themselves or those around them as yet another ethnic or racial group in the United States. Governments (local, state, and federal) and Native communities themselves agree on this implicitly, even though it is seldom phrased in these terms.

This point is often lost outside of Native American communities—appearing too often under the hazy rubric of sovereignty, and thereby encouraging non-Natives to see it as a claim of separateness rather than a claim on a particular type of inclusion. Viewed in this way, the struggle for and recognition of sovereignty has been among the most valuable and most fiercely disputed claims ever made by Native Americans. Much of this is very straightforward and economic. With recognition as Native American, a host of significant political and economic repercussions attaches itself, including tax exemptions and, most importantly, exemption from certain local laws, including those prohibiting commercial gaming and, in some cases, important environmental laws.

But there is both more and less at stake in sovereignty and its recognition than legal loopholes and the recently wild commercial success of some groups exploiting those loopholes. The majority of claims by Native communities are not so complicated, and most involve, instead, actual pieces of property—claims to land and what lies on it or beneath it. From the Southwest to the Southeast, to the Northern Plains, to the Northeast, to the Midwest, to Alaska, to Hawaii; in all of these places and many more, land claims dominate the way that Native Americans see themselves in relation to those around them—most especially in their relationship to non-Natives, but also to other Native Americans with whom they sometimes compete or cooperate for recognition, restitution, recuperation, or simple redress.

PHOTO 16: *A pie eating contest on the Fourth of July. As one resident put it: "I don't know why we [Indians] are so excited about the Fourth of July. It really didn't turn out that great for us." Still, Fourth of July is one of the biggest public holidays in the region.*

This attachment to land is complex, but alongside emotional and spiritual ties, the material value of the land is frequently a necessity for the survival of the community. In places where pressure from the surrounding community has been great or where Native land has held resources deemed especially significant—gold and silver in the 19th century, minerals and oil in the 20th century—the extinguishing of Native claims and often the assault on the Native communities claiming them followed quickly. But as significant as the erosion and elimination of Native title or claims (and generally undiscussed by many anthropologists or Native activists), is the fact that the U.S. government has never sought the full extinguishing of Native American claims, and has in fact participated in the co-production of Native American sovereignty, in large part because of the sorts of flexibility that Native claims have provided the U.S. Government and its corporate allies.

At times, this flexibility takes the form of pliancy. Little more explanation is required to understand the attempt by Murkowski and others to use the landless Natives issue to further an agenda so squarely in the corner of large commercial timber interests. At other times, the uses to which Native communities are put are far more murky.

To see this, we must recognize that U.S./Native American relations continue to be governed by a web of relationships other than those between the government and the Native communities, tribes, or nations themselves.

Perhaps the most important force shaping this relationship is the much broader relationship between the U.S. Government and other, non-Native groups and classes in the United States. This sort of dynamic is particularly obvious when, as during the 18th and 19th centuries, rural whites' clamoring for land caused the continuous redrawing and diminution of Native reservations rather than a redistribution of state land or lands held privately by the wealthy non-Natives that controlled the government. But class politics within the U.S. (outside of Indian Country) has played an equally significant role in *expanding* U.S./Native relations and encouraging the recognition of Native American claims as well.

To give but one obvious example, present-day, widespread government support for Native land claims in upstate New York is fueled largely by local, non-Native interests who hope that the commercial gaming that ensues from the recognition of Native claims in the area will replace the dying horse-racing and dogtrack industries.[30] In such cases the recognition of Native claims amounts to little more than the establishing of joint ventures between tribes and states—with states supplying the land (and reaping their share of the profit in the taxes paid by employees and the political support of the non-Native communities involved) and the tribes supplying the legal justification through sovereignty that is unavailable through other means, while reaping their profits directly through gambling proceeds. The third party to this agreement, the communities of non-Natives struggling to survive the rapid decline of New York's rural areas, hopes only to receive enough jobs to themselves hang on, much as Native American communities had hoped to in the past, and many still hope for today.

ANCSA was remarkable along similar lines for its efforts to avoid recognition of sovereignty but reap the same benefits, and on a much larger scale. It is clear from the framing of the Act and its subsequent implementation and modification that Congress sought to recognize the claims of Native communities in Alaska without seriously empowering the sovereignty of those

---

[30] A recent proposal by New York State includes transferring the use of defunct racetracks directly to Native claimants in satisfaction of Native claims to property lost in the 19th century; see Charles, V. Bagli, 2003. "New deal puts face on proposal for Indian Casino in Catskills." New York Times, April 7: F1; The Post Standard, 2003. "Empire Resorts Agrees to Oversee Casino Venture." Syracuse NY, July 11, 2003, p. B1.

communities. This was the intention behind awarding settlement funds and lands to corporations rather than claimant tribes, clans, and communities. This strategy of quasi-recognition did result in the harvesting of vast amounts of natural resources, most especially, crude oil in the North and commercially valuable timber in the Southeast, though astonishingly few of the economic benefits of either of these harvests ever found their way back to communities that suffered environmental and social disruption caused by their development.

Despite this, strategies of recognizing claims to resources remain central to government/industry relations in Alaska today, and have figured significantly in the strategies pursued by Southeast Alaska Native communities seeking subsequent revisions of ANCSA.

Strategies of development via the recognition of Native claims like these are difficult to see as such, often because they are cast as Native victories by both sides—which, in a very real sense, they are. But the lesson of the post-termination period is instructive. A common sentiment in the federal government in the 1950s was that the government ought to "get out of the Indian business." For reasons that have much to do with the shifting relationship between the federal government and the wider American population, the Indian business has, since the 1970s, undergone something of a boom, to the point that the federal government seems much less rushed in its efforts to divest. What has emerged in place of termination, we might call, a politics of recognition.

***

*The Normalization and Naturalization of Native Marginality.* The second theme in the politicization of Native culture is perhaps the most obvious: the attempt by the federal government to force questions of Native claims (including claims to Native status) into ordinary governmental and bureaucratic channels. This is a politics of normalization, and it has been carried out consistently across the 20$^{th}$ century from the Indian Reorganization Act to creation of the Federal Acknowledgement Program. The strategy itself is perhaps not surprising; the same processes have been applied to other non-white groups in the U.S. with similar consistency and similar intentions. Yet for Native Americans, normalization has been applied to Native culture as well.

As Gerald Sider has noted, in the eyes of the U.S. Government, " 'cultural identification' is necessary for the racial or ethnic identification of Indians (and unthinkable as a criterion for judging the identity of African Americans)."[31] He cites as evidence the "affirmative action race and ethnic categories" used by the federal government (which is also the model for most state programs). Compare how the three categories of White, Black, and Indian, are defined for purposes of the U.S. census:

- White (not of Hispanic origin)—a person having origins in any of the original people of Europe, North Africa, or the Middle East.
- Black (not of Hispanic origin)—a person having origin in any of the Black racial groups of Africa.
- American Indian or Alaska Native—a person having origins in any of the original people of North America, *and who maintains cultural identification through tribal affiliation or community recognition.*

As James Clifford and others have argued, the working definition of "cultural identification" proposed by the Federal Acknowledgment Program and the courts has similarly been construed in very specific, very narrow cultural terms. Yet the attempt to normalize Native culture has many unintended repercussions, among them:

(1)   the success Native groups have had in organizing resistance via culture (here thinking about the Hydaburg protests around illegal fishing);

(2)   fantasies on the part of the powerful about the nature of Native distinctiveness that have often be absorbed by Native groups themselves (here thinking about the Kuiu Court events in Klawock);

(3)   the desire to create more clear distinctions between Natives and other non-white groups (here thinking about Celebration and the "new traditions" it entails); and finally,

(4)   the attempt by power to root Nativeness in something that cannot remain stable for long, and hence to make Indianness an issue that cannot be settled in any lasting fashion.

Each of the first three of these processes has been dealt with fairly extensively in the previous chapters and by other writers. Here I would like to focus on the last of these—the seemingly contradictory fact that the procedures set up to

---

[31] Sider, 1993: xvii; *emphasis added.*

incorporate and bring Native groups into the bureaucratic fold are rooted in a criterion (culture) that seems, even to those in power, to resist lasting or stable definition. This, it seems to me, is a key and often missed element in how Native culture is normalized, naturalized, and simultaneously made marginal to the very processes in which it is invoked.

To untangle the reasons why the U.S. Government has been anxious to root Native recognition in cultural ground (despite the potential it has to empower some local communities, such as Hydaburg, or others in Alaska, such as Venetie,[32] or beyond), one must begin by recognizing that the insistence on the cultural nature of Native American distinctiveness was not accidental. Nor was it simply a reflection of hegemonic ideas concerning racial essentialism prevalent in anthropology at the time.[33]

On the contrary, it turns out that the normalization of Native culture has everything to do with keeping a great many Indian peoples forever between official statuses. A case in point is provided by none other than the Bureau of Indian Affairs (BIA) itself. Up to 1994, tagged on to the end of the lists of officially recognized "Indian Tribes" published periodically in the Federal Register, the BIA for a time included lists of "Unrecognized Indian Groups." While such a status—official lists of unofficial Indians—may strike us as the height of post-modern irony or bureaucratic new speak, for those involved, there was nothing funny about it.

During this same time period, between the enacting of laws governing acknowledgment in 1978 (CFR 25 part 83) and their revision in 1994, Alaska Natives faced a similar sort of ambiguity. While ANCSA seemed to acknowledge their claims to Native status, the federal government remained reluctant to see either the groups that had brought the claims that prompted ANCSA, or the corporations that ANCSA created, as "recognized tribes." Neither were they willing to see them divested of sovereignty altogether. Thus the official rosters of official "tribes" and unofficial "groups" published in the Federal Register between 1988 and 1993 do list *both* tribes and ANCSA

---

[32] ALASKA v. NATIVE VILLAGE OF VENETIE TRIBAL GOVERNMENT (96-1577) 101 F.3d 1286, reversed.

[33] Rather, as anthropologist Gerald Sider points out, for Native Americans it has never been entirely clear whether this criterion was meant to supplement definitions of race (making it harder to become recognized as Native American) or to circumvent definitions of race (making Indians distinct in ways blacks or Latinos never could be). In either case, it is clear that by rooting Native American distinctiveness in cultural as well as, or in place of, racial terms, the U.S. Government was not seeking to clarify or simplify its relationship to Native communities. For more, see: Gerald Sider, *Living Indian Histories: Lumbee and Tuscarora People in North Carolina.* UNC Press, 2003.

corporations and a host of other Alaska Native groups, but not as "tribes," nor even as "groups." Rather, Alaskan communities and corporations and the entire northern grab bag of Indians, Inupiat, Yupik, Aleuts, and the like are listed as "Alaska Native Entities."

Seriously, entities?

This status, as neither official tribes, nor unofficial Indians, seemed doubly ironic to Alaska Natives given the recognition of their claims implicit in ANCSA, and it is thus not surprising that, in the late 1980s, the Alaska Federation of Natives sought to keep the BIA from including lists of Alaska Natives in any capacity in their published register, at least until the full legal status of the groups was settled. These efforts failed, however, and though the question of Indian territory in Alaska has since been settled by the courts, (according to Alaska v. Venetie, there is no Indian Country created by ANCSA) Alaska Natives continue to appear in the Federal Register under a separate heading, as "Native Entities Within the State of Alaska."

Federal requirements for the recognition of tribal status duplicate this process on the level of culture. Federal recognition ordinarily requires those applying for tribal status to provide documentation of a kind of cultural fixity that few, if any, already recognized tribes could meet.

But to see this as pure obstructionism is to miss the point raised by official lists of unofficial groups and entities. Only one aim of requiring such things of Native American communities is that it makes all Native culture look the same (which it does). As importantly, normalization criteria force those who would be recognized to debate their status as Indians in terms that can never fully justify either inclusion or permanent exclusion. Does recognition as a Native entity imply status as a tribe? If so, then why not list them with the tribes? If not, then why list them as Native? Questions like these ensure that would be applicants for official status spend most of their time chasing their own tails, or perhaps better put, tilting at windmills only the Congress and BIA seem to be able to see.

To put it more plainly, the normalization of culture is part of a process of keeping those who claim Native status more or less permanently in-between, such that even the recognition process itself becomes part of the bureaucratic technology for normalizing a status of uncertainty, of marginality, of no status.

Anthropological descriptions of this situation are hard to find, however, in part because anthropology for many years viewed culture as inherently stable, and in part because collaboration with and support of Native American claims often encourages anthropologists and ethnohistorians to lend Native culture a degree of fixity it lacks. This is not done out of dishonesty, but for the very good reason that federal recognition requires it.

However, anthropologists do write about this sort of in-betweenness indirectly (and often unknowingly) when they write about how this unfixity works out in actual practice: as social, personal, or political splits and ruptures within Native communities. This can include splits in tribal courts, political factionalism, contests over development, disagreements over blood and tribal membership, gender struggles, and any number of issues. Fractures like these are frequent, though they vary across communities and shift frequently over time in any single community.

From the outside or individually, these states of immanent fission appear as evidence of the intrinsic "dividedness" of Indian communities. When looked at altogether, the various and ever-shifting divisions that characterize Indian communities seemingly everywhere require a different explanation—one that has everything to do with the fact that the incorporation of Native communities within the larger society has, for Native communities themselves, necessarily entailed fixing their collective identity on unsolid ground. Such a strategy is bound to produce conflict. Both the importance of overall success (the survival or failure of a community, and of some and not other households within that community) and the likely partial failure of just about any strategy (such that the losses are likely to go beyond even those obvious enough to prompt opposition) ensure that no single strategy will ever serve even a single community.

In Southeast Alaska Native communities in the 1990s these fractures have appeared as splits over questions of religion and local culture. At one level, church versus culture divisions in Southeast Alaska appear to be a restatement of class divisions in these same communities: in general terms, the newer, more radical Pentecostal and Evangelical churches tend to find their members among the poorer, more marginal members of every community, while better-off members of these same communities tend to belong to either the Salvation Army, Presbyterian, or Russian Orthodox churches. Alternatively, the splits over church membership in Southeast Alaska could be seen as traditionalists (who gain much more of their livelihood from hunting, fishing, and gathering) versus ANCSA corporation shareholders and those who earn their living by participation in the larger economy—with traditionalists favoring an approach to the local surroundings that promotes livelihood, and others favoring uses that promote identity. Or finally, the divisions between newer churches and those of long standing in the region may simply represent those who oppose the emerging, revived vision of Native culture and those who support it.

PHOTO 17: *Participants at a "choker setting" competition. As is clear here even in sport, the size of the logs is large and resulting work is very difficult.*

In truth, it is probably more likely that church and culture divisions in Southeast Alaska Native villages represented all of these various disagreements, and in any single community, many locally specific ones, such as family politics or memories of past political disputes. In each case, one division simply restates and reforms the others and what is really at stake in the various sides and factions is actually different visions of what each sees as the best (perhaps only) possible future for the village and its members.

On one side (those that attend the more insular, more radical Christian charismatic churches) are those who see the future as intimately caught up with the righting of specific local problems through the remaking of local, community relations. They view their future as depending on those around them to come to terms with the social problems and issues within that community—problems such as high rates of alcoholism, suicide, and family dysfunction.

On the other side are those who see their future as being part of a specific sort of community (a *Native* community) and thus a party to the special relationships that that status entails. For members of this group, it is only by addressing the larger political relationships that surround the community (historically and in the present) that the community can begin to chart a course of its own. This group sees a revival of a sense of Native culture as critical in reconstituting village residents' sense of their distinctive collective future vis-à-vis the surrounding, invasive, non-Native society. They too seek to address the same local problems, but in a different manner.

Divisions like these are common and recurrent, and the communities in which they occur suffer under the weight of their recurrence, while non-Natives around them wonder why Indians seem so incapable of getting along with one another. This is why many Native villages, towns, or reservations appear to those on the outside as hopelessly factionalized by internal strife, while to those involved they look much more like a single community in search of itself.

Such characteristics, however, are intrinsic neither to Native communities nor to Native peoples, but are instead a reflection of the fundamental instability of their situation. In a very real sense, the character of Indian country as it has emerged since the mid-20th century is a very accurate reflection of the position of Native peoples in the larger society—and not simply a reflection of the character of the people who live in the communities. Despite this fact, the opposite is often assumed: the characteristics of life in Native communities are attributed to Natives and their culture. Take, for example, the response of (then) Senator Frank Murkowski to concerns raised by Hoonah resident Ernestine Hanlon before the U.S. Senate Subcommittee on Public Lands during their revisions of logging regulations in Southeast Alaska in 1990:

> *SENATOR MURKOWSKI: If I can briefly go to Ms. Hanlon. In your testimony, which I read and I think it is very well done, you indicate your concern about the effect of floating logs on the fisherman at Hoonah and I can assure you that it is not the intent of the government to destroy the life styles of people at Hoonah. I have been over there several times. I am familiar with some of the road systems. I know the concern of the floating logs. It is my understanding that the Hoonah Native Corporation owns about 23,000 acres of land near the Hoonah Village. Do you know how much of that has been logged?*
>
> *MS. HANLON: The [unintelligible] is completely cut and Sealaska has seven more cuts to go. If you look on your map that you have there, you are going to see that the percentage of the corporation land versus the Tongass National Forest is a very small percentage.*
>
> *SENATOR MURKOWSKI: That is correct, but is the area immediately near the Hoonah area going to get logged up? I was under the impression that you had not quite lost all of the timber, but evidently you have now. I was told that there were*

> *about 18,000 acres that had been logged but not all of it.*
>
> *MS. HANLON: When the total is done.*
>
> *SENATOR MURKOWSKI: I think much of your statement refers to concerns applicable to both Forest Service sales as well as private sales, because you are rafting out of Hoonah, towing to Wrangell; and that is a mixture of, obviously, Forest Service logs and your own logs. I think we should have the record reflect that your concern is primarily with Forest Service sales and not your own sales from your own private land... My point is you have control over what you do with your own lands, if you want to log them, and Hoonah Native people do?*[34]

Murkowski's insinuation here is that Hoonah Natives are advocating a double standard, seeking at once to prevent timber sales on public lands while profiting from sales on their own land. In so doing, Murkowski turns a political condition created by the federal government to facilitate resource exploitation—i.e. the corporate structure and profit incentives of ANCSA—into a characterization of a group of people or even a single individual. It is Ms. Hanlon who is characterized as contradictory, not her condition as both a shareholder in a "Native" corporation and member of a "Native Entity" (?!). Ms. Hanlon's response is clear; she replied: "I oppose the Native logging, too." In so doing, she takes a position within a widening split within Hoonah over the place of ANCSA-based development and the future of the Hoonah community.

***

***Having Culture.*** Beyond the politics of recognition and the normalization of marginality, there is a third process through which Native American culture and politics are conjoined. As noted above, from the beginning of their relationship with the United States and even earlier, Native American peoples have organized their own claims, access, and control over resources largely within the realm that anthropologists have come to call "culture"—the realm of custom, tradition, and the symbolic and practical organization of social life.

In part, but only in part, this is because "culture" continues to describe those areas of Native life that remain outside of the structural constraints of direct U.S. governance. And in part, but again only in part, it is because culture has

---

[34] U.S. Senate, Tongass Land Management Plan Field Hearings, Committee on Energy and Natural Resources, held in Ketchikan and Juneau, AK. Hearing 104-0670, 1990: 477–8.

been made intrinsic to Native claims by the laws governing the adjudication of those claims. Both of these are discussed above, but more than either of these two issues, and essential in understanding the shifting relationship between Native Americans and their culture, is the fact that control of the sorts of resources that Natives possess and claim often means control across lines of internal as well as external divisions.

That is to say, much of what anthropologists and increasingly Native people themselves call "culture" is central to processes of social differentiation and social control *within* Native communities.

Such a thought may strike the reader as strange, but these sentiments are not rare in any of the Native American or Inuit communities in which I've lived. Perhaps its strangeness rests with the fact that anthropologists have seldom focused on this directly, a fact which persists well into the present. Yet in those places where culture remains fundamental to the reproduction of Native communities as *Native* communities, it does so at least in part by virtue of its ability to organize and reproduce relatively autonomous, internal inequalities— inequalities at least partly independent of the sorts of political and economic relationships that tie Native American communities to the surrounding society.

To recognize this is to move beyond a standpoint that sees culture as contributing to the survival of Native American communities ideologically (by the valorization of subsistence-level survival) or materially (by contributing to the maintenance of communities that are otherwise just getting by). Culture does both of these things, but this is not all that it does, and probably not the most important things that it does.

To view local culture for the role that it plays in creating internal inequalities is to move us toward a view of culture that recognizes its ability to routinely organize critical lines of internal cleavage that at once reflect village-level participation in the larger political economy and simultaneously create the potential such communities have to resist incorporation by these same global forces. Let me take one last example from Southeast Alaska that illustrates the ways that questions of culture come to be shaped by both external dynamics and simultaneously by the role culture plays in shaping divisions and inequalities *within* villages. For this, we turn to the role of the potato in traditional Native subsistence.

As above, the question of "subsistence" politics in Southeast Alaska begins with the fact that, from the late 1880s to the early 1960s, Southeast Alaska was home to one of the world's largest fishing industries.

The rhetoric of "subsistence" today emerged almost entirely within the context of the collapse of that industry, for reasons that are both simple and not so simple. We begin to see this by noting that this same collapse caused the abandonment of most of the non-Native towns in the region. Yet even as non-Native towns were abandoned, Native villages remained, and "subsistence" emerged as the main rallying point in local definitions of Native culture. The contrast is striking, and it points us to the role that Native culture plays in creating or facilitating local social reproduction; for by the 1960s, Native and non-Native towns were in the same economic and social straits.

In systemic terms, the closing of a community's single industry means that some of its residents have to pay a higher price for social reproduction if the community is to survive. Some, perhaps all, have to work for lower wages, go without new clothes or choice foods, live with inadequate schools or government services, reliable electricity, adequate housing. Without the same inflow of money, the fund of community wealth shrinks, and some have to be willing to live with a smaller share.

When asked to do so, individuals and families in non-Native villages whose lot was likely to be hardest simply left, causing even those who might have afforded to stay to leave as well. The results were rapid and uniform: virtually all of the non-Native villages outside of the regions larger cities—those towns that lived and worked in ways most similar to the villages of their Native neighbors—all of these towns disappeared.

The Native villages in the region that survived this period did so largely because they contained populations, both generally, and more importantly, unevenly across households, that were willing to bear (or who could be made to bear) the quickly rising costs of socially reproducing the village in the post-cannery era. The role of local culture in redistributing the costs of village social reproduction is critical, for the cultural dynamics put in place during the collapse of the cannery period set the stage for both ANCSA and the subsequent village-based class divisions discussed above. It was not coincidental, therefore, that at the same time that "subsistence" became so closely identified with Native culture, questions of belief, language, religion, social organization, and any number of potential rivals shrunk into the background.

During this time, until the brief timber boom of the late 1980s, most Native villages did lose significant population to outmigration, and all showed the signs of strains in the ability of villages to successfully reproduce themselves: rises in the levels of poverty, the undermining of household health and well-being, the disappearance of almost all commercial fishing and fish processing enterprises, the collapse of village-based tribal governments and Indian Reorganization Act organizations, high levels of suicide and alcoholism, rising levels of welfare dependency, and rapidly decaying housing.

For this reason, the focus on subsistence is perhaps not surprising, for many households were turning to hunting, fishing, and gathering to supplement dwindling cash income at this time. Yet one additional change in subsistence practice is normally left out of this story, perhaps because it so clearly contradicts the main narrative.

In the 1930s, up to the late 1970s or early 80s, coinciding with the height of the cannery period and, bafflingly, ending with the collapse of the commercial fishery, most Native households in Southeast Alaska grew significant amounts of potatoes for their own use.[35] This included, in many cases, more than a 100 pounds for some households, particularly those with limited access to cash income. Later, in the 1990s, people could still point out the locations of the fields.

When asked to explain the presence of potato fields in many of the old accounts, residents point out that with the end of the "camp system" of fall fishing for subsistence, households on the economic margins who lacked access to year-round employment turned to potatoes to supplement the supplies they could buy, and the fish they could catch, to get them through the winter.

Older village residents recalled working in the potato fields right up through the 1970s, but despite these memories, no one I spoke with thought of the disappearance of potato cultivation as a "subsistence" issue. And while potatoes remain a substantial part of village residents' diets today, I was unable to find a single household in Southeast Alaska actively engaged in potato cultivation in the 1990s in any of the six villages where I stayed.

So what happened to them? From what I could tell from walking around with older residents, the bulk of the old potato fields had been built over and are now held as private property, or tribal property controlled by T&H. Many were subsumed in the building era that placed rows of new houses in Southeast villages after tribal recognition of T&H and the first wave of ANCSA cash payouts from the original settlement. This is simultaneously the same period in which subsistence became the major rallying cry for local cultural advocacy.

---

[35] For early sources, see Margaret Lantis and Varden Fuller, (MS) "Economic Needs of Natives of Southeastern Alaska." Draft report to the U.S. Bureau of Indian Affairs. Juneau: Alaska State Historical Library, 1948.

The communal potato production of the past (where the entire village collectively cleared and maintained acre or more fields) seems impossible today, for reasons of both space and because the divisions within most communities make ordinary common cause on such non-cultural issue impossible. Gardening in present-day Native villages is limited to meager kitchen gardens behind a very small number of houses. Yet potatoes continue to be served alongside salmon in virtually every house in every village—often boiled in the same pot.

Today, the right to fish for salmon remains a major rallying point for Native culture, while the right to grow potatoes seems scarcely conceivable in that same role, despite the fact that potato cultivation has far more thoroughly disappeared from the food-producing practices than has either fishing or hunting. Obviously, potatoes are not "indigenous" to the area, while salmon harvesting goes back thousands of years. Yet just as important is the fact that salmon harvesting involves a confrontation with non-Native interests (commercial fishermen, state regulators, federal enforcement officials), while potatoes point us to questions about who gets to live where, and who doesn't, in today's Southeast Alaska Native villages.

In this way, what gets called culture, and in return what does not, matters a great deal in the fault lines that divide even the most uniform-looking communities in Southeast Alaska.

It is worth noting that, with few exceptions, the population of most Southeast Alaska Native villages in the early 1990s were not much larger than they were at the end of the cannery era (i.e. mid-1960s) or at the time when Lantis and Fuller did their survey of household production that included the production of hundreds of bushels of potatoes (in the late 1940s). High birthrates, then and now, make it clear that questions of land ownership and housing are more than symbolic issues in all of the villages in the region.

Given this, the fact that salmon is seen as iconic with Native culture while potatoes are largely forgotten returns us to the fact that culture does things for and to those who live with it. Put more provocatively, a discourse of subsistence that includes some things, such as salmon, and excludes others, such as potatoes, is part of a larger process in which people, not words, are included and excluded, and boundaries around communities are continuously drawn and redrawn.

Returning to the question of village social reproduction, the role of subsistence in holding together Native villages where non-Native villages failed cannot be underestimated. Subsistence practices and their accompanying ideologies created the means for marginal households to remain in villages, increasing the viability of schools and stores and other density-dependent enterprises. These same households continue to gain a limited amount of prestige as well by producing ideologically important items for large events. In the meantime, however other bases for their subsistence, such as the potato, ensured that under the new cultural plan, their ability to stay remained tenuous, at best.

By the mid-1990s, the greatest threat to the subsistence livelihoods of subsistence-dependent households since the 1980s has turned out to be the industrial timber harvest undertaken by members of their own or neighboring Native communities—not surprisingly, under the direction of many of those same folks who sponsor the events at which subsistence plays such a critical ideological role.

In this way (and this is the point raised by the emerging discourse on subsistence), the form that local culture takes—the difference, for example, between advocating subsistence as "lifestyle" rather than "livelihood"—affects social reproduction in direct and indirect fashion, and does so by organizing people across the lines of class division it simultaneously helps to create within communities. The current ways in which subsistence is understood and advocated helps to knit marginal households to their communities by marking them as producers of resources that are, for most Alaska Natives today, emblematic of their Nativeness. By allowing marginal households to remain in Native villages, the valorization of subsistence practices has increased the power of local leaders (swelling their constituencies) and helped promote the social reproduction of village-wide institutions such as schools and medical facilities.

Still, by harnessing the symbolic resonance of subsistence to land claims projects and Native identity (and away from issues of material reproduction for households engaged in the harvest of resources), subsistence advocacy has actually done little for those most dependent on subsistence production and their ability to remain in these communities. In fact, to the extent that local Native land claims, and to that extent, ANCSA, depended on recognition of subsistence use, the symbolic recognition of subsistence practice has done more to end the viability of intensive subsistence harvests by marginal households than anything else in recent years. As ANCSA corporations have, in effect, denuded hundreds of thousands of acres of local hunting and fishing areas throughout the region, hunting and fishing households have simply disappeared. It is in this sense that culture and politics are joined functionally, not simply symbolically or ideologically or even legally.

***

This sort of relationship creates a politics of social reproduction within which local culture is defined and lived quite differently by different members of every community. In contrast to both the politics of recognition and the politics of normalization, the politics of having culture turns the understanding of Native culture away from questions about relations between the local community and the surrounding political economy and back toward questions about relationships within Native communities. The dynamics of the latter are not comprehensible without an understanding of the first two processes. Yet neither is the role of culture in creating and bridging local differences reducible to either the politics of recognition or the politics of normalization.

Village social reproduction (and the visions of culture that emerge from it) remains both the source of Native autonomy in the face of outside domination and the cause of some of the most painful social dynamics present in Native American communities today. It is these dynamics, after all, that can force some households to leave for Seattle rather spend another winter "begging" credit through one more bad winter. It is in this sense that Native culture remains not simply a question of anthropological representation or collaboration, but also, and much more seriously so, a dilemma for Native communities themselves.

***

Pentecostal church membership is a relatively new phenomenon in Southeast Alaska, but one with parallels in many areas of the neocolonial world. Everywhere, it has found special appeal among those made marginal by the history of colonial expansion and by the continuing ebb and flow of capital penetration. It has also, and perhaps surprisingly, inspired in many of its converts distinct anticultural sentiments—feelings that, in Alaska, have encouraged some people to look with suspicion on the Native cultural practices sponsored by corporations bent on industrial development, even when those corporations are ostensibly Native owned and those cultural practices are engaged in by their own neighbors and kin.

They are not alone. Similar churches have had success preaching an anticultural message in Highland New Guinea, to cite but one example. There, Seventh-Day Adventist churches have proved popular despite the fact that (or, if the parallel with Alaska is true, because) they have forbidden their members to have contact with pigs—in an area where pigs have always provided the main means for participation in funerals, weddings, politics, and virtually all cultural events that form the basis *both* for community and for specifically local inequalities.

In these situations, the anticultural activities of church members in Alaska are more than simply the result of theological intolerance. Rather, the roots of Pentecostalism's appeal grow in the increasing internal differentiation that has accompanied the most recent wave of colonial expansion in the region—ANCSA.

Without exaggeration, it is clear that the Alaska Native Claims Settlement Act has laid the foundation for new forms of local economic and political stratification in every Native village in the State. It has done so by invoking and enhancing claims of cultural distinctiveness of Natives in the region, often at the expense of other sorts of identifications (e.g., working status, gender, age, or class). Some in Alaska have advocated the use of this politically reinforced and redefined cultural distinctiveness to overturn ANCSA. Others, specifically church members, have rejected strategies of cultural distinctiveness altogether. On the surface, this puts the more radical culture advocates and church members on opposite sides. Yet it should be clear by now that the two sides share many of the same goals.

Central among these goals is the rejection of the ANCSA-inspired changes, particularly those that have led to a decline in community, regardless of whether that community is thought of as Native or as Christian. Church membership provides new means for expressing dissatisfaction. It also creates and maintains a set of social relations largely outside the political economy in which most of other social relations are embedded (relations of tribe, family, shareholder status, or even subsistence work). This, as much as anything, distinguishes it from its rival. These new relations can and frequently do serve as an alternative to those caught up with ANCSA or family or other, clearly political relationships. Often, and not surprisingly, they find themselves in conflict with those other relationships as a result.

It is easy to see how these same feelings—desires for a set of relations beyond those that have proved themselves so clearly destructive of community—might push some people to embrace and redefine the new traditions of Native culture, which are also, potentially, a set of social practices capable of creating distinctive groups and social dynamics. In many ways the two endeavors are very similar. One critical difference—one that makes the situation something more than simply a set of symmetrical alternatives—is church members' rejection of this very equivalency. Without exception, church members deny that there is any sort of equivalence between the two strategies.

This rejection seems almost incomprehensible to those in the culture group, who are much more willing to accept the idea that there are multiple ways of pursuing the same goals. This is likely the reason why many are so willing to attribute Pentecostal resistance to theological intransigence.

Yet by rejecting the idea of alternative political or social strategies, church members do more than simply advocate a particular theological stand or their own moral superiority. They advocate a strategy of collectivity and connection over one rooted in difference. They advocate collective practice over individual belief in a way that insists upon the mutual interdependency of collective representations. This idea places church members not just against Native culture, but against some of the foundational ideas of Culture itself—which contains, implicitly and explicitly, the assumption that all cultural representations are inherently arbitrary and rooted in tradition, not truth (or Truth).

In seeing themselves, via church membership, as against culture, Native church members are aided in two ways. The first, as we saw in Chapter 1, is rooted in the fact that all people find themselves, at certain times and in certain ways, necessarily against a culture that they simultaneously consider their own (i.e., against a set of locally defined and locally valued meanings and the practices associated with their explanation and reproduction). Those from whom cultural reproduction exacts a particularly high price—i.e. those whose continued participation in the community is the most tenuous and who are forced to absorb the greatest emotional, economic, or political risk in participating in a particular culture at a particular time and place—are apt to be the ones most frequently confronted by their own anticultural feelings. It is no coincidence, then, that radical churches have had their greatest successes among marginal groups, whether in large cities or the rural third world.

Alaska Natives, having already borne the brunt of hundreds of years of colonial extraction and political-economic uncertainty, have been placed at the margins of the Western world and have borne a particularly heavy portion of the burden of reproducing a Western culture that offers them very little in return. Paying the price of generations of subsistence food for the ability to watch Pocahontas or The Indian in the Cupboard (as Disney turns hunters' losses into corporate tax shelters) seems, to put it mildly, a one-sided exchange.

Even here, the costs of the exchange are not distributed evenly among the residents of Kake, Hydaburg, Klawock or any of the other Southeast Native communities. Clear cutting costs some people more, even beyond the fact that the non-shareholders in all of these communities received none of the payouts. When moneys gained by such an exchange are used to support cultural programs, marginal members of these communities continue to bear the burden of the cultural resistance in the form of exodus, hunger, or cold.

Beyond the fact that some people pay a higher price for culture than others, Native Americans are also forced into an even more ambiguous relationship than marginal people elsewhere as they are forced to view their culture in particularly narrow terms, defined mainly by laws (like ANCSA and the Indian Reorganization Act) that have linked their participation *as Native communities* to their ability to maintain an acceptable level of cultural distinctiveness. In Chapter 1, I linked this fact to the recognition that there are no Indian subcultures. Native culture, unlike many other kinds of culture, is an all-or-nothing endeavor for its members, according to the laws of the society in which Indians are embedded. As a result, ordinary tensions between people and the culture they claim as their own are especially exaggerated among Native Americans, who are never entirely free to make of their culture what they otherwise might.

These two factors provide much of the answer to the question of why Pentecostal church practice and not some other form of resistance has proven so popular here and elsewhere.

\*\*\*

Such an approach may strike some as an overly politicized view of culture, one that places an undue emphasis on culture's place in ideology and political-economic power at the expense of questions of meaning. Admittedly, this has not been an ethnography in the conventional sense of the term. Most ethnography is concerned with descriptions of a people's culture per se, its webs of meanings and the insights we might gain by pondering a different way of carving up the world into inter-related, meaningful blocks. But there are critical problems that stem from thinking that "a people" can have "a culture." Important social divisions exist within every group—divisions of class, age, gender, or ethnicity—and these divisions make culture or "local meaning" an issue for struggle, not something unconsciously accepted among those in a particular locality. Sometimes these lines are less obvious in a Native village in Alaska than in other places, but a sense of these divisions and the struggles they create is critical for understanding how people's everyday lives shape and are shaped by themselves and those around them.

In the past, many ethnologists were able to justify a notion of shared culture by ignoring these divisions and choosing instead to look at how aspects of meaning are linked to cosmologies, social organization, traditional beliefs, and so on. The connections they found are interesting and often quite complex. Yet most ethnology stops here, taking these connections to be characteristic of culture in some general sense, rather than viewing them as the outcome of an ongoing set of social processes, located very specifically in a particular time and place. Absent this realization, culture always seems fixed in the past, arriving on the scene preformed, predetermined, or *a priori*—as though all cultures were created at the dawn of time, as anthropologist Gerald Sider notes critically.[36] Culture, in this view, is something that can be lost, but seldom is it considered something that might be, or must be, made and remade if it is to exist at all. And often, even when such questions are asked, most ethnography forgoes asking whether such making and remaking is done at the expense of some more than others.

Looking at culture for its place in ongoing processes of social differentiation is not to eliminate questions of meaning from questions of history or to reduce meaning to political expedience. Putting aside the notion of culture as a fixed way of looking at the world, a viewpoint normally associated with the term "a culture," means only that we begin to think of how people make collective futures. The process is seldom neat, and less often is it peaceful. Rather, in such a view, what seems most important is how people of a particular geographic and historical locale are able to make meaningful the world around them, and, less innocently, how they are also made to accept some meanings they would prefer not to.

Either way, something as seemingly bewildering as all-Native, anticultural Pentecostal churches rising up in Native communities almost immediately after they have been federally recognized and awarded large tracts of valuable timber land—something this different from what we have been taught is "natural" must, as such, be understood from the question of how people make meaning—how they collectively manage that combination of creativity, force, collective negotiation and hope, always in ongoing fashion, over and over again, in ever-changing contexts amid ever-changing desires, and worries. The fact

---

[36] Gerald Sider, "When parrots learn to talk, and why they can't: Domination, deception, and self-deception in Indian-White relations." *Comparative Studies in Society and History* v. 29, n. 01 (1987): 3-23.

that they do these things amidst others trying to do similar things for themselves is equally important. Point in case: without either the oil crisis of the 70s, or the environmental movement of the 80s and 90s, Native land claims in Alaska would likely have turned out very very differently.

Thinking back to Billy in the vignette that began this chapter, if locally produced culture of the sort that emerged in Southeast Alaskan Native villages in the late 1970s allows ordinary people to live with a world they otherwise might not, it still does little to change that world—little to resolve the elements of daily life that make it so close to being unlivable. In making a difficult world livable but no less difficult, this culture becomes something less than an absolute savior. We began the book with the idea that no one (singly or collectively) can live easily with their own culture; neither entirely comfortably nor readily within one's own partly successful ways of lending meaning and incurring hope in exceedingly difficult circumstances.

This, it seems to me, is very much what is at stake for those who join Pentecostal churches—and who in the process lose their place in "family," "identity," and "Native culture." The results they seek, though quite ordinary by middle-class American standards, are extraordinary given the lives they lived before becoming church members. Ironically, while standing "against culture" they must also stand "against" the only lives they have ever known or are likely to know.

The importance of this process was made apparent to me by a recently converted church member named Mary, who, like many of those in the past chapters, had come to church after several years of alcohol abuse. As we stood on the edge of the boardwalk, near the center of town, surrounded by the older downtown houses and the few remaining shops, with the bay in front of us and the mountains beyond, she said, "I'm trying to live where all of this can make sense." As she spoke, her hand swept out in front of her, motioning toward all of what lie before us.

Her thoughts were at once theological and deeply personal—and it was plain that success in this effort, and thus her success in staying "off the bottle," was by no means assured. Nor was it clear how much of what came within the sweep of her hand had to be included for her to make sense of, and successfully remain an inhabitant in, the new life she was living. Her effort to see a world where she might live a meaningful life seemed at the heart of what she sought in church, and what she sought from those around her, for it was clear that the sweep of her hand intended to take in the houses of the village. In this way it seems clear that any success might depend in part on what those around Mary are willing (or unwilling) to have her imagine.

For those in between, then, the consequences are immense. Owen, the subsistence hunter, is one of those people. Owen's wife is a member of the Hoonah prayer group, and most of her family is "saved." Owen is a member as well, though he does not attend quite as regularly as she does. Nor is he quite so ready to be "against culture" as are some other members of the group. "I still got to feed my family," he explains. So he continues to hunt seals in the winter at great personal risk, and to dance in the dance group when he can. Owen is "like a real old-time Indian," I was often told. For this same reason, he is very much a prospect for local church recruiting.

## Epilogue—Beyond Alaska

About the time NOL politics were causing the mass deforestation of much of the land surrounding Indian communities in Southeast Alaska, the United Nations proclaimed 1993 the International Year of the World's Indigenous Peoples. In facing its own questions about what constituted indigenism, the UN was guided by the so-called Cobo definition, named for the director of the original UN Indigenous Peoples project. The Cobo definition laid out five criteria for being considered an indigenous people. Indigenous communities are peoples who:

(1)     have "historical continuity with pre-invasion and pre-colonial societies that developed on their territories;"

(2)     "consider themselves distinct from other sectors" of these societies;

(3)     "form at present a non-dominant sector of society;"

(4)     "are determined to preserve, develop and transmit to future generation their ancestral territories and their ethnic identity;" and

(5)     seek to do so "according to their own cultural patterns, social institutions and legal systems."[37]

The Cobo definition has proven widely influential, helping to put indigeneity in its current form on many political agendas and making it a specter on the horizon for many contemporary nation-states. Yet, as becomes clear from the material discussed here, it is not just the generality of these five criteria that ensures their wide appeal—as though the members of the UN committee had

---

[37] José R. Martinez Cobo, 1987. "Study of the Problem of Discrimination against Indigenous Populations." Vol. 5. UN document E/CN.4/ Sub.2/1986/7/Add.4., p. 48; this division into five criteria follows Richard B. Lee, "Twenty-first century indigenism." *Anthropological Theory* v. 6, n. 4 (2006): 455-479.

somehow hit upon a common denominator of ready-made indigenous peoples. Rather, what marks these criteria and the concept of indigeneity they enshrine as something with real-world political appeal is their ability to bring into focus a host of incipient relationships between potentially indigenous groups, surrounding non-indigenous peoples, and the nations states within which indigenous peoples now find themselves.

When looked at in this way, notions of indigeneity—and its associated rights and claims—are not seen as something emerging entirely from those communities who would claim it. Instead, indigeneity is something of a political middle ground. Like new traditions, indigeneity is a new political territory whose terrain is uncertain and fluid, yet one whose eventual dynamics can greatly affect both those taking up the mantel of indigeneity and the societies and states that surround them.

There is reason to believe that the current dynamics of indigeneity are largely new, distinct from the types of relationships between colonial powers and Native peoples in the past. In the past, states and industries interested in resources claimed by indigenous people have sometimes, perhaps most of the time, simply taken them—by force, by law, by trickery, and by brutality. What makes today different is the nearly complete reversal of this process, not everywhere, but certainly in North America, Australia, and increasingly many other places. Today, in Alaska and elsewhere, states are increasingly willing to recognize and acquiesce to Native claims, where doing so provides them opportunities that are otherwise denied. The example at the center of this book is the Alaskan logging industry, where environmental laws affecting timber cutting on federal lands have encouraged both government and industry to support the recognition and even expansion of Native claims. This would have seemed unthinkable in the 1950s, in the U.S. or anywhere else for that matter.

The logic of this change of attitude is clear. By awarding land to ANCSA corporations, with their partial sovereignty over their own lands, the U.S. government allows land that would otherwise be subject to a host of harvest regulations to be developed without being subject to federal environmental laws. Similar issues regarding Indian lands throughout the United States have allowed the increasing use of reservations for toxic waste dumping, high-stakes gambling, and, as with the notorious Black Mesa projects, strip mining and electricity generation. All of these are destructive and harmful forms of industrial exploitation, both to Natives and to their neighbors. Yet each offers recognition of a sort to the indigenous claims involved. Together, situations like these encourage us to look further into the meaning of indigeneity in the

U.S. than a simple reading of the Cobo definition might suggest, as the current stakes of indigeneity the world over are very high.

Of the five characteristics of the Cobo definition, all are of interest to states and their corporate allies. First, according to criterion 1, indigenous groups are those with claims to what we might call special status political-economic participation based on a priori claims to important resources. That is, what marks potentially indigenous ethnic minorities as distinct from other ethnic minorities (in the eyes of surrounding states and often in their own eyes) are claims to significant resources *other than their own labor*, resources that they still, in some measure, possess. Importantly, these claims are often quite different from the way that property is normally recognized, as reflected in Cobo criteria 4 and 5, where we note that Native claims are supported neither by force nor on obvious legal grounds, but rather through claims of continuity based on tradition. This idea, that indigeneity is intrinsically related to resources held insecurely (but held or claimed nonetheless), is perhaps the main reason why so many groups and surrounding states found much to like, as well as to protest, in the definition.

Beyond this, we note that according to criteria 2 and 3, indigenous groups are defined as not holding state power, nor are they simply one among other ordinary subjects denied access to state power. To be indigenous, that is, one must be neither; though for anyone to be indigenous, the others must exist. This last part is deeply ironic, for it points out that, in contemporary global politics, for anyone to be indigenous there must exist not only a state from which they are excluded, and whose interests are different from those of the indigenous group, but also others who are both excluded from state power and considered by both the state and by the indigenous themselves to be non-indigenous. For Natives in Southeast Alaska, this includes both the non-Native population of the region and, perhaps more importantly, the larger American middle class.

The tie to nature wrought by reference to resources and tradition has lingering effects on what may and may not be done by states to, and on behalf of, Native peoples. One of the key features of Native political sovereignty, as it has been defined and limited by the U.S. courts, is that Native tribes and related political "entities," insofar as they are recognized by the federal government, are considered to be governed by the U.S. criminal code, but to be exempt from the U.S. civil code, in recognition of (what is regarded by the dominant society as) the remaining or "residual" sovereignty of Native peoples.

In looking back at this process, it is worth pondering what is in it for Native peoples themselves. Without a doubt, the new recognition process has created a new class of elite representatives, and more than a few museums and ministries of cultural affairs. But is there more? The answer is yes; though it is more of a qualified yes, and one that rests as much in potential as accomplishment, even after many years of advocacy and protest. While it is certainly true that the first set of Cobo characteristics (an indigenous group's largely unenforceable claims to significant resources) has meant that these groups have often found themselves buffeted by the combination of state power and national populations, this is not invariably the case, in Alaska or elsewhere. Recognition has helped foster an environment in which diverse communities within the more easily defined towns or tribes have been able to produce their own understandings of sovereignty, and to propose their own social relations and legal and political resources. Examples of this from the previous chapters include "the Radicals," the Hydaburg subsistence protest, and, I would argue, the rise of all-Native Pentecostal Churches. None of these succeeded, at least not in any lasting way, and all paid some kind of heavy, long-term price, but the variety of the kinds of sociality and resulting solidarity are perhaps the best antidote to the narrowing of indigenous recognition that ANCSA and similar forms of "recognition" began.

The give and take of this dialogue is ongoing. In cases like these, indigeneity must be seen for the political dynamics it contains, rather than its adherence to imposed stereotypes. This happens when people refuse continuity, without giving in to proposed new traditions that would leave many unable to participate. In this way, responses to the new politics of indigeneity, like those of the Pentecostal church members, must be understood in this broader political context as well. Native peoples have long known this in some capacity, and have, in the midst of their struggles against the imposed reshaping of their lives, continually developed ways of putting the issues that truly matter to them beyond the reach of power. This has often meant that sustaining Native existence both within and beyond domination and exploitation entails continual, and often fundamental, cultural transformations. Pentecostalism, in this perspective, is part of (but not reducible to) the continuity of Native culture, in Alaska and likely beyond.

***

The situation beyond Alaska is, to reverse a familiar phrase, neither much better nor much worse. Indigenous people everywhere remain among the world's poor, and rather unremarkable in this way. Unremarkable except for the fact that somehow their poverty is made to seem more natural. Other than this, they live and die like the 1.5 billion or so people that get by on less than $5 per household per day in the modern world. Their quaint habits and novel languages have long made them an object of anthropological study and a fair bit of anthropological fantasy, but their lives, in any broad social or demographic sense, are typical. They live in overcrowded houses, have disastrously short life expectancies, high rates of substance abuse, equally high rates of domestic and sexual violence, a deep dependence on the state for individual and household reproduction—all when compared with their neighboring middle classes. When compared with others on the margins of capital, the indigenous look like everyone else; their lives make them typical of the global poor, not the exception.

The fact that some indigenous people continue to live in rural areas makes them a bit unique, though only if we decide to neglect the large numbers shed by these same communities to nearby "non-indigenous" cities and, increasingly, the suburbs and ex-urbs of larger metropoles. Of course, indigenous people are not the only ones leaving the countryside these days. Most everyone is leaving: whites, browns, exotics; which ought to prompt the larger question of why or how anyone manages to stay. If indigenous people are remarkable in any sense that distinguishes them from their would-be future neighbors in the city, or their largely unmentioned former neighbors in the country, it is the fact that by and large *indigenous* rural residents have been able to resist the massive dislocation that has swept up most other rural peoples over the last 30-40 years. Why and how those who stay behind manage to do so remains an open question.

Many of these rural places are beautiful, of course; links to kin and kind are strong pulls, and there is the feeling of a connection to place—historical, spiritual, or cultural, or some combination of these things. Though none of these are particularly unique to indigenous peoples. Most rural residents feel the same pull, whether they have been country people for a generation or a millennium. Instead, what seems more important than the various pulls and inertias of rural life in our attempt to understand the lingeringness of indigenous homelands is the extent to which surrounding states seem willing to go to make such situations possible—how far states will go to allow indigenous peoples to remain partly rural, even while not extending such opportunities to their non-indigenous neighbors. It is in this context that the naturalness of indigenous poverty must be interrogated.

One doesn't have to dig too deep for candidate answers to the question of why governments since the 1970s have sought to raise the exceptionalism of indigenous peoples and link it to particular rural locales. Even the most cursory examination of the global business of development over the last four decades reveals that indigenous 'staying behind' has been underwritten by successful land claims, many modeled on ANCSA, which have in turn fed the voracious appetite of capital for the raw material basis of modern manufacturing. Land claims are rarely looked at in this way—as the means through which states and businesses have fractured the rural landscape into communities with claims that are thus allowed to struggle on, and those without claims, who are cast willy-nilly into the world's "bottom billion." Instead, the success of indigenous land claims is chalked up as evidence of local persistence and cleverness, the hard work of indigenous peoples' liberal allies, a rather broad, perhaps world-wide change in the generosity and fairness of national governments toward the recognition of past wrongs, or perhaps even a sudden willingness of colonial governments to obey their own laws.

These sorts of explanations ought to arouse suspicions immediately, but somehow they do not. Yet if one looks at the nature of virtually any of the various indigenous land settlements of the last 40 years, it is abundantly clear that they were, from the beginning, intended only to make indigenous life at the margins marginally more possible—not to make it pleasant or worthwhile. Despite their lack of "success" in producing thriving indigenous towns and settlements, they have managed to get a lot of oil, coal, copper, zinc, diamonds, uranium and so on, out of the ground and into production.

The results of this are easy to see. Life in rural indigenous communities post land claims "success," in Australia, the U.S., Canada, Chile, Argentina, and many other places, is generally just as precarious and beset by social problems as the dreary "urban outback" described by Gillian Cowlishaw, awaiting rural residents on the other end, if and when any particular indigenous person, household, family or town decides to throw in the cultural towel.[38]

We should also note that Indigenous claims world-wide rose significantly about 40 years ago amid the momentum of a host of other "new social movements" such as the environment, gay rights, civil rights, black power, feminism, and so on. Taken together, the movements of the 1960s and early 70s saw an assault on the claims that governments were making to public spaces, public resources, national treasuries, political discourses, public

---

[38] Gillian Cowlishaw. *The City's Outback*. NewSouth Publishing, 2009.

education, on an unprecedented scale. In general, they were remarkably successful; so much so that together they represented the first real challenge to the hegemonic form of the Western Business State since the 1930s. Ironically, indigenous claims were among the most easily dismissed at this time—and many were, backed by notions of modernization and demographic decline and aided by the already marginal place of indigenous peoples in most national imaginaries.

Arguably, the indigenous came out of this period more successfully than other claimants who far outnumbered them and whose claims stood on far more stable legal ground. In large part, this book has been an attempt to explain why this was so. Explanations, like this one, are often overlooked, as are the costs of this "success." Too often we only hear about how the indigenous have gotten a "special deal," or how other rural residents are subject to "reverse discrimination."

In answer to the question of what sort of special deal the new politics of recognition provide, one need only consider the story of Johnny Abel, recently passed, from Canada's Northwest Territory. On August 12, 2009, Johnny Abel was found dead in a day-rate hotel room in Yellowknife, in Canada's Northwest Territories.[39] While having been born on the Lutsel K'e reserve (not far from where global mining giant Rio Tinto now operates the Diavik diamond mine), he was well known in Yellowknife: he'd lived on and off the streets there for nearly 20 years, and despite its regional prominence, Yellowknife is still a small town. He was a drunk, though a friendly one, and for twenty years he hadn't worked, living instead off of the Indian dole. Until he died.

His death having passed rather unremarkably, especially for a small town, his family wanted his story told, the local newspaper reported. Without openly saying so, the family knew that his death would be chalked up to one more sad but inevitable Indian story, in a town where such stories are common enough to be seen as natural. He was an honorable man, they told the paper over and again, a father of two daughters and several grandchildren, despite his young age. He had worked in the Giant Mine as a driller when he was younger, until he was redeployed into the logging industry when mining slowed in the mid-1980s. There he cut timber in the woods for a local contractor for several years until he simply couldn't anymore. The two jobs had left him with what local folks in the North call "white hand," a medical condition known as Hand Arm Vibration Syndrome, caused by working long hours with tools that create

---

[39] T. Edwards, "He really was a good man." *Northern News Service*, 14 August 2009.

constant, hard vibrations. Slowly, but surely, the vibrations sever the smaller blood vessels and nerves in the hands and arms, and then the nerves in the extremities die and the limb becomes functionally useless; the lack of circulation leaves them white and cold. Once Abel got white hand, he never worked again, though surviving on the streets in a place where winter temperatures are regularly -30° C seems to me like an accomplishment in its own right.

In his youth, he had been to residential school which he didn't talk about much, his family said, but where he learned to play the guitar and even had a band called the "Blind Onions" that performed Creedence Clearwater Revival covers at local bars. He was successful, in a general sort of way. By popular acclaim, he was the first person on the Ndilo Reserve to own a pickup truck. He'd been a good father to two daughters, and remained faithful for two decades to his common-law wife. He died what would undoubtedly be perceived as an Indian death, and his family wanted people to know that he had lived an Indian life. The two are related, joined together in this case by the white hand of capitalism that quite happily took what it could get and shed the rest. What struck me most in reading the story in the paper, however, was how hard his family had to fight to counteract the presumed understanding. Case in point: without the slightest hint of irony, the newspaper reported that Johnny Able had died of "natural causes."

Johnny Able wasn't from Alaska, though his story would sound familiar to many who live there. But for a few details, it could be the story of Billy or Tom or any of the others from the past several chapters. They, and others like them from Australia, India, New Zealand or South America, come from very different cultures. But their lives are remarkably similar, and what they make of their lives seems often to be remarkably similar. And though they don't share a culture, in the small sense of that term, they do share a cultural situation, one in which their indigeneity or aboriginality or some such lately-contrived notion of their place in this world pits them between the rock of a marginal past and the hard place of the modern development economy. That they come through it all with such humor and grace is a testament to the power of culture making. That they are forced to do so at the expense of much of themselves—at various times: life, limb, sobriety, family and community—is a testament to a culture politics they would never choose, but which they live and die with nonetheless.

NOTES AND SOURCES

**Chapter 1**

I learned most of what I know about culture politics from Gerald Sider. His work on Lumbee Indian histories and the entire corpus of settler colonialism in North America allowed me to see a world that would otherwise have remained hidden in plain sight. Interested readers should consult:

- Sider, Gerald M. *Living Indian histories: The Lumbee and Tuscarora People in North Carolina.* UNC Press Books, 2003.
- Sider, Gerald M. *Lumbee Indian Histories.* Cambridge University Press, 1993.
- Sider, Gerald. "When parrots learn to talk, and why they can't: Domination, deception, and self-deception in Indian-White relations." *Comparative Studies in Society and History* v. 29, n.1 (1987): 3-23.
- Sider, Gerald M. *Between History and Tomorrow: Making and Breaking Everyday Life in Rural Newfoundland.* University of Toronto Press, 2003.
- Sider, Gerald. "Against experience: The struggles for history, tradition, and hope among a Native American people." *Between History and Histories: The Making of Silences and Commemorations, University of Toronto Press, Toronto* (1997), pp. 62-79.
- Sider, Gerald. "The walls came tumbling up: The production of culture, class and native American societies." *The Australian journal of anthropology* v.17, n.3 (2006): 276-290.

In recent years, a number of important works have followed Sider's in taking up the question of culture in the dialectic of production/self-production, where culture becomes intimately tied up with issues of governance, economy, and racism. This is a vast literature on a global problem; a good place to start would be:

- Cattelino, Jessica R. *High Stakes: Florida Seminole Gaming and Sovereignty.* Duke University Press, 2008.
- Cattelino, Jessica R. "The double bind of American Indian need-based sovereignty." *Cultural Anthropology* v. 25, n.2 (2010): 235-262.
- Cattelino, Jessica R. "One Hamburger at a Time." *Current Anthropology* v. 52, n.S3 (2011).
- Biolsi, Thomas. "Imagined geographies: Sovereignty, indigenous space, and American Indian struggle." *American Ethnologist* v. 32, n.2 (2005): 239-259.
- Cowlishaw, Gillian. "Mythologising culture." *The Australian Journal of Anthropology* v. 22, n.2 (2011): 170-188.
- Jordan, Kurt A. "Colonies, colonialism, and cultural entanglement: The archaeology of postcolumbian intercultural relations." *International Handbook of Historical Archaeology.* Springer New York, 2009, pp. 31-49.
- Starn, Orin. "Here come the anthros (again): The strange marriage of anthropology and Native America." *Cultural Anthropology* v. 26, n.2 (2011): 179-204.
- Austin-Broos, Diane J. *Arrernte Present, Arrernte Past: Invasion, Violence, and Imagination in Indigenous Central Australia.* University of Chicago Press, 2009.

- Austin-Broos, Diane. "Keeping faith with self-determination: Economy and cultural difference." *Indigenous Law Bulletin* v. 7, n.29 (2012): 19.
- Austin- Broos, Diane. "The politics of difference and equality: Remote Aboriginal communities, public discourse, and Australian anthropology." *Transforming Anthropology* v. 19, n.2 (2011): 139-145.
- Li, Tania Murray. "Articulating indigenous identity in Indonesia: Resource politics and the tribal slot." *Comparative Studies of Society and History* v. 42, n.1 (2000): 149-79.
- Beckett, Jeremy. "Returned to sender: Some predicaments of re- indigenisation." *Oceania* v. 82, no. 1 (2012): 104-112.
- Cowlishaw, Gillian. "Culture and the absurd: the means and meanings of Aboriginal identity in the time of cultural revivalism." *Journal of the Royal Anthropological Institute* v. 18, no. 2 (2012): 397-417.

I was fortunate to enter graduate school at the height of "historical anthropology" movement, and to do so in New York, which was its center. I studied with Sider, William Roseberry, and Joan Vincent, took the last graduate course that Eric Wolf taught, and found my way down to the New School to hear Eric Hobsbawm lecture. It was a great time to be working these topics. For those interested in what happens when Anthropology meets History see:

- Wolf, Eric R. *Europe and the People without History*. University of California Press, 1982/2010.
- Wolf, Eric R. "Inventing society." *American Ethnologist* v. 15, n.4 (1988): 752-761.
- Trouillot, Michel-Rolph. *Silencing the Past: Power and the Production of History*. Beacon Press, 2012.
- Roseberry, William. *Anthropologies and Histories: Essays in Culture, History, and Political Economy*. Rutgers University Press, 1989.
- Vincent, Joan. *Teso in Transformation: The Political Economy of Peasant and Class in Eastern Africa*. Berkeley: University of California Press, 1982.
- Smith, Gavin. *Confronting the Present: Towards a Politically Engaged Anthropology*. Berg Publishing, 1999.
- Smith, Gavin. "The production of culture in local rebellion." *Golden Ages, Dark Ages: Imagining the Past in Anthropology and History* (1991): 180-205.
- Smith, Gavin A. "Selective hegemony and beyond-populations with 'no productive function:' A framework for enquiry." *Identities* v. 18, n.1 (2011): 2-38.

The intersection of race, subculture and anthropology is an enormous field, and has shaped my thinking in very important ways. Apart from Sider's work, other worthwhile reads by several scholars that have helped me think through these things including:

- Baker, Lee D. *Anthropology and the Racial Politics of Culture*. Duke University Press Books, 2010.
- Baca, George. *Conjuring Crisis: Racism and Civil Rights in a Southern Military City*. Rutgers University Press, 2010.
- Hebdige, Dick. "Subculture: The meaning of style." *Critical Quarterly* v. 37, n.2 (1995): 120-124.
- Hebdige, Dick. "From culture to hegemony." *The Cultural Studies Reader* (1993):

357-67.

- Crehan, Kate. "Gramsci's concept of common sense: a useful concept for anthropologists?" *Journal of Modern Italian Studies* v. 16, n.2 (2011): 273-287.
- Crehan, Kate. *Gramsci, Culture, and Anthropology.* University of California Press, 2002.

I knew very little about religion before discovering it in Alaska. As is clear in the text, I benefited considerably from the work of Susan Friend Harding, including:

- Harding, Susan F. "American protestant moralism and the secular imagination: From temperance to the moral majority." *Social Research: An International Quarterly* v. 76, n.4 (2009): 1277-1306.
- Harding, Susan F. "Convicted by the Holy Spirit: The Rhetoric of Fundamental Baptist Conversion." *American Ethnologist*, v. 14, n.1 (1987): 167–181.
- Harding, Susan F. *The Book of Jerry Falwell: Fundamentalist Language and Politics.* Princeton University Press, 2001.

As noted in the Acknowledgments, my own work on this topic was developed in my earlier book and a series of articles, portions of which appear in Chapter 1.

- Dombrowski, Kirk. *Against Culture: Development, Politics and Religion in Indian Alaska.* University of Nebraska Press, 2001.
- Dombrowski, Kirk. "Culture and praxis in post-modern times." *Focaal* v. 56 (2010): 81-89.
- Dombrowski, Kirk. "The praxis of indigenism and Alaska native timber politics." *American Anthropologist* v. 104, n.4 (2002): 1062-1073.
- Dombrowski, Kirk. "Reply: what's changed (since 1975)?" *Dialectical Anthropology* v. 32, n.1 (2008): 43-50.
- Dombrowski, Kirk. "Reply to Clifford in "Looking Several Ways." *Current Anthropology* v. 45, n.1 (2004): 23-24.
- Dombrowski, Kirk. "New Perspectives on Native North America: Cultures, Histories and Representations." *Ethos* v. 38, n.1 (2010): 1-3.

## Chapter 2

Much has been written on the history of Alaska and the industrial development of the Pacific Northwest, both generally and as it pertains to Alaska Natives. Some worthwhile general sources are:

- Gibson, James R. *Otter Skins, Boston Ships, and China Goods: The Maritime Fur Trade of the Northwest Coast, 1785-1841.* McGill Queens University Press, 1992.
- Newell, Diane. *Development of the Pacific Salmon-Canning Industry: A Grown Man's Game.* McGill Queens University Press, 1989.
- Crutchfield, James A., and Guilio Pontecorvo. *The Pacific Salmon Fisheries: A Study in Irrational Conservation.* Baltimore: Johns Hopkins University Press, 1969.
- Arnold, David F. *The Fishermen's Frontier: People and Salmon in Southeast Alaska.* University of Washington Press, 2009.
- Haycox, Stephen. *Alaska, an American Colony.* University of Washington Press, 2006.

- Case, David S. and David A. Voluck, *Alaska Natives and American Laws (Third Edition).* University of Alaska Press, 2012.
- Durbin, Kathie, *Tongass: Pulp politics and the fight for the Alaska rain forest.* Oregon State University Press, 1999.
- Arbogast, Dean. "Labor in the Alaskan Salmon Industry." Master's thesis, Faculty of Business, Columbia University, 1947.
- Knight, Rolf. *Indians at Work: An Informal History of Native Indian Labour in British Columbia, 1858—1930.* Vancouver: New Star Books, 1978.
- Morehouse, Thomas A., and George W. Rogers. "Limited Entry in the Alaska and British Columbia Salmon Fisheries." A report from the Institute of Social and Economic Research, University of Alaska-Anchorage, 1980.
- Price, Robert E. *The Great Father in Alaska: The Case of the Tlingit and Haida Salmon Fishery.* Douglas AK: First Street Press, 1990.

On the Alaska Natives of Southeast Alaska, some conventional ethnographic/ethnological approaches can be found in:

- Thornton, Thomas F. *Being and Place among the Tlingit.* University of Washington Press, 2012.
- Dauenhauer, Nora, and Richard Dauenhauer. *Haa shuká, Our Ancestors: Tlingit Oral Narratives. Vol. 1.* Seattle: University of Washington Press, 1987.
- Dauenhauer, Nora Marks, and Richard Dauenhauer. *Haa Tuwunáagu Yís, for Healing Our Spirit: Tlingit Oratory. Vol. 2.* Seattle: University of Washington Press; Juneau: Sealaska Heritage Foundation, 1990.
- Dauenhauer, Nora Marks, and Richard Dauenhauer. *Haa kusteeyi, Our Culture: Tlingit Life Stories. Vol. 3.* University of Washington Press, 1994.
- Kan, Sergei. *Symbolic Immortality: The Tlingit Potlatch of the Nineteenth Century.* Vol. 51. Washington, DC: Smithsonian Institution Press, 1989.
- Kan, Sergei. *Memory Eternal: Tlingit Culture and Russian Orthodox Christianity Through Two Centuries.* University of Washington Press, 1999.

A fascinating historical window is available via a series of unpublished or historic government reports, see:

- Cobb, John N. "Pacific Salmon Fisheries." Bureau of Fisheries Document no. 1092. Washington DC: Government Printing Office, 1930.
- U.S. Department of the Interior, Bureau of Education. (MS) Village reports to the U.S. Commissioner of the Bureau of Education. Microfilm. Juneau: Alaska State Historical Library, 1907-15.
- Goldschmidt, Walter R., and Theodore H. Haas. "Possessory Rights of the Natives of Southeast Alaska: A Report to the Commissioner of Indian Affairs." Washington DC: U.S. Bureau of Indian Affairs, 1946. Republished as Goldschmidt, Walter Rochs, and Theodore H. Haas. *Our Land.* Univ of Washington Press, 1998, with an introduction by Thomas F. Thornton.
- Bureau of Indian Affairs. (MS) "Economic Survey." Photocopied manuscript in possession of Alaska Historical Library, Juneau, 1938—41. .
- Camarot, Henry, and Marjory Wentworth. "A Report and Recommendations on the Study of the Problems in the Fishing Industry." Compiled for the Alaska

Legislative Council, 1958.

- Lantis, Margaret, and Varden Fuller. (MS) "Economic Needs of Natives of Southeastern Alaska." Draft report to the U.S. Bureau of Indian Affairs. Juneau: Alaska State Historical Library, 1948.
- LaVerdure, George A. (MS) "A Study: Alaska Native Cannery Operations and Allied Activity." Juneau: Alaska State Historical Library, 1961.
- Paul, William L., Sr. Papers. Microfilm. Juneau: Alaska State Historical Library.

More detailed reading on several aspects of this chapter, including the politics of negotiating these changes at the local level see:

- Philp, Kenneth R. "The New Deal and Alaskan Natives, 1936-1945." *Pacific Historical Review* v. 50, n.3 (1981): 309-327.
- Pegues, Juliana Hu. "Rethinking relations: Interracial intimacies of Asian men and Native women in Alaskan canneries." *Interventions* v. 15, n.1 (2013): 55-66.
- Reedy-Maschner, Katherine. "Salmon politicians: Mapping boundaries, resources, and people at the Bristol Bay–Aleutian border." *Society & Natural Resources* ahead-of-print (2012): 1-14.
- Dombrowski, Kirk. "Totem poles and tricycle races: The certainties and uncertainties of Native village life, coastal Alaska, 1878—1930." *Journal of Historical Sociology* v. 8, n. 2 (1995): 136—57.
- Cooley, Richard A. *Politics and Conservation: The Decline of the Alaska Salmon.* New York: Harper and Row, 1963.
- Dinneford, E., and K. Cohen. "Changes in the Distribution of Permit Ownership in Alaska's Limited Fisheries: 1976—1988." Commercial Fisheries Entry Commission, Report no. 89-3, 1989.
- Masson, J., and D. Guimary. "Pilipinos and unionization of the Alaskan canned Salmon Industry." *Amerasia* v. 8, n. 2(1981): 1—30.
- Rogers, George W. *Alaska in Transition: The Southeast Region.* Baltimore: Johns Hopkins University Press, 1960.

The court decisions on several issues pertaining to this chapter can be found in:

- (1879) *Reynolds v. United States,* 98 U.S. 146.
- (1902) Proclamation no. 37, 33 Stat. 2025, creating the Alexander Archipelago National Forest in Southeast Alaska.
- (1944) *"Hanna Opinion":* Report of the Presiding Chairman, Richard A. Hanna. Hearings on Claims of Natives, of the Towns of Hydaburg, Klawock, and Kake, Alaska, Pursuant to the Provisions of Section 201.21b of the Regulations for Protection of the Commercial Fisheries of Alaska.
- (1952) *"Folta Decision":* United States of America v. Libby, McNeil & Libby, District Court for the Territory of Alaska (no. 6445-A).
- (1968) *Tlingit and Haida Indians v. United States,* 177 F.Supp. 452 (Court of Claims, 1959) and 389 F.2d 788 (Court of Claims, 1968).
- (1971) *Alaska Native Claims Settlement Act,* Public Law 93-203. 85 Stat. 689; 43 USCA 1601 et seq.
- (1975) *Indian Self-Determination and Education Assistance Act,* 25 USC 450 et seq.
- (1980) *Alaska National Interest Land Conservation Act of December 2, 1980,* 94 Stat.

2371.

- (1987) *Alaska Native Claims Settlement Act Amendments of 1987*, Public Law 100-241. 101 Stat. 1788.
- (1990) *Tongass Timber Reform Act*, Public Law 101-626—November 28, 1990.
- (1994) *Alaska Wilderness Recreation and Tourism Association; Organized Village of Kake; Southeast Alaska Conservation Council; Natural Resources Defense Council; and the Wilderness Society v. U.S. Forest Service.* No. J94-033-CV (JWS), U.S. District Court for the District of Alaska.


## Chapter 3

The Alaska Native Claims Settlement Act of 1971 changed much in Alaska. In other ways it offered more of the same—another large scale land grab driven largely by people who were concerned with everything but people. My interest in ANCSA is for the role it played in marking a change in the way that states and industries dealt with the problem of indigeneity. Much of this book is dedicated to this idea. But there were many aspects of ANCSA, and many books and articles have been written on it. Those I found most helpful in framing my own views are:

- Alaska Federation of Natives. 1988. "1991—Making It Work: A Guide to Public Law 100-241, 1987 Amendments to the Alaska Native Claims Settlement Act." Anchorage: Alaska Federation of Natives.
- Berger, Thomas R. *Village Journey: The Report of the Alaska Native Review Commission.* New York: Hill and Wang, 1985.
- Federal Field Committee of Development Planning in Alaska. 1968. "Alaska Natives and the Land." Washington DC: Government Printing Office.
- Knapp, Gunnar. "Native Timber Harvests in Southeast Alaska." U.S. Forest Service/Pacific Northwest Research Station General Technical Report PNW-GTR-284, 1992.
- Ganapathy, Sandhya. "Alaskan neo-liberalism: Conservation, development, and Native land rights." *Social Analysis* v. 55, n. 1 (2011): 113-133.

Other sources on ANCSA that cover aspects not specifically addressed here are:

- Arnold, Robert D. *Alaska Native Land Claims.* Anchorage: Alaska Native Foundation, 1978.
- Berry, Mary C. *The Alaska Pipeline: The Politics of Oil and Native Land Claims.* Bloomington: Indiana University Press, 1975.
- Berardi, Gigi. "Alaska Native Claims Settlement Act (ANCSA): Whose settlement was it? An overview of the salient issues" *Journal of Land Resources & Environmental Law* v. 25, n. 2 (2005): 131-137.
- Case, David S. *Alaska Natives and American Laws.* Anchorage: University of Alaska Press, 1984.
- Chance, Norman A. *The Inupiat and Arctic Development.* Chicago: Holt, Rinehart and Winston, 1990.
- Ford, Marilyn J. Ward. "Indian country and inherent tribal authority: Will they survive ANCSA." *Alaska Law Review* v. 14 (1997): 443-470.

- Jorgensen, Joseph, et al. *Native Americans and Energy Development*. Cambridge MA: Anthropology Resource Center, 1978; and *Native Americans and Energy Development II*. Cambridge MA: Anthropology Resource Center, 1984.
- Kendall-Miller, Heather. "ANCSA and sovereignty litigation." *Journal of Land Resources & Environmental Law* v. 24, n. 3. (2004): 465-474.

And finally, sources for the local politics around the implementation of the Act and its subsequent revision can be found in:

- Alaska Department of Fish and Game (Division of Subsistence). "Report on Implementation of 1992 Subsistence Law." Juneau: Alaska Department of Fish and Game, 1995.
- Barsh, Russel L. "The international legal status of Native Alaska." *Alaska Native News*, July 1984.
- Bernton, Hal. "Logging hard against debt." *Anchorage Daily News*, August 11, 1985; "Hope fuels expanded cut." *Anchorage Daily News*, August 12, 1985; "Ecology impact debated." *Anchorage Daily News*, August 13, 1985; "Tax amendment proves boon for Native logging." *Anchorage Daily News*, June 21, 1987; "Logging takes toll on habitat in Southeast." *Anchorage Daily News*, August 23 1987; "Native groups turn losses into assets." *Anchorage Daily News*, December 20, 1987.
- Colt, Steve. "Financial performance of Native regional corporations." *Alaska Review of Social and Economic Conditions* v.28, no. 2 (1991).
- Ellana, Linda J., and George K. Sherrod. "Timber Management and Fish and Wildlife Use in Selected Southeastern Alaska Communities: Klawock, Prince of Wales Island, Alaska." Technical Paper no. 126. Juneau: Alaska Department of Fish and Game, 1987.
- Goldbelt Inc. "1989 Annual Report." Juneau: Goldbelt Inc., 1989.
- Gorsuch, Lee, Steve Colt, Charles Smythe, and Bart K. Garber. "A Study of Five Southeast Alaska Communities." Washington DC: U.S. Department of Agriculture, U.S. Forest Service, U.S. Department of the Interior (Bureau of Land Management and Bureau of Indian Affairs), 1994.
- Huna Totem Corporation. "Huna Totem Corporation and Subsidiaries, Consolidated Financial Statements and Schedules for January 1, 1987 and 1988." Hoonah AK: Huna Totem Corporation, 1988.
- Kake Tribal Corporation. "Kake Tribal Corporation and Subsidiaries Consolidated Financial Statements and Supplementary Information for Years Ended December 31, 1988 and 1989." Kake AK: Kake Tribal Corporation, 1988-89
- Leghorn, Ken, and Matt Kookesh. "Timber Management and Fish and Wildlife Utilization in Selected Southeast Alaska Communities: Tenakee Springs, Alaska." Technical Paper no. 138. Juneau: Alaska Department of Fish and Game, 1987.
- Ortega, Bob. "Sealaska Posts Record Income." Anchorage Times, September 11, 1988.
- Schiller, Robert. "Overview of the Timber Industry in Southeast Alaska." Department of Commerce and Economic Development, State of Alaska, Research Monograph no. 84-013. Juneau: State of Alaska, 1984.

- Southeast Alaska Conservation Council. "Senator Murkowski's New Native Claims Bill: A Destructive Raid on Public Lands." Juneau: Southeast Alaska Conservation Counci, 1995.
- U.S. Forest Service. "Timber Supply and Demand, 1988 Report." ANILCA, section 706(a), Report no. 8, R10-MB-78. Juneau: U.S. Department of Agriculture, 1989. *And* "Timber Supply and Demand, 1989 Report." ANILCA, section 706(a), Report no. 9, R10-MB-113. Juneau: U.S. Department of Agriculture, 1990.
- McGee, Jack B. "Subsistence hunting and fishing in Alaska: Does ANILCA's rural subsistence priority really conflict with the Alaska constitution." *Alaska Law Review* v. 27, n. 2 (2010): 221-255.

Portions of this chapter have appeared previously in:

- Dombrowski, Kirk. *Against Culture: Development, Politics and Religion in Indian Alaska.* University of Nebraska Press, 2001.
- Dombrowski, Kirk. "The praxis of indigenism and Alaska native timber politics." *American Anthropologist v. 104, n. 4 (2002): 1062-1073.*
- Dombrowski, Kirk. "Reply: what's changed (since 1975)?" *Dialectical Anthropology* v. 32, n. 1 (2008): 43-50.
- Dombrowski, Kirk. "Reply to Clifford's 'Looking Several Ways'." *Current Anthropology* v. 45, n. 1 (2004): 23-24.


## Chapter 4

Kinship is one of the oldest topics in anthropology, and I was happy to have the opportunity to study it with Abe Rosman and Paula Rubel at Columbia in the early 1990s. What follows here is inspired by two very different sorts of takes on kinship, Eric Wolf's concept of the kin-ordered mode of production described in *Europe and the People without History* (1982) and David Schneider's (1984) *A Critique of Kinship.* Ann Arbor: University of Michigan Press. Classical sources on Tlingit and Haida kinship include:

- Emmons, George Thornton, and Frederica De Laguna. *The Tlingit Indians.* Vol. 70. Seattle: University of Washington Press; New York: American Museum of Natural History, 1991.
- Lowie, Robert H. "The relationship systems of the Tlingit, Haida, and Tsimshian." *American Anthropologist* v. 32, n. 2 (1930): 308-309.
- Drucker, P. "Rank, wealth, and kinship in Northwest Coast society." *American Anthropologist* v. 41, n. 1 (1939): 55-65.
- De Laguna, Frederica. "Some dynamic forces in Tlingit society." *Southwestern Journal of Anthropology* v. 8, n. 1 (1952): 1-12.
- McClellan, Catharine. "The interrelations of social structure with northern Tlingit ceremonialism." *Southwestern Journal of Anthropology* v. 10, n. 1 (1954): 75-96.
- Allen, Rosemary A. *Changing Social Organization and Kinship among the Alaskan Haidas.* University of Alaska, 1955.
- Rosman, A., and Rubel, P. G. "The Potlatch: A Structural Analysis." *American*

*Anthropologist* v. 74, n. 3 (1972): 658-671.

- De Laguna, F. *Under Mount Saint Elias: The History and Culture of the Yakutat Tlingit.* Smithsonian, (1972).

More recent sources on employment and the transformation of the Alaska economy since the 1970s can be found in:

- Rogers, George William, Richard F. Listowski, and Judith Brakel. "A Study of the Socio-economic Impact of Changes in the Harvesting Labor Force in the Alaska Salmon Fishery: Final Report." Institute of Social, Economic and Government Research, University of Alaska, 1972.
- Adasiak, Alan. 1977. "Limited entry in Alaska." *In Pacific Salmon Management for People*, ed. D. V. Ellis. Western Geographic Series, vol. 13. Victoria BC: University of Victoria Press.
- Knapp, Gunnar. "The Economic Outlook for Rural Alaska." Institute of Social and Economic Research, University of Alaska Anchorage, 1988.
- Colt, Steve. "Financial Performance of Native Regional Corporations." *Alaska Review of Social and Economic Conditions* v. 28, n. 2 (1991).
- Betts, Martha F., and Robert J. Wolfe. "Commercialization of fisheries and the subsistence economies of the Alaska Tlingit." *Society & Natural Resources* v. 5, n. 3 (1992): 277-295.
- Boucher, John. "Sitka: Coping with Structural Change." *Alaska Economic Trends*, Juneau, 1998.
- Robertson, Guy C. "A test of the economic base hypothesis in the small forest communities of Southeast Alaska." U.S. Department of Agriculture, Forest Service, Pacific Northwest Research Station, 2003.
- Colt, Steve, Darcy Dugan, and Ginny Fay. "The regional economy of Southeast Alaska." Institute of Social and Economic Research University of Alaska Anchorage, 2007.
- Beier, Colin M., Amy Lauren Lovecraft, and F. Stuart Chapin. "Growth and collapse of a resource system: an adaptive cycle of change in public lands governance and forest management in Alaska." *Ecology and Society* v. 14, n. 2 (2009); article 5.
- Ganapathy, Sandhya. "Imagining Alaska: Local and Translocal Engagements with Place." *American Anthropologist* v. 115, n. 1 (2013): 96-111.
- Dombrowski, Kirk. "Culture and praxis in post-modern times." *Focaal* v. 56, n. 1 (2010): 81-89.
- Dombrowski, Kirk. "Reply: what's changed (since 1975)?" *Dialectical Anthropology* v. 32, n. 1 (2008): 43-50.

The topic of social differentiation remains among the more taboo topics in the Anthropology of Native North America. It clashes with concepts of culture, history, and people-hood, and in so doing it gets in the way of ordinarily more important issues like land claims and sovereignty. Obviously, one of the main points of this book is that issues of internal differentiation stem from these larger political projects, and that they shape how those processes can, and at time cannot, succeed. My own work in this area would include:

- Dombrowski, Kirk. "The white hand of capitalism and the end of Indigenism as we know it." *The Australian Journal of Anthropology* v. 21, n. 1 (2010): 129-140.
- Dombrowski, Kirk. "Subsistence livelihood, Native identity and internal differentiation in Southeast Alaska." *Anthropologica* v. 49, n. 2 (2007): 211-229.
- Dombrowski, Kirk. "Billy Budd, Choker-Setter: Native Culture and Indian Work in the Southeast Alaska Timber Industry." *International Labor and Working-Class History* v. 62, n. 1 (2002): 121-142.
- Dombrowski, Kirk, Emily Channell, Bilal Khan, Joshua M Moses, Evan Misshula. "Out on the Land: Income, Subsistence Activities, and Food Sharing Networks in Nain, Labrador." *Journal of Anthropology* vol. 2013 (2013): 1-9.
- Dombrowski, Kirk, Bilal Khan, Joshua Moses, Emily Channell, Nathaniel Dombrowski, "Network sampling of social divisions in a rural Inuit community." *Identities, forthcoming* v. 21, 2014.
- Dombrowski, Kirk, Bilal Khan, Joshua Moses, Emily Channell, Evan Misshula, "Assessing Respondent Driven Sampling for Network Studies in Ethnographic Contexts." *Advances in Anthropology* v. 3, n.1 (2013):1-9.

For further reading on this, the reader may wish to consult:
- Strong, Pauline Turner. "Recent ethnographic research on North American indigenous peoples." *Annual Review of Anthropology*, v. 34 (2005): 253-268.
- Markstrom, Carol A. "Identity formation of American Indian adolescents: Local, national, and global considerations." *Journal of Research on Adolescence* v. 21, n. 2 (2011): 519-535.
- McMillan, L. Jane. "Colonial Traditions, Co-optations, and Mi'kmaq Legal Consciousness." *Law & Social Inquiry* v. 36, n. 1 (2011): 171-200.
- Wolfe, Patrick. "After the Frontier: Separation and Absorption in U.S. Indian Policy." *Settler Colonial Studies* v. 1, n. 1 (2011): 13-51.
- Sider, Gerald. "The walls came tumbling up: The production of culture, class and native American societies." *The Australian Journal of Anthropology* v. 17, n. 3 (2006): 276-290.

## Chapter 5

For reasons that I hope this chapter makes clear, the history of subsistence hunting, fishing and gathering in Southeast Alaska, and in Alaska in general, has received a lot of attention. In large part, non-Native commentators and researchers have focused on the historical and cultural aspects of this use, and the results have figured significantly in land claims politics since at least the late 19th century. Sprinkled throughout the historical records, though, are other voices—chiefly those of Native residents themselves—that talk about the importance of the land to basic survival. The latter, the literal meaning of subsistence, is often lost in the effort to validate the property relations they produced, though it is not lost to those who are having trouble getting by. This chapter approaches the topic of subsistence in holistic fashion, moving between and within these various levels. As such, the sources it draws from (beyond those of direct observation gained during my fieldwork) are mixed as well. One can learn a great deal from some of the older sources including:

- Goldschmidt, Walter R., and Theodore H. Haas. 1946. "Possessory Rights of the Natives of Southeast Alaska: A Report to the Commissioner of Indian Affairs." Washington DC: U.S. Bureau of Indian Affairs. Republished as Goldschmidt, Walter Rochs, and Theodore H. Haas. *Our Land*. Univ of Washington Press, 1998, with an introduction by Thomas F. Thornton.
- Berger, Thomas R. *Village Journey: The Report of the Alaska Native Review Commission*. New York: Hill and Wang, 1985.
- Langdon, Stephen. "Technology, Ecology, Economy: Fishing Systems in Southeast Alaska." Ph.D. diss., Stanford University, Palo Alto, 1977.
- Moss, Madonna L. "Outer coast maritime adaptations in southern Southeast Alaska: Tlingit or Haida?" *Arctic Anthropology* v. 45, n. 1 (2008): 41-60.
- Thornton, Thomas F. *Being and place among the Tlingit*. University of Washington Press, 2012.
- And an interesting recent summation of research by Wheeler and Thornton: Wheeler, Polly, and Thomas Thornton. "Subsistence Research in Alaska: A Thirty Year Retrospective." *Alaska Journal of Anthropology* v. 3, n. 1 (2005): 69-103.

Perhaps more important to my overall understanding, however, is the series of community reports created over the last several decades by the Alaska Department of Fish and Game, Subsistence Division. As seen in the chapter, some of these suffer from what I think are methodological difficulties (high among those being the inherent conflict in the eyes of many village residents that goes with research by an organization better known to many for its enforcement of highly restrictive hunting and fishing laws). Never the less, the total work, and many individual elements, are inspiring and likely represent a far greater data archive that will be of lasting importance. See, for example:

- Ratner, Nancy C., Morgen Smith, Jesse A. Dizard, Amy Piage, and Michael Francis Turek. "Local knowledge, customary practices, and harvest of sockeye salmon from the Klawock and Sarkar rivers, Prince of Wales Island, Alaska." Alaska Department of Fish and Game, Division of Subsistence, Technical Paper No. 308, 2006.
- Schroeder, Robert F., and Mathew Kookesh. "Subsistence Harvest and Use of Fish and Wildlife Resources and the Effects of Forest Management in Hoonah, Alaska." Alaska Department of Fish and Game, Division of Subsistence, Technical Paper No. 142, 1990.
- Leghorn, Ken, and Matt Kookesh. "Timber Management and Fish and Wildlife Utilization in Selected Southeast Alaska Communities: Tenakee Springs, Alaska." Alaska Department of Fish and Game, Division of Subsistence, Technical Paper No. 138, 1987.
- George, Gabriel D., and Robert G. Bosworth. "Use of Fish and Wildlife by Residents of Angoon, Admiralty Island, Alaska." Alaska Department of Fish and Game, Division of Subsistence, Technical Paper No. 159, 1988.
- Cohen, Kathryn A. "Wrangell Harvest Study." Alaska Department of Fish and Game, Division of Subsistence, Technical Paper No. 165, 1989.
- Firman, Anne S., and Robert G. Bosworth. "Harvest and Use of Fish and Wildlife by Residents of Kake, Alaska." Alaska Department of Fish and Game,

Division of Subsistence, Technical Paper No. 145, 1990.

- Ellana, Linda J., and George K. Sherrod. "Timber Management and Fish and Wildlife Use in Selected Southeastern Alaska Communities: Klawock, Prince of Wales Island, Alaska." Alaska Department of Fish and Game, Division of Subsistence, Technical Paper No. 126, 1987.

- Alaska Department of Fish and Game (Division of Subsistence). "Report on Implementation of 1992 Subsistence Law." Juneau: Alaska Department of Fish and Game, 1995.

On the links between subsistence, land and local culture, some useful sources beyond those listed above are:

- Dauenhauer, Nora, and Richard Dauenhauer. *Haa shuká, Our Ancestors: Tlingit Oral Narratives. Vol. 1.* Seattle: University of Washington Press, 1987.

- Dauenhauer, Nora Marks, and Richard Dauenhauer. *Haa Tuwunáagu Yís, for Healing Our Spirit: Tlingit Oratory. Vol. 2.* Seattle: University of Washington Press; Juneau: Sealaska Heritage Foundation, 1990.

- Dauenhauer, Nora Marks, and Richard Dauenhauer. *Haa kusteeyi, Our Culture: Tlingit Life Stories. Vol. 3.* University of Washington Press, 1994.

- Langdon, Steven. "From communal property to common property to limited entry: Historical ironies in the management of Southeast Alaska salmon." In *Cultural Survival Report 26: A Sea of Small Boats*, ed. John Cordell, 304—32. Cambridge MA: Cultural Survival, 1989.

- Vaughan, James Daniel. 1985. "Toward a New and Better Life: Two Hundred Years of Alaskan Haida Culture Change." Ph.D. diss., University of Washington.

- Oberg, Kalvervo. 1973. *The Social Economy of the Tlingit Indians.* Vancouver: J. J. Douglas.

The effect of ANCSA on local subsistence is difficult to gauge. As argued in the chapter, subsistence history underwrote many of the claims that ANCSA was forced to settle, and which allowed many Native people to stay in local communities that would otherwise have had to leave when the salmon canning industries collapsed. On the other hand, ANCSA-inspired logging in Southeast Alaska has had a devastating impact on subsistence livelihoods. These often have to be read indirectly, as many of those who would complain have long since disappeared from Native communities…forced to leave by the very forces that made the most of their claims. For some of the impact of clear cutting on local ecology see:

- Deal, Robert L. "The effects of partial cutting on forest plant communities of western hemlock Sitka spruce stands in southeast Alaska." *Canadian Journal of Forest Research* v. 31, n. 12 (2001): 2067-2079.

- Deal, Robert L., Chadwick Dearing Oliver, and Bernard T. Bormann. "Reconstruction of mixed hemlock-spruce stands in coastal southeast Alaska." *Canadian Journal of Forest Research* v. 21, n. 5 (1991): 643-654.

- Murphy, Michael L., and Alexander M. Milner. "Alaska timber harvest and fish habitat." *Freshwaters of Alaska.* Springer New York, 1997, pp. 229-263.

- Sigman, Marilyn J. (ed) "Impacts of clearcut logging on the fish and wildlife resources of southeast Alaska." Vol. 85, no. 3. Alaska Department of Fish and Game, Habitat Division, 1985.

- Milner, Jos M., Floris M. van Beest, and Torstein Storaas. "Boom and bust of a moose population: a call for integrated forest management." *European Journal of Forest Research* v. 132, n. 5-6 (2013): 959-967.

- Durbin, Kathie,1999. *Tongass: Pulp Politics and the Fight for the Alaska Rain Forest.* Corvallis: Oregon State University Press.

- Gorsuch, Lee, Steve Colt, Charles W. Smythe, and Bart K. Garber. "A Study of Five Southeast Alaska Communities." Report prepared for the U.S. Department of Agriculture, Forest Service by the Institute of Social and Economic Research, University of Alaska Anchorage, 1994.

- Haycox, Stephen. "Tongass Timber: A History of Logging and Timber Utilization in Southeast Alaska." *Environmental History* v. 16, n. 4 (2011): 719-720.

- Eagleton, Matthew, et al. "Impacts to Essential Fish Habitat from Non-fishing Activities in Alaska." Appendix G update to the 2005 Environmental Impact Statement for Essential Fish Habitat Identification and Conservation in Alaska. National Marine Fisheries Service, NOAA, 2011.

- Schwan, Mark, Steve Elliot and John Edgington, "The impact of clearcut logging on the fisheries resources of Southeast Alaska." In *The Impacts of Clearcut Logging on the Fish and Wildlife Resources of Southeast Alaska.* Technical Report 85-3. Marilyn J. Sigman, ed. Pp. 1-105. Juneau: Alaska Department of Fish and Game, 1985.

- Schoen, J.W., M.D. Kirchoff and O.C. Wallmo. "Sitka Balcktailed Deer/Old Growth Forest Relationships in Southeast Alaska: Implications for Management." In *Proceedings of the Symposium on Fish and Wildlife Relationships in Old Growth Forests.* Pp. 315-319. Morehead City, NC. American Institute of Fisheries Biologists, 1984.

- Chen, J., J.F. Franklin and T.A. Spies. "Contrasting Microclimates among Clearcut, Edge, and Interior of Old-Growth Douglas Fir Forests." *Agricultural and Forestry Meteorology* v. 63, n. 2 (1993) :219-237.

- Salo, E.O.,and T.W. Cundy,. "Streamside Management: Forestry and Fishery Interactions" *Contribution 57, Institute of Forest Resources.* Seattle: University of Washington, 1987

- Larson, David P Philip R. Kaufman, Thomas Kincaid and Scott Urquhar. "Detecting Persistent Change in the Habitat of Salmon-Bearing Streams in the Pacific Northwest." *Canadian Journal of Fisheries and Aquatic Sciences* v. 61, n. 2 (2004): 283-291.

- Brosofske, K.D., J. Chen, R.J. Naiman, and J.F. Franklin. "Harvesting Effects on Microclimatic Gradients from Small Streams to Uplands in Western Washington." *Ecology Applied* v. 7 (1997): 1188-1200.

- Yeo, J.J., and J.M. Peek. "Habitat Selection by Female Sitka Black Tailed Deer in Logged Forest of Southeast Alaska." *Journal of Wildlife Management* 56 (1992): 253-261.

Some portions of this chapter appeared previously as:

- Dombrowski, Kirk. "Subsistence livelihood, Native identity and internal differentiation in Southeast Alaska." *Anthropologica: The Journal of the Canadian Anthropology Society* v. 49, n. 2 (2007): 211-230.

## Chapter 6

The contrast between the everyday lives of Alaska Natives and the political version of their culture is seldom discussed, in part because of the value placed on "authenticity" by the land claims process. One result is that many young people in Native communities find themselves whip-sawed between feelings of not living up to their culture or of living in a culture that does not represent their lives, and the feeling of having to hold on to that same culture in the face of tremendous forces that seek to take away what little life they have left. On the contradictions of "being" Indian, some important sources that have shaped my thinking are:

- Sider, Gerald M. *Living Indian Histories: The Lumbee and Tuscarora People in North Carolina.* UNC Press Books, 2003.
- Cattelino, Jessica R. "The double bind of American Indian need-based sovereignty." *Cultural Anthropology* v. 25, n. 2 (2010): 235-262.
- Biolsi, Thomas. "Imagined geographies: Sovereignty, indigenous space, and American Indian struggle." *American Ethnologist* v. 32, n. 2 (2005): 239-259.
- Cattelino, Jessica R. *High Stakes: Florida Seminole Gaming and Sovereignty.* Duke University Press, 2008.
- McCormack, Fiona. "Indigeneity as process: Maori claims and neoliberalism." *Social Identities* v. 18, n. 4 (2012): 417-434.
- Thomas, Deborah A., and M. Kamari Clarke. "Globalization and race: Structures of inequality, new sovereignties, and citizenship in a neoliberal era." *Annual Review of Anthropology* v. 42 (2013): 305-325.
- Austin-Broos, Diane. "Three points and three replies." *Anthropological Forum* v. 22, n. 1 (2012): 67-93.
- Barker, Joanne. *Native Acts: Law, Recognition, and Cultural Authenticity.* Duke University Press, 2011.
- Carlson, Keith. *The Power of Place, the Problem of Time: Aboriginal Identity and Historical Consciousness in the Cauldron of Colonialism.* University of Toronto Press, 2010.
- Richland, Justin B. "Hopi tradition as jurisdiction: On the potentializing limits of Hopi sovereignty." *Law & Social Inquiry* v. 36, n. 1 (2011): 201-234.
- Cowlishaw, Gillian. "Culture and the absurd: The means and meanings of Aboriginal identity in the time of cultural revivalism." *Journal of the Royal Anthropological Institute* v. 18, n. 2 (2012): 397-417.
- Reedy-Maschner, Katherine L. *Aleut Identities: Tradition and Modernity in an Indigenous Fishery.* Vol. 61. McGill-Queen's Press-MQUP, 2010.

My own thinking has been extended by my recent fieldwork in Labrador, Canada. **See:**

- Dombrowski, Kirk, Bilal Khan, Joshua Moses, Emily Channell, Nathaniel Dombrowski, "Network sampling of social divisions in a rural Inuit community." *Identities, forthcoming* v. 21, 2014.

## Chapter 7

As mentioned in the introductory chapter, much of my thinking on Pentecostalism and conversion more generally was influenced by the work of Susan Friend Harding, to which I would add the recent work of James Bielo. Useful sources include:

- Harding, Susan F. "American protestant moralism and the secular imagination: From temperance to the moral majority." *Social Research: An International Quarterly* v. 76, n. 4 (2009): 1277-1306.
- Harding, Susan F. "Convicted by the Holy Spirit: The Rhetoric of Fundamental Baptist Conversion." *American Ethnologist* v. 14, n. 1 (1987): 167–181.
- Harding, Susan F. *The Book of Jerry Falwell: Fundamentalist Language and Politics.* Princeton University Press, 2001.
- Bielo, James. *Words Upon the Word: An Ethnography of Evangelical Group Bible Study.* NYU Press, 2009.
- Bielo, James S. "The 'emerging church' in America: Notes on the interaction of Christianities." *Religion* v. 39, n. 3 (2009): 219-232.
- Bielo, James S. "Purity, danger, and redemption: Notes on urban missional evangelicals." *American Ethnologist* v. 38, n. 2 (2011): 267-280.

To understand how religious conservatism and social radicalism come together under capitalism, the following sources go beyond the language discourse approach that generally frames Harding's work:

- Mahmood, Saba. *Politics of Piety: The Islamic Revival and the Feminist Subject.* Princeton University Press, 2005/2012.
- Hendershot, Heather. *Shaking the World for Jesus: Media and Conservative Evangelical Culture.* University of Chicago Press, 2004.
- Rudnyckyj, Daromir. "Spiritual economies: Islam and neoliberalism in contemporary Indonesia." *Cultural Anthropology* v. 24, n. 1 (2009): 104-141.
- Bialecki, Jon, and Eric Hoenes del Pinal. "Introduction: Beyond Logos: Extensions of the Language Ideology Paradigm in the Study of Global Christianity (-ies)." *Anthropological Quarterly* v. 84, n. 3 (2011): 575-593.

On the nature of relationship making through speech acts and related notions of exchange, there is a long anthropological history. One can start with Mauss and Austin, and simply go from there, or go even further back to Hegel, of course. A couple of more edgy, popular, and recent applications of these ideas include those at the bottom of the list.

- Hegel, G.F. *The Phenomenology of Spirit* (trans A.V. Miller). Oxford: Clarendon Press, 1977.
- Mauss, Marcel. *The Gift: The Form and Reason for Exchange in Archaic Societies* (trans. WD Halls). New York and London: WW Norton, 1990.
- Austin, John Langshaw. *How To Do Things with Words,* Vol. 1955. Oxford University Press, 1975.
- Schechner, Richard. *Performance Studies: An Introduction.* Routledge, 2013.

***

- Edgar, Kimmett, Ian O'Donnell, and Carol Martin. *Prison Violence: The Dynamics of Conflict, Fear and Power.* Cullompton, Devon: Willan, 2003.
- Seabright, Paul. *The Company of Strangers: A Natural History of Economic Life* (Revised Edition). Princeton University Press, 2010.

- Tsing, Anna. "Sorting out commodities: How capitalist value is made through gifts." *HAU: Journal of Ethnographic Theory* v. 3, n. 1 (2013): 21-43.
- Salmond, Anne. "Ontological quarrels: Indigeneity, exclusion and citizenship in a relational world." *Anthropological Theory* v. 12, n. 2 (2012): 115-141.
- Moore, Gerald. *Politics of the Gift: Exchanges in Poststructuralism.* Edinburgh University Press, 2011.


## Chapter 8

This chapter restates many of the themes of Chapter 7, but attempts to situate them in process of self-making and individual identity, as these come to be caught up in the events of life and global processes of historical change. On these notions, I have found the work of Thomas Csordas helpful. His and related works include:

- Csordas, Thomas J. *The Sacred Self: A Cultural Phenomenology of Charismatic Healing.* University of California Pr, 1997.
- Csordas, Thomas. "Explorations in Navajo poetry and poetics." *American Anthropologist* v. 114, n. 1 (2012): 170-170.
- Several contributions to: Csordas, Thomas J., ed. *Transnational Transcendance: Essays on Religion and Globalization.* University of California Press, 2009.
- Luhrmann, Tanya M., Howard Nusbaum, and Ronald Thisted. "The absorption hypothesis: Learning to hear God in evangelical Christianity." *American Anthropologist* v. 112, n. 1 (2010): 66-78.
- Porcello, Thomas, Louise Meintjes, Ana Maria Ochoa, and David W. Samuels. "The reorganization of the sensory world." *Annual Review of Anthropology* 39 (2010): 51-66.
- Kapferer, Bruce. "Beyond Ritual as Performance. Towards Ritual as Dynamics and Virtuality." *Paragrana* v. 19, n. 2 (2010): 231-249.
- Jansen, Eva, and Claudia Lang. "Transforming the Self and Healing the Body Through the Use of Testimonies in a Divine Retreat Center, Kerala." *Journal of Religion and Health* v. 51, n. 2 (2012): 542-551.
- Wortham, Stanton. "The objectification of identity across events." *Linguistics and Education* v. 19, n. 3 (2009): 294-311.


## Chapter 9

Whereas Chapter 9 restates many of the main themes of the book, many of the above works apply as both sources of inspiration and avenues for further thinking. Some others grappling with these same ideas, though not necessarily in the same way, include:

- Starn, Orin. "Here come the anthros (again): The strange marriage of anthropology and Native America." *Cultural Anthropology* v. 26, n. 2 (2011): 179-204.
- Strong, Pauline Turner. "Cultural appropriation and the crafting of racialized selves in American youth organizations: Toward an ethnographic approach." *Cultural Studies↔ Critical Methodologies* v. 9, n. 2 (2009): 197-213.
- Simpson, Audra. "On ethnographic refusal: Indigeneity, 'voice' and colonial

citizenship." *Junctures: The Journal for Thematic Dialogue* v. 9 (2011).

- Dinwoodie, David W. "Prophetic Identities: Indigenous Missionaries on British Colonial Frontiers, 1850–75." *Ethnohistory* v. 60, n. 2 (2013): 322-324.

- Lea, Tess. "When looking for anarchy, look to the state: Fantasies of regulation in forcing disorder within the Australian Indigenous estate." *Critique of Anthropology* v. 32, n. 2 (2012): 109-124.

- Cattelino, Jessica R. "The double bind of American Indian need-based sovereignty" *Cultural Anthropology* v. 25, n. 2 (2010): 235-262.

- McCormack, Fiona. "Indigeneity as process: Maori claims and neoliberalism." *Social Identities* vol. 18, no. 4 (2012): 417-434.

- Austin-Broos, Diane. *Different Inequality: The Politics of Debate About Remote Aboriginal Australia.* Allen & Unwin, 2011.

# INDEX

www.ingramcontent.com/pod-product-compliance
Lightning Source LLC
Chambersburg PA
CBHW072122270326
41931CB00010B/1635